H. H. Wilson

Essays

Analytical, Critical and Philological on Subjects connected with Sanskrit Literature

H. H. Wilson

Essays
Analytical, Critical and Philological on Subjects connected with Sanskrit Literature

ISBN/EAN: 9783741181900

Manufactured in Europe, USA, Canada, Australia, Japa

Cover: Foto ©Andreas Hilbeck / pixelio.de

Manufactured and distributed by brebook publishing software
(www.brebook.com)

H. H. Wilson

Essays

WORKS

BY

THE LATE

HORACE HAYMAN WILSON,
M.A., F.R.S.,

MEMBER OF THE ROYAL ASIATIC SOCIETY, OF THE ASIATIC SOCIETIES OF
CALCUTTA AND PARIS, AND OF THE ORIENTAL SOCIETY OF GERMANY;
FOREIGN MEMBER OF THE NATIONAL INSTITUTE OF FRANCE;
MEMBER OF THE IMPERIAL ACADEMIES OF ST. PETERSBURGH AND VIENNA,
AND OF THE ROYAL ACADEMIES OF MUNICH AND BERLIN;
PH. D. BRESLAU; M. D. MARBURG, ETC.;
AND BODEN PROFESSOR OF SANSKRIT IN THE UNIVERSITY OF OXFORD.

VOL. V.

LONDON:
TRÜBNER & CO., 60, PATERNOSTER ROW.
1865.

ESSAYS
ANALYTICAL, CRITICAL AND PHILOLOGICAL

ON SUBJECTS CONNECTED WITH

SANSKRIT LITERATURE.

BY THE LATE

H. H. WILSON, M.A., F.R.S.,

BODEN PROFESSOR OF SANSKRIT IN THE UNIVERSITY OF OXFORD,
ETC., ETC.

COLLECTED AND EDITED BY

DR. REINHOLD ROST.

IN THREE VOLUMES.

VOL. III.

LONDON:
TRÜBNER & CO., 60, PATERNOSTER ROW.
1865.

CONTENTS OF VOL. III.

		Page
	Table of Contents	v
XI.	Review of Sir F. W. Macnaghten's 'Considerations of the Hindu Law, as it is current in Bengal'	1–98
XII.	Review of A. W. Schlegel's edition of the Bhagavadgítá. Bonn: 1823	99–157
XIII.	Preface to the Sanskrit Dictionary. First Edition, Calcutta: 1819	158–252
XIV.	Notice of European Grammars and Dictionaries of the Sanskrit Language	253–304
XV.	Review of Professor Max Müller's 'History of Ancient Sanskrit Literature'	305–348
	Index	349–387
	Additional Note	387–388
	Corrections	388–390

XI.

CONSIDERATIONS ON THE HINDOO LAW,

AS IT IS CURRENT IN BENGAL,

by the Honorable Sir FRANCIS WORKMAN MACNAGHTEN, Knt. One of His Majesty's Justices of the Supreme Court of Judicature at Fort William in Bengal.

"Misera est servitus, ubi jus est vagum aut incertum." 4th Inst.

Serampore Mission Press, 1824.

From the Quarterly Or. Magazine, Vol. III (1825), p. 171—240.

A WORK on the Laws of the Hindus by the eminent authority which had long administered them, excited our highest expectations, and we opened the volume with the fullest confidence of its yielding us the most satisfactory information. No common motives had operated on the learned author to induce him to become thoroughly master of his subject: the rights of individuals depended upon his accurate interpretation of the institutes on which they rested, and with the known intelligence and feeling of an English judge, we felt assured that he would never have been satisfied with the hurried or partial investigation of those arguments by which such important decisions were to be justified to the public and himself.

How far our expectations have been realised will appear, as we proceed; but the preface is of evil augury: it is wholly occupied with charges of inconsistency, and uncertainty against the Hindu code. We should have thought these qualifications would have pleaded in its favour with an experienced practitioner in our own jurisprudence, and should scarcely have supposed them serious grievances to one to whom the glorious uncertainty of English law must have afforded, in earlier life, no unfrequent opportunities for the display of acumen and research. The case, however, is otherwise, and Sir F. Macnaghten complains that "the contradictions of Hindu law reduce it to a nullity; that there is hardly any question that may not be either affirmed or denied under the sanction of texts which are held to be equal in point of authority; and that research is productive of little more than perplexity, for the conflict of lawgivers is endless, and they can never be reconciled."

To these assertions, however, we must confess we hesitate in giving unqualified assent. That conflicting authorities may be cited on many subjects may be conceded, but their being held to be of equal weight is by no means universally the case, although a mere English lawyer may be unable to determine which should preponderate: neither is it in our estimation so arduous a task as the learned judge seems to apprehend, to appreciate the reasons why lawgivers disagree, or to reconcile their differences. If that is impracticable, it is seldom difficult to give them that consideration to which they are justly entitled, upon reference to common sense, to obvious analogies, and the unquestionable and, in general, rational principles of Hindu Law. Again, the history of the authorities, the probable dates of their existence, the conditions of Hindu Society to which their institutes apply, and the local character of their influence, ought all to be taken into account in estimating the value of their dicta. Now all this, the criticism of Hindu Law, appears to us to form no part of the studies of the Calcutta Court, and we cannot wonder that its brightest ornaments should often be sadly puzzled. It is quite impossible that it should be otherwise as long as pleaders and judges are wholly at the mercy of the Pandits.

Sir Francis Macnaghten seems rather reluctant to admit the unfavourable testimony of Sir William Jones; as, although he cites that really learned Judge's opinion, that the Pandits have it in their power to mislead the court whenever they please, he holds that "the translated Hindu law-books contain enough, without being aided by the craft or cunning of a Pandit, to mislead any man." This is rather a singular mode of defending the Pandits, but if it be the case, of which by the way we are not at all assured, it must be from other causes than that stated by Sir Wm. Jones. In a translation, the reader has an opportunity of seeing the texts of the law in their proper places, applied to what they relate to, bearing upon the subject to which they belong, and corroborating or contradicting others of a similar tendency; but, as Sir Wm. Jones observes, "*a simple obscure text, as explained by the Paṅdits themselves, might be quoted as express authority, though perhaps in the very book from which it was selected it might be differently explained, or introduced only for the purpose of being exploded.*" In a translation, the entire passage of the original is given, whilst in a Paṅdit's *vyavasthá* it is not unfrequently perverted by incomplete or garbled citation, so as to bear a totally different meaning from that which it really conveys. We have no desire, more than the learned judge, to cast any reflexion upon the Paṅdits of the Supreme Court, or of any other court, but we have seen too much of them, not to be satisfied that they are the authors of many of the irreconcileable contradictions of Hindu law.

The circumstances in which the Hindu legal advisers of the courts of justice in this country are situated, are perhaps not so familiar to many of our readers as to preclude the necessity of our offering some remarks upon the subject. A Paṅdit, attached to a court in that capacity, is placed in it by personal favour entirely, without being subjected to any examination, and without producing any credentials;—who shall say then that he is 'learned in the law'? There is every probability against it, for until very lately neither means nor encouragement were offered to the Brahmans to study their own laws, and the assistance latterly given is much too recent to have produced any effect. There are no public establishments amongst the natives themselves, and they are too poor to pay for education: a teacher must feed as well as instruct his scholars, and such 'virtue is no longer extant.' In fact, an instructor was formerly enabled to maintain his pupils, and to glean a surplus for himself by the bounty of Rájás, and even of Nawábs, who gave him a village or two for that purpose, but grants of this description have long been out of fashion: without education there can be no learning, and as Paṅḍits are at best but indifferently taught, they are very rarely indeed learned men.

If the uncertainties of the English law are less perplexing than those of the Hindu law, we doubt if its *delays* are not something more interminable. A long time elapses before a cause comes for decision, and abundant opportunity therefore is afforded for the traffic of underhand negociation, intrigue and corruption; it is needless to cite instances to prove the consequences, or to make any individual application: public events have rendered the fact notorious. It can scarcely be otherwise. The Paṅḍits are in all cases ill paid, and the sums offered to their acceptance are in general equal to many years' purchase of their salaries: they are but men, and where the temptations are so great, they must be more than men to resist them. But is not every opinion to be received with reasonable distrust, emanating from parties over whom, whether proven or not, we cannot doubt undue influence operates, when a cause comes to be adjudged, and when the Paṅḍits are desired to report their opinions on the points of Hindu law?

Besides the opinions of the court Paṅḍits, given in reply to the queries of the court, it seems to be the practice of the Supreme and Sadr Courts at least, to receive the opinions of other Paṅḍits on either part. Need we wonder that these differ? What are counsel retained for in English courts? If opinions on the law were uniform, at least if the utterance of them were never to vary, what would become of the bar? The Paṅḍit in such a circumstance is an advocate, feed to make out the best story he can for his client, to adduce whatever can be pleaded in his favour, and overturn or explain away whatever appears to make against him. This trial of skill matters nothing with us, because we have Judges who know the law as well as the pleaders. In Hindu law, however, unluckily, the case is otherwise, and the Judge who is to decide the cause, knows nothig *per se* of the merit of the arguments which are to regulate his decision, not even of the language in which they are enforced. As long as this is the case, and every judge cannot be a Sir William Jones, we need not be surprised at the difficulty which attends the reconciliation of the contending doctrines of the Hindu law.

The mere question of the consistency of the Hindu law would be a matter of little importance, but that it leads to the serious consideration of the expediency of maintaining that law in force. If it be a nullity, as the learned judge remarks, what advantage follows its administration? At the same time, he recognises the policy and equity of governing the Hindus by their own laws, and consequently advocates a perseverance in the present plan, recommending however means "by which we may hope in time to cleanse the system of its aggregate corruptions and to *defecate the impurity of ages.*" And what are these means? The decisions of the Supreme Court; an appeal from Hindu law to an English bench: a preference of the opinion of foreign judges, and those but superficially conversant with the subject, to the laborious discussions of native law-givers, and scholars; and the substitution of common for written law, of that law which the historian of British India pronounces oral, traditionary, and barbarous, and describes as 'any thing which the judges choses to call law, under no other restriction than certain notions, to a great degree arbitrary, of what has been done by other judges before them." We doubt very much whether the Hindus will not fare better amongst the contradictions of their own texts, admitting that they exist, than the frequently conflicting decisions of different judges, and the very commonly opposite awards of the Sadr Díwání, and Mufassal Courts, in which we believe the judgements of the Supreme Court are regarded as any thing but infallible. At any rate, before hazarding such an experiment, we should be desirous to behold one much more obvious put to the test, and before the Hindu law is irreprievably condemned, we should wish to see it studied.

There are many other assertions in this preface which we think much too generally, if not incautiously and erroneously, advanced. We shall satisfy ourselves, however, with adverting to but one more, that we may not disproportionately delay our examination of the work itself. Sir F. Macnaghten, speaking of the translations that have been made, observes: "that they admit of different explanations it would be folly to deny, because there is hardly a passage in any one of them which has not been differently explained." We must be guilty of the folly of denying the inference, as we have no proof whatever of the fact. By whom have these passages been differently explained? certainly not by different translators, for we have no one work on Hindu law translated by two different hands. We are not aware that the translators are at variance with themselves, and although obscure sentences, no doubt, occur in which variety of translation might be defensible, yet these are comparatively few, and unimportant. The leading texts, which are repeated in different works are almost always short, simple, and precise, and are rendered in a similar manner wherever they occur. Upon what proof therefore the learned judge's assertion is founded, we are wholly at a loss to conjecture: unless he refers to the explanations of the Pandits; and then indeed we concede the fact, although we are at issue as to the cause. The unfavourable impression of translations, which the learned judge seems inclined to convey, appears to us wholly unmerited, and, if implicitly credited, calculated to do much harm. We can have no expectation that the Gentlemen of the Calcutta Bar will waste their valuable hours upon the unprofitable study of Hindu law-books in the original Sanskrit: and upon translations therefore they must depend for any knowledge of Hindu law: but if they are told from high authority that these translations are only calculated to mislead them, and that the interpretations are in almost every passage disputable, they will of course not think it worth their while to consult such defective guides, and will prefer ignorance to error. In this, however, they will err most egregiously. The translations of Jones, Colebrooke, Wynch, and Sutherland are fully entitled to their confidence, and if read with attention and rendered familiar by frequent reference, they will convey very accurate notions both of the determined, and the doubtful points of Hindu law. Sir F. M's appropriation of the two last chapters of his own book to the publication of part of the translation of the Mitákshará by his son, Mr. W. Macnaghten, is rather at variance with the opinion he would seem to inculcate of the worthlessness of translations.

The first chapter of Sir F. Macnaghten's work is dedicated to the law of inheritance, and starts oddly enough with a paragraph declaring, once for all, that a widow cannot claim any property in right of her husband, of which he was not actually possessed. We have no objection to the law of the declaration, but its abrupt appearance in the van of the laws of inheritance is rather a violent and unnecessary dislocation.

The learned judge next lays down the following as the course of Inheritance.

1st. The primary rules of Inheritance are these—A (the original acquirer) shall be succeeded
  1st. By his son, or sons—if no son, by
  2d. His widow, or widows—if none, by
  3d. His daughter, or daughters—if none, by
  4th. His daughter's son or sons—if none, by
  5th. His Father—if dead, by
  6th. His mother—if dead, by
  7th. His uterine brother or brothers—if none, by
  8th. His brother or brothers of the half blood—if none, by
  9th. Sons of uterine brothers—if none, by
  10th. Sons of brothers of the half blood—if none, by
  11th. Grandsons of uterine brothers—if none, by
  12th. Grandsons of brothers of the half blood.

Here the succession in this line ceases. A's Estate will now go-back to the son or sons of his sisters, and their heirs; failing them, to his paternal grandfather,—then to his paternal grandfather's widow,—then to the paternal grandfather's sons and their heirs.

The order of succession, thus laid down by the learned Judge, appears to us to be very far from full or precise. The first article, for instance, states that the deceased is succeeded by his son or sons, and the second, if no son, by his widow or widows; but unless the term son implies also grandson, and great grandson, the statement is exceedingly inaccurate; for a widow inherits only if neither son, grandson, nor great grandson be in existence.*

The list, also, is much more brief than the detail

---

* [See Sir W. H. Macnaghten's Principles of Hindu and Mohammedan Law. London edition (1860), p. 18.]

required, and the learned Judge admits this, as upon closing it he states, he believes he has set forth a sufficient number of reversioners for all the purposes of utility, and refers to Mr. Wynch's table*, a very useful one no doubt, for the rest of the course; but it is in remote succession that disputes chiefly originate, and opinions differ: and in a work emanating from such a quarter we should have expected to have found such cases less summarily disposed of.

Upon the line of inheritance the learned judge observes, it is perhaps less disputable than any other part of the Hindu law, and this admission is rather irreconcileable with his previous assertion, that the whole is a nullity. In truth all authorities are agreed in the main series of inheritance, and the chief contradictions and incongruities arise out of what must be allowed to be an ample field for their occurrence, partition of property. As far, however, as the claimants are immediate, and exclusive, there is no more conflict of opinion amongst Hindu law-givers than our own: the same may be safely said on every other subject, and in all the leading features, in whatever light the learned Judge may have contemplated them, the aspect of the Hindu code is very reasonably uniform, and consistent.

With respect to the law of inheritance amongst the Hindus, it is regulated generally by the performance of funeral oblations: these consist in the first degree

---

* [Translation of the Dáya Krama Sangraha. Calcutta: 1818, ad ch. I.]

of the presentation of a cake of rice and meat to the manes of a father, grandfather, and great-grandfather, and the individual who offers the gift to all or any of these bears the same proportionable degree of affinity to the deceased. A son, for instance, offers them to all three, a grandson to two, a great-grandson to one, and a great-great-grandson to none, for which reason the direct line of succession does not come to him, a peculiarity noticed but not explained by our text.

2d. There is a peculiarity in the *Hindoo* law, as it relates to descent in the right line. The estate cannot descend to a *great-great*-grandson, unless there be an intermediate heir, through whom it may be conveyed. For instance, If A have a son B, B have a son C, C have a son D, and D have a son E; E will then be the *great-great*-grandson of A. Supposing then B, C, and D to die in the life time of A, E shall not upon A's death take the estate—nor shall he ever take it, if it does not come to him through a long course of reversioners. Yet if D had survived A, D would have taken as A's great-grandson, and E would have taken as D's son. If C had survived A, C would have taken as A's grandson, and E would have taken as C's grandson —or if B had survived A, B would have taken as A's son, and E would have taken as B's great-grandson.

The principle does not seem indeed to have been familiar to the learned judge, and he has therefore been led into ambiguity and error in his 28th rule: (p. 8) he says that

It does not follow that a person whose duty it is to perform the *irdddha*, or funeral rites, shall succeed as heir to the estate; or that the person succeeding to the estate shall have the duty of performing the *irdddha* cast upon him—

An assertion in which we believe all Hindu writers to be at variance with him—except that we may suppose him to intend to say, the heir is not obliged to give the funeral offering to the deceased. That is by no means necessary, but he must share in some of those which the deceased should have offered, as to the father or grandfather, or even more remote kinsmen: the relationship involving the presentation of a funeral cake extending to seven persons, and that of offering libations of water comprehending fourteen. Under one or other of these denominations, therefore, it is highly probable that the heir will come, and he will consequently perform *Funeral rites.*

In illustration of his remark, Sir F. states that the

<small>Sons of a sister may succeed to the estate, but they cannot perform the *śrāddha* except in the absence of relations in the male line, or except in a case in which it may be performed by any person of the same *caste* or tribe. So if there be sons of a sister, the sons of a male cousin cannot succeed to the estate, and yet it will be their duty to perform the *śrāddha* in preference to the sister's sons.</small>

But this passage is far from accurate. The sons of a sister in Bengal inherit before the son of a male cousin, precisely because they do offer funeral oblations in closer connexion with the deceased than the latter, as stated in the *Dáya Krama Sangraha*, where accordingly the following rules are expressed:

"On failure of the brother's grandson the succession goes to the father's daughter's son, for he presents *three* funeral oblations", D. C. S. p. 18;—again,

"Failing the uncle's son, the uncle's grandson succeeds, for he presents *one* oblation",—Ibid. 21.*

---

* [Calcutta edition (1828), p. 8 & 9.]

A rigid regulation of the right to succession by the funeral oblations is, however, peculiar to Bengal, having been adopted as a general principle by Jímútaváhana. In other parts of India the criterion is admitted only partially, and in the very case under examination is not allowed to regulate the order of the inheritance. The law, therefore, as stated by the learned Judge, is defined as loosely as the principle, for it is *only in Bengal* that a sister's son succeeds in preference to the son of a male cousin.* The authorities of the Benares and Maithilá schools do not admit the claims of a sister's son, and remove him very far from the succession. In fact, his rights are not noticed at all, and can only come under the class of cognate or remote kinsmen—those sprung from a different family, but connected by funeral oblations. The reason why a sister's son is thus excluded is, that he belongs to a different family: at the same time the participation in funeral rites, and the argument of analogy induce some of the commentators on the text of the Mitákshará, as Bálambhatta, and Nanda Pandita, to endeavour to explain away the omission of a sister's son by supposing the term Brother's sons to imply sister's sons also: the rationale however of the opposite arrangement is sufficiently obvious, and no doubt of the real purport of the authorities can be entertained: a sister's son carries the property of the family away from it into that of her husband; whilst by a descent in the male

---

* [Dáyabhága. Calcutta: 1829, p. 326.]

line it accompanies the name and direct derivation,—
and although, therefore, in harmony with provincial
and modern notions, the learned Judge's definition
of the law of succession in this case, as connected with
a share in the funeral rites, appears to have been
founded on an imperfect and partial view of both questions.*

The remainder of this chapter is occupied with the
discussion of the question as to the rights of a widow
over property to which she succeeds upon the death
of a husband, illustrated by the answers of the Pundits
to the enquiries of the court. It is stated, that by
former decisions the widow took *moveable* property
absolutely, and *immoveable* property *for life only*, but
it has been since thought, that there is not any ground
for such a distinction, and that the widow takes but
a life estate in moveable as well as immoveable property. There is no doubt of the object of the law,
which declares that a widow succeeding to her husband's estate shall enjoy it until her death, and that
the husband's heirs are to succeed to it; nor have we
any objection, nor is there any in the *spirit* of the
Hindu law for the court to interfere, to control the
widow's expenditure of her property**: at the same
time we are not satisfied that this assumption of power
is warranted by the *letter* of the law.

---

* [Sir Th. Strange, Hindu Law. London: 1830, I, 146 f.]
** [ib. I, 134. 176. 246 f. II, 250 ff. Sir W. H. Macnaghten,
I. I., 19 ff.]

There are but two ancient texts which bear positively on the widow's power over the property which she inherits as her husband's sole heir. One is attributed to Kátyáyana, and states "Let the childless woman preserving (inviolate) the couch of her lord, and obedient to her spiritual guide, enjoy, resigned, her husband's wealth until her death: afterwards let the heir take it."* The other is from the Mahábhárata, which as law, by the bye, is no authority at all. "Enjoyment is the fruit which women derive from the heritage of their Lords,—on no account should they make away with the estate of their lords."¹ Such are the ancient injunctions; which can scarcely be interpreted to mean, that if a widow gives away or sells her estate, such gift or sale is invalid. Even the later writers who entertained less reverence for the female character than the ancient sages, have stopped short of such declaration, and Jímútaváhana is content to say that "a widow shall only enjoy the estate; she *ought not* to give it away, mortgage or sell it."† He

---

* [अपुत्रा शयनं भर्त्तुः पालयन्ती व्रतौ स्थिता
भुञ्जीतामरणात्क्षान्ता दायादा अर्द्धमाप्नुयुः ॥

Viramitr., 194, r, 7. Vivádachint., p. 140, 7. Dáyakramasangraha, p. 2.]

¹ Apahri, Take off or away: it is translated in the Digest and elsewhere, "waste", which perhaps scarcely renders its due import. [According to the Dáyakramasangraha the passage is taken from the Dánadharma of the Anusásanaparva (?):

स्त्रीणां सपतिदायदं उपभोगफलं स्मृतं ।
नापहारं स्त्रियः कुर्य्युः पतिदायात्कथञ्चन ॥]

† [See Dáyabhága, p. 265.]

allows her also, if unable to subsist otherwise, to mortgage or even to sell it, and to make presents to her husband's relatives and gifts or other alienations for the spiritual benefit of the deceased. It is not till we come to the third generation of lawyers, the commentators on the commentators, that the restriction is positive, and Śrí Kríshńa Tarkálankára expounding Jímútaváhana's text declares, "a widow shall use her husband's heritage for the support of life; and make donations, and give alms in a moderate degree for the benefit of her husband, but not dispose of it at her pleasure like her own peculiar property." The utmost that can be inferred from all this, is, that originally the duty of the widow was only pointed out to her, and she was left in law as she was in reason, a free agent, to do what she pleased with that which was her own; but that in later times attempts of an indefinite nature have been made to limit her power. The eagerness with which this latter doctrine is urged by the Scholiasts of the present day is ascribable in all probability to that contempt for the female sex which they have learned from their Mohammedan masters. The willingness with which it has been admitted by English Lawyers is owing no doubt to a conviction of the expedience of the doctrine, unbiassed, we trust, by prejudices either of Indian or English growth.

The learned judge observes, that with regard to immoveable property, so far as a widow is concerned, he has been unable to trace any distinction in Hindu law. We agree with him in as far as her *absolute* right is admitted over *both;* but if this is not conceded, then there is a very easily traceable distinction, for it is made by the same authorities, the modern lawyers, and it is on the very same grounds, those of analogy, that the limitation of a right over immoveable, and absolute right in moveable property, are maintained. The author of the Vivúda Ratnákara, and Vivúda Chintámañi, for example, assert that a wife may give moveable effects, gems, and the like, devolving on her by succession to her husband. Jímútaváhana is only *supposed* to hold a different opinion because he uses the word *Dhanam,* wealth in general, in restricting the widow's authority over wealth she inherits to a life interest; to which, however, as noticed, he admits the exception of charitable donations, and actual necessity: but the chief argument made use of against a widow's aliening her husband's estate is a law attributed to Nárada, that she may enjoy at her pleasure property *given her* by her husband, *or give it away* after his death, *except land or houses;* therefore, say the lawyers, *she cannot give away land or houses which she inherits.* Of course, if the exception applies to both cases, the permission holds equally good in both, and the same analogy that restricts the widow in immoveable effects recognises her right over moveable or personal property: notwithstanding, therefore, the court thought proper to reverse their own decree in the case of Hurasundari and Casinath Baisakh, and after acknowledging in 1814 her absolute interest in the moveable property of her husband, rescinding that admission in 1819; and notwithstanding the opinion declared from the bench that with respect to a widow's right there is no distinction between moveable and immovable property, and that she has no more than life interest in either, we believe it to be established by undeniable analogy, and the declared opinion of at least equal authorities, that there *is* a distinction between moveable and immoveable property, as regards a widow's rights, and that if we are guided by the old Hindu law, unsophisticated by modern subtlety, and forced analogies, a widow has *an absolute interest* in both. As to the Vyavasthá on which the opinions of the court, we presume, were formed, we never saw more superficial law nor palpable contradiction in any we ever perused. It may be worth while to examine it at some length.

1. The Court Pandits asserted that "the Dáyabhága and *other* Sástras current in Bengal make no distinction between moveable and immoveable property." Without knowing what these other Sástras are, we cannot estimate the value of this reply: we have no objection to admit that Jímútaváhana makes no distinction.

2. "A widow has a life interest in both." The texts of ancient sages are equally current everywhere, and as far as their obvious acceptation extends, of which we have as good a right to judge as Jímútaváhana, they do not oppose the widow's absolute right over both: consequently,

3. "A widow is entitled to dispose of the same by

"gift, mortgage, sale, or otherwise for the benefit of "her husband's soul."

4. "It is incumbent upon a widow to act as her hus-"band's kinsmen direct."

The Vivāda Bhangārnava, a Bengal authority, declares "a widow has no lord, and may therefore do as she likes."

5. "The gift of immoveable property is not valid "against herself or the next heir: the same of move-"able property and jewels which might be recovered "by her, or the next heir, the same as money."

Now this we deny in toto— whatever a widow may be recommended not to do, as she is not commanded not to do, she may do, and a breach of a moral injunction is punishable only in the breakers: the person who receives the donation, having received that of which the alienation is not expressly forbidden, has done no wrong: why punish him? the gift of the whole estate, therefore, is valid. The learned judge observes very correctly that it seems exceedingly absurd, that persons should be able to make a valid disposal of property which they have no right to dispose of at all, and that that which is immoral, and sinful, and prohibited, should still be good in law. We wonder it never occurred to him that the *validity* of the gift was an argument in favour of the *legality:* but this is really the case.

The old lawyers have said, 'let a widow enjoy a husband's wealth, afterwards let the heirs take it': what obligation does this involve that she *must leave* it? But she is told she should not waste it,—granted: but suppose she sells it, is that waste? Now as to the gift, the same authorities, from whom there is no appeal, define what things are alienable as gifts and what are not. Amongst the things not alienable no mention is made of a widow's inheritance. The *whole* estate of a man, if he have issue living, or if it be ancestral property, he cannot give away, without the assent of the parties interested, and this may indeed be thought to apply to the *immoveable* property inherited by a widow, but it is the only law that can be so applied: there being, therefore, no law against the validity of her donation, it follows that she has absolute power over the property: at least such was the case, till a new race of law-givers, with Jímútaváhana at their head, chose to alter it; but they only tampered with the law of inheritance, and the law respecting legal alienation being untouched, remains to bear testimony against their interpretation of a different branch of the law.

6. "A widow has not absolute interest in either "moveable or immoveable property. She has not an "uncontrolled interest, she can do nothing of her own "authority."

This last position is contradicted by a Bengal authority, as we have seen, and by the daily practice of all India. Who controlled Ahalyá Bháí?

7. "The widow has a right to the *possession of the* "*moveable property*, to which she succeeds, subject to "the control before mentioned."

We presume by possession is meant having it in her hands, or at her command. How else can she enjoy it. There is nothing that can be tortured into an assertion that her husband's relations, or any other individuals, private or public, have a right to withhold from the widow's own coffers whatever jewels or money she inherits—and, having such property in her hands, who is to prevent her making away with it? Such are the absurdities in which an attempt to limit a widow's absolute right over 'moveable' property has involved the modern Hindu law: the ancient lawgivers were too wise to attempt impossibilities—they gave the widow good advice, but abstained from legislating what it was impossible to enforce.

8. "The relations of her husband cannot dispossess "her of that property, but they may control her in the "use of it."

If they cannot do the one, they cannot do the other: if they cannot take the money from her, how is it possible they can prevent her spending it? By an injunction of the *Supreme Court*, indeed, and the consignment of the funds to the care of the *Master*, it may be, and has been done: this we know: but we have yet to learn that it is *Hindu* law.

9. "There *is no difference* in the interest taken by "a woman in property derived from partition with her "sons, and what she inherits upon her husband's death "without issue." On this point we shall join issue presently—in the mean time, see what immediately follows.

10. "We are of opinion that the most eligible mode "would be to consider it as *Stridhana.*" That is *property over which a woman has absolute power.*

These learned sages, therefore, in the course of half a dozen replies, assert that a widow has a life interest only over property which she solely inherits, and an absolute interest in property which she divides with her sons, and *yet there is no difference.* Oh wise and consistent expounders of the law, we have done with your Vyavasthá!

Next came a knot of five Bengali Paṅdits, who are made to say: The Paṅdits of the Court have quoted the Dáyabhága as their authority; *therefore we differ from them in opinion.* Now really we cannot conceive these Paṅdits ever used any such expression: the Dáyabhága is unquestionably very high authority in Bengal, and for a Paṅdit of this province to make its citation the ground of dissent surpasses our conception. They might indeed decline to admit its authority as far as inconsistent with older works, as would seem to be implied in what follows. "There are older treatises of law by which donation of property by a person who has not uncontrolled authority over it is declared void." Granted, but to what except moral control is a widow subjected? In fact, they admit that, although a widow ought not to aliene her husband's property, yet that the disposal is valid, and they also assert the widow's absolute power over the moveable part of the property.

Two other Paṅdits agreed with the Court Paṅdits:

that is, they admitted there was no difference between life interest, and absolute interest; they asserted, however, that a gift was not valid against the heir—"who might reclaim it". We should like to know upon what authority.

We quite agree with the learned judge, that with such guides it was not easy to arrive at the right conclusion: but this was not the fault of the Law. The spirit and the text of the original law, in our estimation, recognise the widow's absolute right over property inherited from a husband, in default of male issue.* In Bengal the authorities that are universally received have altered this law and restrict a widow to the usufruct of her husband's property. They have not, however, provided for its security, nor for its recovery if aliened, and by such neglect have virtually left the law as they found it, or the power if not the right of alienation with the widow: it is open to the court, therefore, to make what regulations on this subject they please, as far as their jurisdiction extends, and as far as they are authorised by the Charter; and the regulation most conformable to reason, to analogy, and the spirit of the Hindu code, would be to give the widow absolute power over personal property, and restrict her from the alienation of the estate, except with the concurrence of her husband's heirs.

The second division of Sir F. Macnaghten's work

---

* [Mitáksh. ad Yájn. II, 135. Vivádachintámani, p. 151. Víramitrod., p. 193, a. Vyavahára Mayúkha, IV, 8, 2 ff.]

treats of the partition of property, made amongst the parties themselves,—partition amongst others, by the sole owner in possession, being, in our opinion not very methodically, transposed to a future chapter. The learned judge then seems to take it for granted the subject is familiar to his readers; for, without stating either the law or the practice, he begins with considering a case which he admits he does not know ever to have occurred, the right of a great-grandmother to share with her great-grandsons,—on which after a discussion, which appears to us very unprofitable, and very unnecessary, he allows the old lady a share, provided some more immediate descendant is a party. It is scarcely worth while to discuss the case, but it seems to us very easily settled. If the partition is made of a husband's property, his widow and his mother have a right to their shares,—but whenever the character of that property is changed by transmission to persons not inheriting of the deceased husband in the degree of son or grandson, their right ceases. There is another criterion, too, by which the question may be settled, "partition is co-ordinate with the gift of the funeral cake,"* and that extends to the great-grandson. A great-grandson taking a share of his great-grandfather's undivided property, of course implies the great-grandmother's participation, and then she will share as he does. The learned judge does not seem

---

* [Yájnav., I, 132. Dáyabh., p. 326. 157. पितर्दौ ३ बारः, पितामहानंतिसमवायिधिकारः, and the like.]

to have been put in possession of the principle, nor even of the letter of the law by the Pandit of the court, who in reply to his queries, "invariably said the law is silent." For the author of the Digest propounds and answers the very question. "When property left by "the paternal great-grandfather is divided, should not "a share be allowed to his wife? That is admissible "from parity of reasoning, and the particle in the "phrase, "and wives of the grandfather", connects the "terms with what is understood but not expressed": 3, 24. The case, however, is of very unlikely occurrence, and to legislate for improbabilities is a work of supererogation. It seems, however, to be a favourite topic with the learned judge, for he twice recurs to it in this chapter, in rules 13 and 27, and after all, in our estimation, gives the law incorrectly.

The learned judge then proceeds to examine the rights of a woman derived from partition with her sons, and declares it as his opinion, that they are of precisely the same description as those with which she is invested as sole heir, and that she has but a life interest in both moveable and immoveable property so acquired.

In the case of the widow's sole inheritance, we have granted that the Bengal lawyers limit her in all respects to a life interest, whilst the *Mithilá* writers maintain her absolute right in moveables, and the old law authorities oppose nothing to her absolute right in every kind of property. In the case of property, however, acquired by partition, the arguments in favour of absolute right are infinitely stronger, in as much as the Bengal authorities lean to the same view of the subject. Jímútaváhana starts no objection to such power, his remark being confined entirely to the case of sole inheritance, and the Viváda Bhangárnava concludes a long and satisfactory discussion of the question by the corollary, "Therefore a wife's sale or donation of her own share is valid." We are, therefore, very much at a loss to conceive upon what grounds the learned Judge has assimilated a widow's rights as derived from inheritance or partition, or on what the "Supreme Court has considered them on the same footing." We cannot help being amused with the additional remark, "if it ever had been doubted, the "two decisions of which I have spoken are sufficient "to set the question at rest." (p. 45.) For what are those decisions? "That the parties take both moveable and immoveable property —*according to the rules of the Hindoo law*;" leaving the task of establishing the Hindu law for another law-suit. If these are the decisions that are to take the place of Hindu law, Heaven help the litigants.

It is asserted, indeed, that a husband's heirs succeed to such property in preference to a woman's own heirs, and therefore her enjoyment of it is only for life: but the postulate is supported only by analogy, not by any positive law, and therefore the inference is by no means proved: besides, even if admitted, preference of succession does not imply restriction of right in possession: our law of primogeniture does not preclude, under ordinary circumstances, the father's right to sell, give, or bequeath his property as he pleases; and why should any order of succession exercise such influence here, when not specially provided for? "Heritage, and partition" are included by the text of the Mitákshará, which is good law in every part of India, even in Bengal, amongst the constituents of "woman's property", and a woman is acknowledged by all to be mistress of her own wealth. It is argued, that lands and houses *given by a husband* to his wife must not be aliened by her after his death: *therefore,* a share of land and houses *given by his sons* on partition of his wealth, must not be made away with by their mother; but this is surely a different case. A husband, in undue fondness, might bestow upon a wife the *heritage of his sons,* and they would be deprived of that patrimony in which *they have a joint interest with the father:* it is not unwise, therefore, to secure to them the reversion of such effects. In the case of partition, however, they are already secured: they cannot be left destitute, and if the property is ample, as it always is in contested causes, they are fully provided for by the possession of their respective shares. Again, as the partition is their own act, a mother cannot enforce it, although it cannot be made without her consent. In acquittance then of her claims, in order to induce her to forego her lien upon the whole, the sons give her up her part: they then only become fully masters of their own shares, and it would be an unfair bargain if they did not admit the mother's free disposal of what may be considered the purchase money of their privileges.*

Sir F. Macnaghten admits that if it could be considered as an act of free will, the widow's share in a partition might be recognised as the gift of her sons, and consequently "as the gift of kind relations" would be placed at her absolute disposal: but he observes, she may be influenced by one son in contradiction to the will of the rest, and as partition takes place at the desire of any one of the co-heirs, they will then be compelled to relinquish the mother's share against their consent. This may be granted as a possible evil resulting from the law, but it does not alter the character of the law, and therefore, whatever may be the case in a widow's sole inheritance, we see no grounds whatever for restricting her interest in the property which she derives from partition, to a life interest only, whether the property be real or personal. It is absurd to say that a woman was not intended to be a free agent, because the old Hindu legislators have indulged in general declarations of her unfitness for that character. Manu, it is true, says of women "Their fathers protect them in childhood, their husbands protect them in youth, their sons protect them in age. A woman is never fit for independence":** but what does this prove in respect to their civil rights? Nárada goes farther, and asserts, that "after a husband's decease the nearest kinsman should control a widow, who has no

---

* [See also Sir T. Strange, l. l. I, 246 ff.]   ** [XI, 3.]

sons, in expenditure and conduct."* But as we have observed this is neither the law, nor the practice of the present day. Besides it does not apply to the case of partition, as there the widow has sons, and they surely abandon a right to control property which they themselves have given. To sanction any other mode of procedure would only tend to perpetuate the degraded condition of the female sex in India. Admit that at present widows are generally unfit to be entrusted with the absolute disposal of property that devolves upon them by virtue of partition with their sons. Is not that to be mainly ascribed to the restrictions with which they are already fettered? Accustom them to consider themselves as likely to be invested with important trusts; accustom their kinsmen and parents to contemplate them in the same capacity, and all parties will become interested in qualifying them to discharge with ability and conscientiousness the duties to which they may be called. Sir F. M. thinks that "a life interest will secure to the mother a greater degree of peace, and contentment than she is likely to enjoy after having a proportion of the family property at her own absolute disposal." If neglect be essential to peace and contentment, she may certainly expect their enjoyment: her sons and grandsons, secure of the reversion of the principal upon her death, will think it very immaterial how they treat a mother during life who has no power to reward affection or punish undutiful-

---

* [quoted in the Dáyabhága, p. 269.]

ness: the bands of domestic life are already too lax in India to be further unloosed with advantage, and the authority of parents, particularly that of the mother, is too tottering to be further undermined without being utterly subverted. Although, therefore, we give the learned judge full credit for the humanity of his intentions, we think he has adopted a hasty and partial view of a mother's rights, and that the restriction to the extent he proposes would be productive of infinitely more evil than good.

A number of rules, affecting chiefly the rights of females in the case of partition, then follow. In general we believe the law is correctly stated, although there is any thing but distinctness in the detail or method in the arrangement; the rules seem to have been laid down at random, with little regard to order, and with abundant carelessness of repetition. Thus we have the same question as to a great-grandmother's rights discussed in three different places, as we have already noticed, and the argument of the identity of a widow's rights by inheritance, or partition, which had twice been most fully discussed, p. 11, to 27, and p. 31, to 37, is again the subject of animadversion in p. 73, 74, and 93, 97. We shall not imitate the learned judge's example, nor again go over the principles, on which we offer his doctrine. We are satisfied that in the cases in which the decisions of the court, awarding an absolute interest in moveable property to a widow sharing on partition, have been reversed, the tenor of authority, the guide of analogy, and the spirit of the law, have been entirely misconceived.

The laws of partition amongst the Hindus have been always the fruitful source of family dissension. The perusal of this section of Sir Francis Macnaghten's work removes all astonishment at this circumstance; for the conflicting claims become in time so complicated, that it is almost impossible to unravel them. It is evident, however, that the difficulty really arises not from the mere law of partition, but the delay of the practice. It is the attempt to maintain unanimity that engenders disputes; if Hindu families would take our advice, they would never attempt to hold property in common, but make an absolute and final division, the moment they became possessed of it. It is quite impossible as descendants multiply, that they should not disagree, and in proportion to their number, and variety of relation, is the intricacy of their pretensions. Then, as Sir F. remarks of the cause of Govindchurn Baisakh, *v.* Casinath, Ramnath, and Bishonath Baisakh, "come bills, cross bills, and pleadings, in every variety of litigation, and the contest only ceases with the funds of the litigants." That cause, for example, began in 1808, and is still carried on between the sons of Govindchurn and their Cousins, with unabated pertinacity. The following case is illustrative of the complex interests involved in these disputes.

IN EQUITY.

Sree Mootlee Jeromony Dossee, the widow and legal representative of *Gungachurn Ghose*, deceased, and *Sree Mootlee Dossee Dossee*, widow and legal representative of *Buddenchunder Ghose*, complainants,

AGAINST

Attaram Ghose and *Callachund Ghose*, defendants.

The bill stated, and it was proved, that *Corrunnamoyee Dossee* and *Luckapriah Dossee* were resident at *Chandernagore*, and not subject to the Jurisdiction of the Supreme Court.

The prayer of the bill was for an account and partition of the estate of *Kissenmohun Ghose*, deceased,—and that one-fourth equal part or share of the said estate might be allotted to each of the complainants.

The bill also prayed an account and partition of the estate of the said *Kissenmohun Ghose*, as against the defendant *Callachund Ghose* in particular,—and of all profits and purchases made by *Callachund Ghose*, with, or out of the estate of, *Kissenmohun Ghose*, since the death of the said *Kissenmohun Ghose*; and that each of the complainants be decreed one-*third* equal part or share of the said last mentioned estate, to be held in severalty by them the said complainants.

The state of the family was as follows:— *Kissenmohun Ghose* died in the Bengal year 1193, leaving two widows, viz. *Corrunnamoyee Dossee* and *Luckapriah Dossee*, who are still living.

By *Corrunnamoyee Dossee*, *Kissenmohun Ghose* left three sons, viz. *Gungachurn Ghose*, who died in the month of *Ithadur* in the Bengal year 1207; *Buddenchund Ghose*, who died in the month of *Joistee* in the Bengal year 1216, and *Callachund Ghose*, who is still living and one of the defendants. By *Luckapriah Dossee* he left *Attaram Ghose*, who is still living and the other defendant.

Gungachurn Ghose had married two wives, first *Joyah Dossee*, who died in the life time of her husband, and in the Bengal year 1201. She left one son, *Sumboochunder Ghose*, who survived his father *(Gungachurn)* and died in the month of *Shrabun*, in the Bengal year 1215. The other wife of *Gungachurn* is the complainant, *Jeeomonee Dossee*. She had a daughter *Roopah Dossee* by *Gungachurn*, and *Roopah Dossee* is since dead.

Buddenchund Ghose left one widow, the complainant *Dossee Dossee*, by whom he had one daughter only (*Doyamoyee Dossee*). *Doyamoyee Dossee* is still living and married to *Kissenchunder Cowar*. *Callachund*, the other son of *Kissenmohun* by *Corrumamoyee*, and *Attaram*, the only son of *Kissenmohun* by *Luckapriah*, are the two defendants.

The defendant *Attaram Ghose* not only refrained from opposing the partition as between him and the other claimants under *Kissenmohun*, but alleged that a partition had already been actually made.

An account and partition of the estate of *Kissenmohun* was in the first place ordered as between the other claimants under *Kissenmohun* and him (*Attaram*), he being declared entitled to one-fourth part or share thereof as one of the four sons of *Kissenmohun*. *Attaram*, then, being solely entitled to a fourth separate part of the estate of *Kissenmohun*, it was understood and admitted, that his mother *Luckapriah* was not entitled to any separate property upon a partition made between her only son and his three half brothers, and that she was to look to him for her maintenance.

If *Sumboochunder*, the son of *Gungachurn* and *Joyah Dossee*, had died in the life time of his father, it seemed to be agreed, (*Joyah Dossee* having died before her husband,) that *Jeeomonee* the surviving wife of *Gungachurn* would have been entitled to his estate; but *Sumboochunder* having survived his father, it was held that his father's estate vested in him, and that *Jeeomonee*, (not being his mother, although the wife of his father) could not take from him, (*Sumboochunder*) but that his father's mother, (*Corrunnamoyee*) was his heir.

It was also declared that *Dossee Dossee*, the widow of *Buddenchund*, he (*Buddenchund*) not having left a son, succeeded as his heir, and was in his right entitled to one-fourth part of *Kissenmohun's* estate.

It was therefore ordered that a partition be made of the estate of *Kissenmohun*, that it be divided into four equal parts or shares and that *Attaram*, the only son of *Kissenmohun* by *Luckapriah*, do take one of the said *four* parts or shares in severalty.

Of the other three parts it was ordered that *Corronnamoyee* do take one as the heir of her grandson *Sumboochunder*, that *Dossee Dossee* do take one as the heir of her husband *Buddenchund*—and that *Callachund* do take one as the survivor of *Kissenmohun's* son.

This partition having been made, it was further declared *Corrunnamoyee* was entitled to a *fourth* part of the *three* which had been so divided, the *third* part which she had taken upon partition contributing to make up the said *fourth* part. It then stood thus,—*Corrunnamoyee*, the representative of *Sumboochunder*, *Dossee Dossee*, the representative of *Buddenchunder*, and *Callachund*, the surviving son of *Kissenmohun*, having come to a partition—*Corrunnamoyee* as mother of *Sumboochunder's* father, as mother of *Dossee Dossee's* husband, and as mother of *Callachund*, became, upon a partition, entitled to a share equal to that of the several partitioners.

The *three* parts were therefore again to be consolidated and then divided into *four*, of which *Corrunnamoyee* as mother was to have one,—the same *Corrunnamoyee* as representing her grandson, one—*Dossee Dossee* as representing her husband, one—and *Callachund* in his own right, one.

Supposing then the three parts (*Attaram* having taken the fourth) to be divided into *twenty-four* parts, *Corrunnamoyee* would have eight, *Dossee Dossee* eight, and *Callachund* eight;—*Corrunnamoyee* then for the purpose of converting the *three twenty-fourths* into *four twenty-fourths* must contribute *two* parts out of the *eight* she had taken,—and *Dossee Dossee* and *Callachund* must each contribute *two* parts out of their *eight*. Then each (*Corrunnamoyee* in her different characters being considered as two) will have *one-fourth* or six twenty-fourth parts. The result will be, that two-eighths of the share of *Dossee Dossee* and two-eighths of the share of *Callachund* will be added to the eight twenty-fourths of *Corrunnamoyee*, who will thereby have eight twenty-fourths and four twenty-fourths, or one half of that part of *Kissenmohun's* estate which went immediately from *Kissenmohun* to her own sons. She is now entitled to twelve twenty-fourths or one half of three parts of *Kissenmohun's* estate.

It was also ordered that *Corrunnamoyee* (not being a party to the suit) be at liberty (if she shall please to do so) to come in as a complainant before the Master in taking the account, and before the commissioners in making a partition of *Kissenmohun's* estate.

It is to be observed that on the death of *Dossee Dossee*, her daughter *Doyamoyee* will succeed through her *(Dossee Dossee)* to the estate of her *(Doyamoyre's)* father *Huddenchund*.

As to *Jeeomonee*, she has a right to maintenance out of her husband's estate, and may follow it for the purpose of obtaining her right into the hands of *Corrunnamoyee;* but from what has been already said, it is needless to state that she may now, if she has just cause, require security as to her rights—or perhaps the Court would have been, at the hearing, justified in ordering her maintenance to be secured. It was not asked, and she having gone for a specific proportion, and having failed in that, was I presume not apprehensive of the want of a maintenance during her life. If she has grounds for fear, she may yet come in for it upon petition.

Another case which arose out of disputes in Muddun Baisakh's family is cited in this chapter as illustrative of the effect given to a will, in the Supreme Court, and the right of a widow as heir to a husband: it is of considerable interest, but too long to be cited. We notice the result for the "grave and important question" it involves, as stated by the learned judge. Sentence was given in favour of the widow Hura Sundari, and she was declared entitled to her husband's estate, to be possessed, used, and enjoyed by her in the manner prescribed by Hindu law. Accordingly it was ordered that the principal, and accumulated interest then in the hands of the Accountant-general

should be paid over to her. Her husband's brothers
appealed against the decree for various reasons, but
chiefly "because the decree declared Hura Sundari *entitled* to the *possession* of her husband's estate, whereas,
she being entitled to the *use* and *enjoyment* only, it
ought to be secured *in the hands of an officer of the
court*, or *deposited with the relations* of Bishonath,
who will after the death of Hoorasoondaree be entitled to it", assumptions that speak for themselves,
as it is clear the Hindu law could not recognise *an officer* of an *English* court of justice, and common sense
would deprecate the consignment of property to interested relations.

The Supreme Court, however, thought differently,
and,

> The petition of appeal having been filed, it became necessary,
> if she took the money, to give security for its restoration in case
> the order should be reversed. She did not do so, and the prin-
> cipal sum with its accumulations up to the date of the order are
> still in the Accountant General's hands.

The learned judge observes,

> That it has been usual to give a widow, or a mother, *posses-
> sion* of the property to which she may succeed, must be admitted
> —and that the money of her husband's estate would, had it not
> been for the appeal, have gone into the hands of *Hoorasoondures
> Dossee*, is certain. Yet the right of her husband's heirs to it after
> her death is indisputable, and the justice of restraining her from
> waste is a necessary consequence of this right.
>
> What then is to be done? Possession will enable her to do all
> the mischief, before any restraint can be applied.

In our opinion this case is conclusive of a widow's
rights to moveable or personal property. If it is not

to be placed in the widow's own hands, to whom is it to be entrusted? certainly not to those, who are interested in dispossessing her of it. Does the Hindu law enact that it shall be deposited with any other person?—if not, it follows it must go to the widow herself, and she must have the power to do what she pleases with it. The original Hindu Legislators never brought themselves into such a dilemma: they conceded a right where they could not prevent its exercise. Lands and houses could not be made away with without formalities that admitted the interposition of authority, but money and jewels could not be restrained, and therefore they did not attempt to legislate for their appropriation. The learned Judge argues that the discipline of Hindu widows is relaxed, and that they are not under the same control as formerly: what proof have we of this, and even if true what right has the Supreme Court to legislate for this new state of things? They are to administer justice to the Hindus according to the laws and usages of the Hindus, and we believe it would be difficult to fancy any allusion in either to a Master in Chancery or Accountant General. If the laws are bad, abrogate them: substitute English Law at once; but it is mockery to regulate decisions by institutions and arrangements wholly foreign to the Hindu system, and call the hybrid monstrosity Hindu Law.

The learned Judge observes that the reversioner's right is as well founded as that of the widow; but he has by no means proved the nature of that right. In our estimation it is not absolute, but contingent. The law is simply "after her death let the heirs take it." So with us it is said "inheritance shall lineally descend to the issue of the person, who last died, actually seized", but does not therefore render it imperative that the property must be transmitted to the heirs. The rule in either case applies to property left, and cannot be said to give to the reversioners a right or control over the acts of the possessor.

Again who are these reversioners whom the learned Judge is so anxious to protect? and in answering this question we do not wish to dispute the equity, but the necessity, of their being made the objects of legal protection. Where a widow inherits as sole heir, there can be no nearer heir than a daughter, who in the constitution of Hindu society, we may be well assured, is married or will be at the mother's charge: she is therefore in her own person provided for, and if the property goes to her, it is transferred to another family, unconnected probably by name or descent with that of the deceased. In this case we should think it very immaterial whether the integral inheritance was preserved or not, as far as the interests of general society, the only interests that should be looked to, are concerned.

If there be no daughter nor daughter's sons, the estate will go to the husband's brothers: here it remains in the family, but what necessity is there for the apportionment? The brothers should not be in want, as they have already divided during the life time of the owner the patrimonial property, and have received a share severally equal to that of which the posthumous apportionment is in question: it will be no very great hardship upon them, therefore, to be excluded from a remotely contingent share in that, to which as a whole they had long before foregone all claim.

The same argument applies to a widow's rights upon partition. The sons and grandsons, and even great-grandsons, have had their shares, and the final alienation of a fraction, to which they assented for their mother's life, cannot expose them to distress—unless, indeed, the certain reversion of additional property at the end of the mother's life time, an event which they will be then tempted to desire, if not to expedite, should render them less careful of what they actually possess, and thus operate as a bounty upon extravagance. On the ground, therefore, of necessity, and in our estimation of expediency also, we deny the claim of the reversioners to that peculiar protection, which the learned judge is inclined to extend to them.

In page 56 the learned judge has explained the law relating to the portions of sisters, and concludes that they have a claim rather than a right. In page 97 he reverts to the subject thus:

> I do not expect that the value of what I now add will compensate for the irregularity of introducing it here. After my manuscript had gone to the press, I prepared this to be introduced at page 56, but it was mislaid; and when discovered, the printing had advanced too far to admit of its insertion in the proper place.

His conclusions are to the same effect, and whatever

may be the law, we admit the practice: originally, however, a sister claimed a fourth of a son's share. The commentators have made this simple law very indistinct by their explanation, supposing it to be necessary first to set apart a son's share, and then to give a daughter one fourth of that: thus they say in the case of a brother and sister sharing, the estate shall be divided into two equal parts: the son shall take one of these; the other is to be again divided into four, and one of those subdivisions shall go to the daughter; the rest shall devolve upon the son: consequently he will have seven-eighths, and the sister one-eighth, but we cannot conceive the law to sanction any such clumsy construction. It is true it does not authorise a sister's sharing in the whole estate to the extent of one fourth: because, in that case supposing six sons, and one daughter, the son would only take one-eighth, or half as much as the least worthy. Now this would be quite contrary to the spirit of the Hindu law. Again, a daughter cannot be said to take only one-fourth of one actual share equal to that of a son, because in the case of there being five or more daughters, all above four would go without any share at all. The inconsistencies of the law as thus understood are too obvious to have escaped the learned judge's notice; he has accordingly detailed them at considerable length, but he has offered no solution of the difficulty, nor attempted to explain, what is evidently the purpose of the law, and what involves no absurdity nor contradiction. A sister shall have the fourth part of a brother's own share: that is she shall divide with a brother in the proportion of one to three, or to state it more distinctly, a brother shall take seventy-five in the hundred, and the sister twenty-five. It is clear that, be the number of sisters, or brothers, what it may, this principle is of unvarying and ready application, and it is not the law, but the arithmetic of the case that has created any perplexity. We shall not dwell upon the subject here, as we shall have again occasion to advert to it, when we examine the similar principle which regulates the portion of adopted after the birth of natural sons. We may observe that, if the Court were to do what Sir F. M. supposes (p. 104) it might by virtue of the laws of Manu[*], it would be just as bad arithmetic as that of the Hindu Scholiasts, and worse law: he states that, if there were three brothers, and one sister, and the estate 24,000 rupees, the court would declare the sister entitled to one-fourth or 6,000, placing the female heir on a par with the male in contradiction to the spirit of both English and Hindu law; the purport of which latter is clearly, that the brothers in such a case should receive each 7,200 rupees, and the sister 2,400 rupees. We have a mighty simple rule called Single Fellowship, which is the best comment upon the Hindu law that can be offered."[**]

---

[*] [IX. 118. Yájnav., II. 124.]
[**] [Sir W. H. Macnaghten, l. l., p. 54. Sir T. Strange, l. l., l., p. 173.]

The next division of Sir F. M.'s work is upon reunion, the return of a separated brother to the co-parcenary enjoyment of property: in fact, however, the chapter treats only of one circumstance connected with reunion or the rights of a separated uterine brother and united half-brother to inherit; it being held by some lawyers, that a connexion by blood confers priority of right whether united or separated, and by others, that reunion places a half-brother on a par with a whole brother and entitles him to an equal division of the inheritance. The learned judge admits that he knows no instance of such reunion, and the chief object of the section seems to be an attack upon the digest of Jagannáth, an exceedingly useful work, although it does not profess to save those who consult it the trouble of judging for themselves. As little practical benefit would result from the investigation of this subject, we shall not dwell upon it further.

The next section treats of a subject of great importance in Hindu law as giving rise to almost daily discussion, *Adoption*. A Hindu *must have* a son to extricate himself and his ancestors from a kind of purgatory, and if he have no children of his own he must adopt one. It is said indeed by Manu, that "amongst several brothers if one have a son they are all pronounced fathers of a male child"[*], and it might be supposed unnecessary, therefore, for the uncles to adopt sons for themselves. Upon this Sir F. M. observes,

---

[* [IX. 182, quoted and discussed in the Dattakamimánsá, II, 29 ff.]

Upon this particular point, the sum of all I have been able to collect out of books, or from living authorities, is, that in the three superior classes, if there be *brothers of the whole blood*, a son of *one* of them, *for religious purposes*, will be the son of *all*; and that, while this son exists, the childless brothers by the same father and mother need not adopt one for the performance of *sacred rites*. But that, in a secular point of view, a male child is not considered as the son of his father's brethren—and that to take the heritage *as a son* of his uncle, he must be adopted; that, temporally considered, he does not, as a son, derive any benefits from them, and that the son of a brother is *recommended*, in preference to all others, for adoption.

I find this explained, and I think satisfactorily, in an opinion given by *Govardhana*, some time since a *Pandit* of the Supreme Court. He quotes *Vrihaspati* as follows*:—If among several *uterine* brothers *one* have a son born, the *whole* are considered as fathers. These authorities declare a nephew even as a son to a childless uncle—*effecting, as a son would do,* the relief of his soul from the hell called *put.* It therefore follows that the adoption of any other son during the existence of such nephew *ought not* to take place, and that *he ought* to be preferred. *It must not* however be inferred that, because such nephew be equal to a son in *this one respect,* he is so in *any other without being qualified by adoption*—us, according to the following stanza of *Yájnavalkya*, *his title to inherit* his uncle's estate comes *after* that of the widow, daughter, daughter's son, father, mother, and uncle—whereas, *were he adopted,* he would *precede all these.*

There is another view of the subject, however, to which neither Govardhana nor the learned Judge has adverted, and which appears to us to afford a much more satisfactory conclusion, even than the arguments of the former. The son of a brother is only in a subordinate or subsidiary capacity of benefit to his uncle

---

* [See the Dattakamimánsá. Calcutta: 1834, p. 15, II, 71.]

in his own person, in the matter of religious rites. That is, he offers no funeral cake to his uncle's spirit, except under a special rule, the exact purport of which is not admitted, but is supposed to imply only a confirmation of the undisputed doctrine that the son of a brother should be preferably adopted: he benefits his uncle mediately in as far as he offers cakes to his grandfather and great-grandfather, the common ancestors of his father and his uncle. In these oblations the latter has a share, but if he die without a natural or adopted son, he loses the certainty of his own oblation, and will consequently run the risk of purgatory. To escape this chance, from which it is doubtful if the oblations of a nephew can secure him, he must adopt a son for himself, and it is therefore not only on secular but religious grounds that such adoption is imperative.* The text of Manu does not contradict this view of the case, and the expression occurs merely in illustration of the figurative application of the term *Son* to an adopted son, who can bear such relation *actually* only to his natural father, although he is considered to bear it *legally* to his adoptive parent. The conclusion affecting the right of uncles to adopt sons is Kullúka Bhatta's, not Manu's, and in this case and every other it may be observed, that the remarks of a scholiast, however high his character, do not debar the exercise of independent reasoning. A Paṅḍit of the present day, who should bring superior talent to

---

* [Sir T. Strange, l. l., I, p. 84 ff. Duttaka Chaudriká I, 21 ff.]

the task, would be entitled to a preference over all preceding expositors. As to the legend from the Kúliká Puráńa cited by Sir F. M. from the Dattaka Mímánsú*, it does not seem to us to bear materially on the question, and if it did it would signify little; for the *Puráńas* are not authorities in law. They may be received in explanation or illustration, but not in proof.

The right of an adopted son, to inherit collaterally, which has been the subject of much difference of opinion amongst the Pańdits, and variety of decisions in the courts, is next discussed by the learned Judge: with his usual disregard to arrangement however, he has made the same topic the subject of discussion in his preface, whilst in the same chapter, after some interval, he narrates the case of Gourbullukh v. Jagannath Prasad in which this subject was the question at issue, and illustrates it in the appendix by the opinions of 51 Pańdits belonging to the different Courts. We agree with him in his conclusions, that an adopted son, or the son given, has the right of collateral succession, and that its ever being contested shewed but a partial appeal to the authorities or the principles of Hindu law. The following is the view of the question we are disposed to advocate.

Twelve kinds of sons are enumerated by Manu and other writers. These sons are divided into two classes: those who are heirs and kinsmen (Dáyádás and Bán-

---

* [See Orianne, Droit Hindou. Paris 1845, p. 274. Dattakamímánsá. Calc. 1834, p. 11 f., and Sutherland's notes ad II, 45.]

dhuvás), and those who are not heirs but kinsmen. It is agreed that a son of one kind or other, there being no son of a superior class in his way, takes the inheritance of his adoptive father, and the specification of them as heirs does not apply to his wealth, but to that of such persons as the father would be heir to in the event of their deaths; as "uncles and the rest", according to Maheśwara, and as Sapińdas, or the paternal grandfather and others connected by the funeral cake, according to Jímútaváhana. There is no difference of opinion on these subjects, but the question is, which of the adopted sons inherit thus collaterally, and which do not, and here we have some difference of classification. We have taken some pains to ascertain the notions of the different authorities with respect to the comparative grade of the different sorts of adopted sons, and they seem to us to run as follows*:

Authorities.	Manu.	Kátyáyana.	Baudháyana.	Ujmana Pur.	Kálika Pur.	Yájnaralkya.	Yama.	Hárita.	Devala.	Nárada.	Vishnu.
The natural son (Aurasa)	1	1	1	1	1	1	1	1	1	1	1
A daughter's son (Putrikáputra)	0	0	2	0	0	2	3	5	2	3	3
Son of a wife (Kshetraja)	2	2	3	2	2	3	2	2	3	2	2
A son given (Dattaka)	3	3	4	3	3	7	9	7	9	9	8
A son made (Kŕitrima)	4	5	5	4	4	9	10	9	11	11	12

* [See Sir T. Strange, I. l., II, 194 ff. Manu IX, 166 ff. Yájnav. II, 128 ff. with the Mitákshará. Dattakachandriká, p. 60. Vivádachint., 147, 5. Vyavahára Mayúkha IV, 41 ff. Viramitrod., p. 184, v., 6 ff. Sir W. H. Macnaghten, I. l., p. 65 ff.]

Authorities.	Manu	Kátyáyana	Rawdháyana	Vámana Pur.	Kálikd Pur.	Vyavaháriya	Yama	Hárita	Devala	Nárada	Vishńu
Son of unknown parentage (Gúdhotpanna)	5	9	6	5	5	4	6	6	5	6	6
Son rejected (Apaviddha)	6	7	7	6	6	12	7	12	6	8	11
Son of an unmarried Girl (Kánína)	7	8	8	7	7	5	5	4	4	4	5
Son of a pregnant bride (Sahodha)	8	10	9	8	8	11	8	10	7	5	7
Son bought (Krita)	9	4	10	9	9	8	11	8	12	10	9
Son of a remarried widow (Paunarbhava)	10	11	11	10	10	6	4	3	8	7	4
Son self-given (Swayamdatta)	11	6	12	11	11	10	12	11	10	12	10
Son of a Súdra or a Slave (Saudra)	12	12	13	13	12	0	0	0	0	0	0

This enumeration extends to thirteen kinds of sons, but they are regarded usually as but twelve, a daughter's son, or a son by a female Súdra, being excluded from some of the lists. It is immaterial, however, to adjust the scale throughout, for in the present age there are but three descriptions of sons admitted, the natural son, the son given or Dattaka, and in some places the Kŕitrima or son made. The learned judge in concluding (p. 132), that there are but two kinds known at present to Hindu law, the son begotten in wedlock, and the son given in adoption, seems to have lost sight of the case he had particularised but a few pages before, and which he states in p. 128 was a Kŕitrima adoption. This mode of adoption, however, is of restricted currency, and limited in Gangetic Hindustan, at least, to Mithilá; it is therefore sufficient here to fix the place of the *Dattaka* or the son given.

On the above authorities, four concur in placing him the third on the list, and besides these Gautama, Vasishťha and Vṛihaspati as quoted in the Digest, assign him the same place. Baudháyana, who makes him fourth, does so only by inserting the daughter's son, and a text of the Vedas, an authority that should be final, as cited in the Dattaka Chundriká, assigns him a similar grade.* The weight of authority therefore clearly recognises the classification of the Dattaka amongst the first six, or those who are declared to be heirs to collateral kinsmen, as well as to their adoptive father.

There is no doubt that the worthiest sons are entitled to the highest privileges. This is conformable to common sense, as well as the manifest purport of the authorities. That the Dattaka is amongst the most respectable, is admitted even by some of the authorities, who seem to give a preference to others in their enumeration; and Vishnu who places him below the son of an unmarried girl**, &c. states [?] that they are not reputable (Aprasasta), and share neither the funeral oblation nor estate. The very acknowledgement of the Dattaka, or son given, as co-existing almost, if not quite alone, with the son begotten in wedlock, in the present age, is an admission favourable to his character, and consequently to his claims.

---

* [V, 26.]   ** [ch. XV.]

Notwithstanding these considerations, however, a text of the sage Devala is adduced by Jímútaváhana* unfavourable to the collateral succession of the Dattaka, and he seems to have been usually considered, in Bengal, as classed with sons who are kinsmen but not heirs. An opinion so opposite to that which is derived from the text of Manu and other legislators is certainly startling, and it might be supposed impossible to offer any satisfactory explanation of such a difference, or any attempt at the reconciliation of these contradictory positions. To us, however, it appears by no means difficult to understand how the difference of doctrine has arisen, or to solve the inconsistency of Devala's text with principles that are uncontested, and to shew its utter inapplicability to the existing circumstances of Hindu Society.

The classification of the Dattaka, or son given, below several of the others, by which he is reduced to the lowest grade, depends upon a principle more subtle than just, and one contrary to established doctrines. It is argued that, whilst the son given, and his like, may be of *a different caste* from the adoptive father, the son of an unmarried daughter, of a widow remarried, and of concealed birth, may be, by the female side at least, of *the caste of the deceased*, and are *possibly* his own sons. The affinity, however, is not proven, and if it were, what would be the result? they would as bastards be excluded from all class and tribe what-

---

* [Dáyabhága, p. 227. Dattakachandriká. p. 61.]

ever: it is on this account in all likelihood that Manu ranks them lowest in the scale, Vishńu calls them Aprasasta, or not reputable, and Vŕihaspati declares they are contemned by all good men. Kátyáyana* is more explicit, for he declares that they are Asavarńas, not of the same Varńa or caste with the father, and the author of the Mitákshará observes "that although they may be deemed of the same class through their natural father, yet they are not so in their own character, for they are not within the definition of tribe and class**." In fact, as far as the question turns upon this point, and it is the only thing like an argument in the way, it may be easily settled. Whatever might have been the difficulty in ancient times, there is none now; for whilst the mere possibility of affinity of tribe gave the three sorts of sons above named a contingent advantage over the son given, to whom such an affinity might not apply, that is not the case at present, as the Dattaka's being of the same caste is in the present age an indispensable condition of the validity of the adoption.

The principle, on which the opposition, therefore, to the collateral succession of a son given rests, being fallacious, or inapplicable, the objection grounded on it becomes unsubstantial, and there can be no doubt, that the Dattaka inherits mediately as well as immediately from his adoptive parent: he stands in fact in every respect in the place of a natural son; he presents

---

* [Dáyabhága, p. 229.]   ** [XI, 39.]

the funeral cake to his adoptive father and his ancestors, and he foregoes all claims upon his peculiar birthrights. On the ground of equity and of equivalent, therefore, his claims are further corroborated, and the decision of the court in the case of Gourbullubh &c. was perfectly consonant with the reason and spirit of the Hindu law.

The learned Judge next proceeds to consider other contingencies of the act of adoption, and discusses the right of the adopted son in the event of a natural son being born after his adoption. In that case he says, it is the general if not the universal opinion of the Pandits, that the adopted son is entitled to a third part of the estate; upon a text of Devala who lays it down that the adopted son shall in this case take one third, and the begotten son two thirds of the estate.

In quoting texts of law, it is very necessary to adhere to the precise expressions as any partial change may alter the colour of the whole. Now neither in the original nor translation is there a word about the *estate*, or the two thirds to be taken by the begotten son: neither is the law so generally admitted as the learned judge seems to imagine. If it were, indeed, what is the meaning of the next page and a half, complaining of the uncertainty of Hindu law and abusing Jagannáth's digest? At the same time, setting aside the texts of Manu regarding a fifth or sixth share as no longer applicable, we believe the only difference in the law in this case arises, like that in the case of a sister's portion, from want of a knowledge of the elements of arithmetic.

Devala says, adopted sons after the birth of a natural son are dividers of *a third share**, which Jímútaváhana explains, a third part of the share of a natural son."* According to our notions of computation this does not mean *a third of the whole*, but a part equal to *one third of the portion* of the natural son, and consequently *a fourth* of the *whole* dividend: accordingly, the Mitákshará*** awards a fourth share upon the authority of Vasishťha, and the doctrine is precisely the same as that of Devala, according as the application is made; for it is clear that, if out of 100 parts the natural son takes seventy-five and the adopted son twenty-five, he may be said to take a fourth or a third share, according as the assertion is absolute or relative. In no case, however, can it be argued that the adopted son is to have one-third, and the natural son two-thirds: the proportion is not as *two to one*, but as *three to one*, and conclusions to the former effect are not warranted by any interpretation of the law; the supposed inconsistency of which lies, in our estimation, not in the law, nor even its commentators, but its living interpreters.

The next consideration is the age at which a boy may be adopted, and which the learned judge con-

---

* [औरसे पुत्रजन्यते तेषु धीर्यं न विद्यते ।
तेषां सर्वत्वे ये पुत्रास्ते तृतीयांशभागिनः ॥]

** [औरसपुत्रमानस तृतीयांशभागी ।]

*** [I, XI, 24.]

ceives Hindu authorities to have limited to that of five
years. He cites however a decision of the Sadr Dewání, in which the adoption of a boy of eight was declared valid, and he expresses a hope, that henceforth
that may be acknowledged as the limit, because it has
once been so decided: a very odd reason, supposing
the decision to have been incorrect.

The real spirit of the Hindu law, however, leaves
the age of the boy a matter of perfect indifference. It
is true, that authorities founded on a contested passage of the Káliká Puráña prohibit the adoption of a
boy whose age exceeds that of five years; but even if
the passage be authentic*, we deny its competency to
constitute the ground-work of a positive law. But the
text of the Puráña does not prohibit the adoption; it
says, "after the fifth year sons given, and the rest
are not sons but slaves"—and why? because a son, having been initiated under the family name of his own
father unto the ceremony of tonsure inclusive, does
not become the son of another man: "the ceremony of
tonsure and other rites of initiation being indeed performed under his own family name, sons given, and
the rest may be considered as issue, else they are
termed slaves."—Even on this very authority, therefore, the initiatory ceremonies are all that is essential,
and the age of five years is specified only, because it

---

* [Colebr. ad Mit. I. XI; 18. Vyavahára Mayúkha, IV, 5, 20.
Sutherland's transl. of the Dattaka Mimánsá. Madras: 1825,
p. 225 f. 237.]

is taken for granted that by that age tonsure, which should be performed in the 2d or 3d year, must have been performed. But here again the authority invalidates its own assertion, that tonsure in the family of the adopted father is essential to adoption, for that rite will be performed probably in the 3rd year at latest, and the period of adoption is extended to five, or *after* tonsure is performed. These inconsistencies, however, arise from chusing to consider the passage as law: it is no such thing, it is merely an exposition and recommendation of the practice, and should no doubt be thus understood: initiation completed in the natural family disqualifies a boy for adoption into any other, and the greater the number of initiatory rites performed in the family into which he is adopted the better; he cannot therefore be adopted at too early an age, and it is very desirable that he should be adopted before tonsure is performed; but if that is not possible, then the age of five may be regarded as a fair average limit, because that anticipates the period of investiture with the sacrificial string, which would be a disqualification. Although the upanayana is performed usually in the eighth year from the conception of a Bráhmaña, it may be, and not unfrequently is, anticipated in the fifth. On the other hand it may be delayed till the sixteenth year, and accordingly adoption may be proportionately extended. The Hindu law refers here to a positive principle, and is neither inconsistent nor contradictory. As to the arguments in favour of early adoption suggested by the learned judge, (p. 145) they are manifestly exotics,—the growth of an English, not of an Asiatic soil. We are not aware either of the necessity, or the existence of any distinction in the age of a son who is adopted, whether he is nearly related, or not, to the adopter.

In rule 8th Sir F. M. lays it down, that the gift of an only son is absolutely prohibited, acknowledging, however, that an only son may be so given, the donor being content to suffer the consequences. Those consequences relate to his condition after life, and no Hindu will, very readily, incur them. The evil, however, is only to the prepetrator, and as the measure does not affect the peace or well-being of Society, it seems rather superfluous to have legislated upon the subject—except that it gives the learned judge an opportunity of impugning an extra judicial opinion of the Recorder of Madras. Sir F. M. has not adverted here to the allowable arrangement, by which a case of the kind is provided for, and an only son, though not absolutely given in adoption, may be affiliated as the son of two fathers—fulfilling the double capacity of a son to his natural, as well as to his adoptive father.

The law of adoption, as it stands in the Hindu code, is of itself a sufficiently fertile source of dissension, but it appears that in practice it has become still more so, and that the decisions of the courts have authorized innovations not contemplated, and therefore not only prohibited by Hindu law, but foreign to its objects, and productive of additional intricacy and doubt.

A man requires a son, to perform his funeral ceremonies, and save him from purgatory. This being done, the necessity for adoption ceases, and his *multiplying* adopted sons is an act of supererogation. It has, however, been recognised in a decision of the Sadr Court, founded chiefly on the doctrine that "many sons are desirable, and that the wish for many is meritorious"; but such an admission can scarcely constitute law. The practice may be suffered, because it is not prohibited, but the principle will equally authorise adoption, where natural sons exist, and in many respects is likely to produce mischievous results;—to lay it down as a rule, as is done by the learned judge, (rule 23d) is only likely to promote litigation.

Again the adoption is for the benefit of the father, and where a widow adopts a son, she does so under his instructions, and as his representative, and in no case is she supposed to adopt a son *for herself*, though permitted by her husband so to do, except, agreeably to the form of adoption practised in Mithilá, that of the Kŕitrima, or son made, which is especially for the purpose of performing the woman's Sapińdí Karańa. In this case a husband's assent is not necessary, and the widow therefore acts for herself, not as a husband's representative, as she does under all other circumstances: the three rules therefore, advanced (p. 156) upon the authority of the Sadr Dewání reports, tend only to sanction anomalies incompatible with the spirit of the Hindu law.

Another contingent perplexity attached to the subject arises out of the innovation of wills, by which the regulation of adoption is made the matter of posthumous caprice. We shall have more to say on the subject of wills hereafter, and it may be sufficient here to remark that, if the Hindus are to be authorised to make wills, they should be instructed how to make them, and not be suffered to bequeath absurdities, or to make the arrangements which they contemplate subject to improbable or impracticable conditions.

Finally another source of perplexity is the arbitrary interference of the Courts.

The following case singularly illustrates the mischief of all these innovations.

*Luckinorain Tagore** (a *Brahmin*) died possessed of considerable property, *moveable* and *immoveable*; mostly, I believe, ancestorial; but that circumstance was not relied upon in any stage of the cause. Three wives, viz. *Sree Mootee Taramonee Dabee, Sree Mootee Bhagabuttee Dabee, Sree Mootee Dagumbaree*** survived him; and at the time of his death, he had not a child.

Luckinarain made a will, by which he left 5000 rupees to each of his wives, and 1000 rupees, in addition to the 5000, to his second wife *Bhagabuttee*.

In his will he recited the pregnancy of his younger wife *Dagumbarre*, and declared that her *(son or daughter)* should be the possessor of his wealth. He constituted *Juggomohun Mullick**** his executor; *Juggomohun Mullick* some time after this died, having made a will, and constituted *Bustom Doss Mullick* † his executor. In this state of things it was assumed, and received as a matter of course, that *Bustom Doss Mullick* became the executor of *Luckinarain Tagore*. I am particular in noticing this, because

---

* [लक्ष्मीनारायण ठाकुर.]
** [श्रीमतीतारामणि देवी. श्रीमतीभगवती देवी, श्रीमती दिगम्बरी.]
*** [जगमोहन मल्लिक.] † [पैचदास मल्लिक.]

it may serve to show the extent to which the wills of *Hindoos* are recognized in the Supreme Court.

Juggomohun, as executor of *Luckinarain*, had possessed himself of *Luckinarain's* property - and *Bustom Doss*, as executor of *Juggomohun*, possessed himself of it, after *Juggomohun's* death.

On the 7th of November, 1818, and thirteen days after the death of *Luckinarain Tagore*, his youngest wife *Dagumbaree* was delivered of a son. This son died in seventeen days after his birth.

If *Luckinarain* had died intestate, this son must have succeeded to his property as *heir at law*; and *Dagumbaree*, his mother surviving him, would incontestably have succeeded to the property as his heir. *Luckinarain*, however, made a provision by his will, in case of the death of this child with which his wife was *enceinte*. In the event of its death, he directed that his *widows* should *adopt a son*. If they could not *all* agree in the selection of a boy for adoption, he directed that one should be chosen by his *first* and *second* widows, *Taramonee* and *Bhagabuttee*. If the *first* and *second* widows could not agree in the selection, he then directed that a boy should be chosen by his *second* and *third* widows, *Bhagabuttee* and *Dagumbaree*. It will be seen, that the *second* widow, *Bhagabuttee*, was in any case to have a voice in the selection of a son for adoption. From this provision, and from the additional thousand rupees which he gave to her, it clearly appears that she was the favorite, and the one in whom he had most confidence.

In 1818, *Dagumbaree*, the youngest widow, and mother of the child, of *Luckinarain*, filed her bills against *Taramonee* and *Bhagabuttee*, the other two widows, and against *Bustom Doss Mullick*, the executor of her husband's executor.

By this bill the complainant, *Dagumbaree*, affirmed her right to the estate of her late husband, in consequence of her having had a son by him, whose heir she stated herself to be by the *Hindoo* law. She prayed an account and to be put into possession of the estate of her husband, *Luckinarain*.

To this bill an answer was put in by *Bustom Doss Mullick*, admitting that as the executor of *Juggomohun*, who was executor of *Luckinarain*, he, *Bustom Doss*, did possess himself of *Luckinarain's* estate, and that he was then in possession of it. He admitted also the birth of a son, and his death, as the bill set forth; but he denied that the complainant was entitled to the estate of *Luckinarain*, and he *relied upon the will* by which the adoption of a son was directed. He denied the complainant's right to an account of *Luckinarain's* estate, and insisted that no person had a right to such an account, except a son to be adopted *according to the terms of Luckinarain's will*. The other two defendants put in a joint answer to the same effect with that of *Bustom Doss Mullick*.

The will was established, and directions were given for the adoption of a son according to its provisions. Such vexation as might have been foreseen was the consequence. The widows could not be brought to concur in the selection of a boy for adoption. A reference was then made to the master, who was directed to enquire and report to the Court concerning the fitness of a boy to be adopted as the son of *Luckinarain Tagore*. The master reported in favour of *Taracomar Surmono** who had been nominated for adoption by the *second* widow *Sree Mootee Bhagabuttee Dabee*. *This boy was the son of Bhagabuttee's* UNCLE.

The Master's report was confirmed, and this furnished matter for further contention. The boy *Taracomar* was to be adopted; but the question was, which of the three widows had a right to receive him in adoption. The law is clear, and was undisputed. The boy could not be received by the *three widows jointly*. He must be received by *one* of them—and would then be considered as the son of *Luckinarain and the widow by whom he had been received*: about this there was not, because there could not be, any dispute.

Had it not been for the *natural* relation in which the child stood to *Bhagabuttee*, the second widow, the Court, considering the preference which had been given to her by her husband, might probably have declared her the properest person to act as adopting mother. But it was a family of *Brahmins*, and her claim was impugned upon the ground of relationship, it being argued that she could not without incest be the mother of her uncle's son.

---

* [नारांकुमारबर्मञ.]

The argument was supposed to be conclusive, for she withdrew her pretensions.

There was no dispute as to the eligibility of this boy. He might have been adopted by *Luckinarain* himself, *but not as the son of Bhagabuttee*, who was his first cousin.

The first widow, *Taramonee*, founded her claim to receive this child upon seniority. The *third*, *Dagumbaree*, founded hers upon the fact of her having borne a son to her deceased husband.

The Master reported in favor of the *first* widow, and the Court confirmed his report; not from a *conviction* of its having been right, but because it was not opposed, and because it did not appear that the *third* widow ought to have been preferred.

I have added the will of *Luckinarain*, the Master's report, and the opinions which were given by the *Pandits* in his office, to the appendix. If those opinions do not impart knowledge, satisfy curiosity, or remove doubt, they will at least prove the deplorable state in which ministers of justice are placed, when they have recourse to *Pandits* for an exposition of the *Hindoo* law in a depending cause.

We shall content ourselves with a few remarks on this case.

The learned judge admits, that if Luckinarain had died intestate, the infant would have succeeded to the property, and Digambari, his mother, would incontestably have succeeded to his property as his heir; the will therefore on the learned judge's own showing violated the law of inheritance.

The learned judge states also that the greater part of the estate was ancestorial property. In the following chapter on unequal distribution, he endeavours, it is true, to maintain a father's right to assign immoveable ancestorial property unequally *to his sons;* but admitting this, which is more than doubtful, he has *no right to give it away to others:* consequently the will of Luckinarain could not invalidate his own infant's claim to the ancestorial immoveable property at least, and the decree that gave it away from his heir was a violation of the law.

The idea of compelling two of the widows to agree in the choice of a son was an absurdity, and as it was a condition that could not be enforced, it ought of itself to *have invalidated the will,* in which case the whole of the property, subject to deduction for the maintenance of the other widows, would have reverted to the younger widow.

No *two* of the widows agreeing, the court assume the power of sanctioning *one* to adopt. Did this assumption emanate from the will, or from the Hindu law?

The widow makes a choice, and it is declared to be within the proscribed degree of consanguinity: to whom? not to her husband on whose behalf, and for whose benefit she acts, but herself: a matter wholly irrelevant in regard to property on which she has no claim.

This adopted son is then declared by the court not to be the adopted son of the mother who adopted him, but the adopted son of the mother, who did not adopt him: a stretch of power that we certainly can find nothing in Hindu law, nor we imagine in English law, to justify.

"Those who acted for the second widow would have held fast by her claim, if they had not known it to be untenable", so says the learned judge near the bottom of page 172: at the top of page 173, however, we have, "I now hear that the right of Bhagubuttee to receive the child in adoption was not abandoned by her adviser",—quære how long an interval had elapsed between the penning of these two passages.

"Dagumbaree being excluded, however, the second widow forbore to oppose the judgment of the court."

But allowing to the will of the deceased the power, which it cannot have in law or reason, of subverting the most positive and undoubted provisions of the Hindu code, has it not been virtually cancelled by the authoritative interposition of the court in enforcing an arrangement *contrary to the terms* of the will, and in that case has not Digambari a right to inherit as she would have done, if no such will had existed?

The adopted son has since died: without issue it may be presumed from the date of his adoption and his age at the time. Who has succeeded to the inheritance? if the elder widow be held to be his adoptive mother, she now claims the whole succession, and if Bhágavatí's advisers have not been long-sighted enough to anticipate such a contingency they have very imperfectly advocated her interests.

Sir F. M. seems to anticipate a new adoption on the part of the widows and suggests the question of its validity (p. 175). He has forborne from answering it, but it may be safely asserted, that the Hindu law has not provided for the case; the widows have no authority from their husband to make a second choice, and in Bengal they cannot adopt without such authority*: it might be argued upon the reason of the case, that "if a man desires one son to be adopted, this is clearly expressive of his wish to be at all events represented, and that the adoption is therefore to proceed toties quoties, until this object shall have been finally accomplished." But it is not so written in the bond, and we are not aware, that the courts of judicature are authorised to make the constructive wishes of deceased parties law. If the adoption is tenable, the mother, whichever it may be, is heir, and she will have very good grounds therefore to resist a second adoption. The cases referred to by Sir F. M. as proving the validity of successive or several adoptions, do not bear upon this, as in them special authority from the husband was established; that authority being held legal, of course, the acts emanating from it were legal also.

Above 40 pages are next occupied with a critical review of a division by Sir Thomas Strange, in the case of Virapermah Pillay *v.* Narain Pillay. and we shall content ourselves with this reference, as we have already dwelt too long on this chapter. It is impossible however to avoid drawing a very important inference from the result of the investigation. The Chief Justice of Bengal declares that a decision pronounced and argued with great pains by the Chief Justice at Madras *will mislead those by whom it may be followed, and that the doctrines which it inculcates are con-*

---

* [See Sutherland, 1. 1., p. 233 ff. Notes VI & VII.]

trary to law (p. 229). Can we then wonder that Paṅdits differ, or can we consent to take the decisions of the judges as substitutes for Hindu law?

At the end of this section, we have "Addenda to the chapter on inheritance", the insertion of which in this place is thus adverted to:

> Although I ought, perhaps, to apologize for the great defect in point of arrangement, which will be found throughout my publication, I hope an acknowledgement of the fault will be deemed sufficient from a gratuitous labourer—from one whose thoughts must have been chiefly directed to other avocations, and who has hardly had a single day which he could devote to this work with undivided attention.

The next chapter on gifts and unequal distribution regards the father's absolute power over his property, or his right to divide or bequeath it unequally amongst his sons. The learned judge admits, that the law is tolerably precise with regard to property acquired by a person himself, and the moveable portion of his patrimonial inheritance. Of this there is little question, although a distribution of such effects dictated by prejudice or partiality is considered immoral. He endeavours however to shew, that the unequal distribution of ancestorial immoveable property, if not legal, is not valid, and he here avails himself of the doctrine which he sturdily resisted as applicable to the rights of a widow, *quod fieri non debet, factum valet:* he endeavours (p. 301) to make out a difference in the nature of the cases, but we think without success.

> When I noticed it first, I was upon a subject very different from the present. There the question was, whether or not a

woman (who was certainly entitled to no more than a life interest in the property she possessed) could lawfully deteriorate that property to the prejudice of him, who had an unquestionable title to succeed to it after her death. Here the question is, whether or not the man in possession of *ancestorial immoveable* property, has a right to dispose of it according to his own will. If I could venture to draw a conclusion, it would be that he is invested with the temporal right, subject to the spiritual consequences, of its exercise.

If a man has this right, why has not a woman? because, it is said, she has no more than a life interest in the property. But how is this proved? because others have an unquestionable right to it after her death. But who are these others? the *husband's remote heirs* Surely a son has a more unquestionable right to it than they, and the rights of a son in ancestorial property being unquestionable, the rights of the father are as much restricted to a life interest in it as those of a widow, and by the very same course of reasoning adopted by the learned judge the same absolute power must be conceded to or withheld from both.

But the fact is that the father's control over ancestorial property *is* restricted by positive texts, whilst that of the widow or mother is only limited by analogy and general declarations, as we trust we have satisfied our readers. On the contrary the authorities are clear and consistent with respect to a father's power, and although they do not invalidate *unequal* distribution, they declare that the gift of the *whole* is illegal and invalid. We shall cite a few of these texts.

What is bailed for delivery, what is lent for use, a

pledge, joint property, a deposit, a son, a wife, *and the whole estate of a man who has living issue*, the sages have declared unalienable, even by a man oppressed with grievous calamities, and what has been promised to another. *Nárada.**

The prohibition of giving away is declared to be eight fold, a man shall not give joint property, nor his son, nor his wife, nor a pledge, nor *all his wealth, if he have issue living. Vrihaspati.***

A wife, or a son, or *the whole of a man's estate*, shall not be given away or sold without the assent of the persons interested. *Kátyáyana.*

Joint property, deposits for use, bailments, in the form called Nyása, pledges, a wife, her property, deposits for delivery, bailments in general, and the whole of a man's estate, if he have issue alive, are things which the learned have declared unalienable even in times of distress. *Daksha.*

The ample support of those who are entitled to maintenance is rewarded, but hell is the portion of that man, whose family is afflicted with pain by his neglect. Therefore let him maintain his family with the utmost care. *Manu.****

Even those who are born or yet unborn, and they who exist in the womb, require food for subsistence;

---

* [Vyavahára Mayúkha IX, 2.]
** [F. E. Sicé, législation Hindoue. Pondichéry: 1857, p. 130.]
*** (quoted in Dáyabhága, p. 57. Cf. Man. IX, 202 and Viramitr. p. 291, v.)

the deprivation of the means of subsistence is reprehended. *Nárada*.*

We might multiply these citations abundantly, and of whatever modifications or qualifications they may be susceptible, they leave no doubt that a man has neither temporarily nor spiritually an absolute command over the whole of any description of his property: he may certainly make away with a great part of it, but there is a limit, although the learned judge thinks it difficult to assign one. That limit is an adequate provision for his family, and we can conceive no more difficulty as to the determination of this provision by the court, than there is in the ascertainment of the sum a widow is entitled to for her maintenance.

In the above texts also is to be understood the existence of no distinction between self-acquired and inherited property, and they all apply to a man's wealth generally, making it imperative upon him to secure provision for his family before he alienates even self-acquired wealth. With this reservation, he may dispose of property he has gained during his own life time, as he pleases, as according to Kátyáyana "except his whole estate and his dwelling house, what remains after the food and clothing of his family, a man may give away **." Food and clothing are however not to be understood in their literal acceptation only, but imply maintenance, as appears from other texts.

---

* [Dáyakramasangr. IV, 25.]   ** [Vyavah. May. IX, 4.]

With regard also to moveable ancestorial property, there is authority for considering that to be at the father's disposal, according to the text of Yájnavalkya: "Of precious stones, pearls and corals, the father is master of the whole, but of the whole immoveable property neither father nor grandfather is master"[*]. The text of Vishńu, however, goes further and declares that "the father and son have equal ownership in the whole of the grandfather's wealth." As however the control over moveable property, consisting at least of money or jewels, is a nullity, the distinction may be admitted, and the power if not the right of a father to dispose of such property at his pleasure is in general undisputed; at the same time it may be safely said that the alienation of this property, like that of self-acquired wealth, is only allowable after provision made for the family, and that the unequal partition of both amongst sons, which is authorised by special considerations, may be set aside, if the least favoured son can establish undeniably, that he has been deprived of a due share of his father's wealth by that father's unjust anger towards himself, or undue partiality for another son. We think the dialogue between the learned judge, and the court Pańdits on the subject quite inconclusive. It proceeds in the first place upon the inaccurate assertion of the latter, that a father may give a larger share of the ancestorial immoveable

---

[*] [quoted from the Mitákshará in the Vyavahára Mayúkha IV, 1, 5, Dáyakramasangraha, VI, 19 f., and Dáyabhága, p. 56.]

property to one son than to another, and that he may do this on account of being better satisfied with that son's conduct, of which, the learned judge observes, the father alone can judge, and that accordingly the act must be taken as proof of the equity of the preference. The first position is certainly contrary to the conclusions even of the Bengal lawyers, and the second is unfairly stated. The mere satisfaction of the father is not receivable in proof. Where all his sons have notoriously acted towards him in the like manner, and have been treated by him, during life, with no marked difference, he would not be justified in making unequal distribution; but if it could be proved in justification, that the son preferred had alone discharged his filial obligations to his father, and that his brethren had been notorious for contumaciousness, and had been known to have incurred the father's severe displeasure, the unequal partition of the father's own property should be upheld. In like manner, if the son excluded from a due share of his patrimony could shew, that he had never deserved the displeasure of his father, he would have a good right to such addition to his portion, as should provide for his support. There are other conditions, under which unequal distribution is allowable, but all are susceptible of proof, and this proof should be required, where the proportions are wholly inadequate. The mere unequal distribution of self-acquired or inherited moveable property by which one gets more and another less, but in which all are provided for, is not matter of litigation.

The learned judge states truly (p. 247), that the right to make an unequal partition of ancestorial immoveable property is unequivocally denied. He asks, 'will such a partition be valid, if made'? and he adds in the course of the chapter decisions and opinions, to shew that 'factum valet' has overcome the law, that the whole ancestorial lands were given to one son, that the illegality of the act was admitted, that it was declared to be immoral and sinful, but that having been done it was valid; and throughout the whole of the argument he evidently leans to an opinion founded on what he admits to be an absurdity, that a man may make what disposition he pleases of his property both ancestorial and self-acquired, and personal or real: a doctrine which is wholly at variance with the letter and spirit of the whole Hindu law, whether as laid down by Manu, and ancient legislators, or as expounded by modern Scholiasts. It is therefore worth while to examine this doctrine of the validity of illegal acts.

In the first place then, where is the distinction found? In the most recent commentators, and those of a peculiar province only, those of Bengal, whose explanation is founded on a general position laid down by Jímútavāhana; "therefore, since it is denied that a gift or sale should be made, the precept is infringed by making one: but the gift or transfer is not null, for a fact cannot be altered by a hundred texts."[*] This remark refers, however, to the alienation of property

---

[*] [Dáyabhága, p. 60.]

of which the aliener is undoubted proprietor, as a father, of immoveable property if self-acquired, or a coparcener of his own share before partition: but he himself concludes that a father cannot dispose of the ancestorial property, because he is not sole master of it. "Since the circumstance of the father being lord of all "the wealth is stated as a reason, and that cannot be "in regard to the grandfather's estate, an unequal dis- "tribution made by the father is lawful only in the in- "stance of his own acquired wealth." Nothing can be more clear than Jímútaváhana's assertion of this doctrine, and the doubt cast upon it by its expounders Raghunandana, Śrí Krishńa Tarkálankára and Jagannátha is wholly gratuitous. In fact the latter is chiefly to blame for the distinction between illegal, and invalid acts.

The distinction has clearly arisen from a confusion between the notion of acts, and rights: to say that an act is not altered by a hundred texts is an obvious truism, as Raghunandana illustrates it; "it is highly criminal to kill a cow; but if she be killed, the deed is done." That is incontestable, but there was no *right* to kill her, and the killer may be punished. So though a thing be immorally given, the person had no right to make the gift, and the misdemeanour must be dealt with accordingly. There arises something like a difficulty in determining who is the object of punishment. The donor is the culprit, but by revoking the gift the donee who has committed no crime is punished. Revocation of gift, however, is obviously the most ready mode of preventing such alienations, and the enforcement of this is fully justified by the sort of discretionary power confided in this case to the ruling authority, as "he who foolishly receives what is deem-"ed ungiven, and he who gives what may not be le-"gally aliened, should be punished by a king who "knows the law." *Nárada.* And "he who receives a "thing which ought not to be given, and he who be-"stows it, both these are to be punished as thieves, and "amerced in the highest penalty." *Mitákshará.* The *Vivada Chintámani, Vira Mitrodaya,* and other works of authority, declare also that illegal gifts shall be resumed.* Besides this the ruling power is specially enjoined to enforce the observance of the legal code, and of all local usages or institutes not in contradiction to that code, and it is absurd to say, therefore, that the judge is to acknowledge as valid, or to permit the validity of, that which sacred institutes and universal feeling denounce as immoral and illegal. That the practice has been authorised and decisions passed accordingly, has arisen from a mistaken delicacy as to the right of authority to interpose. The only argument of any weight adduced has been this: the law certainly prohibits the practice, but it has not provided for its prevention or punishment, and therefore being done, it must be recognised. But this is a very incorrect view of the case, and would, as observed by

---

* [Mitáksh. ad Yájn. II, 176. Vivádachint., p. 35—61. Viramitrod., f. 121 r. ff.]

Sir F. M., authorise the perpetration of a vast variety of crimes. The law has not been so improvident. It has stated what ought and what ought not to be done, and has left the enforcement of its prescriptions to the discretion of the executive power. We are confident, that the question between illegality and validity would never have been agitated under a Hindu administration.

Notwithstanding, therefore, "the right of a man to make any unequal distribution amongst his sons of *ancestorial immoveable* property seems never to have been doubted in the Supreme Court" (p. 268,) we cannot admit, that it exists, and the learned judge acknowledges that the law cannot be considered as finally settled. We cannot admit either, that the owner has more than a contingent right to make a very unequal distribution of any description of his property, without satisfactory cause. The onus of disproving such cause, it is true, rests with the plaintiff, and unless the proof were too glaring to be deniable, it would not of course be allowed to operate. We only mean to aver that it is at the discretion of the court to determine, whether an unequal distribution has been attended with such circumstances of caprice or injustice as shall authorise its revisal. It should never be forgotten in this investigation, that wills, as we understand them, are foreign to Hindu law; for there is clearly a bias in favour of full testamentary power in the practice of the Supreme Court, and in the arguments of Sir F. M., which cannot fail to introduce many innovations into the law, and many new and vexatious sources of perplexity and litigation which are unknown to the Hindus, in the unsophisticated condition of their native code. The following case was a clear violation of the law under this feeling.

Soorjeecomar left a widow, but no child; and he made a will by which all his property, consisting in part of *ancestorial immoveable* estate, was given to his brothers. By this will he had made a provision, which he considered to be a suitable one, for his widow.

The will set up was alleged to have been forged, and upon that ground alone it was contested by the widow. It was found to have been duly executed, and here the case ended.

But why should it have ended thus? The widow's advocate was not staunch to her cause, unless indeed he felt, that it was vain to dispute the determination of the court to maintain a will at all hazards. Then he acted wisely; but his prudence does not justify the sentence. Nothing is more positive in Hindu law, than that a widow shall succeed to her husband's estate, in failure of direct issue. Here is no inconsistency nor perplexity; the law is precise and positive, and yet the will of an individual is to be maintained against it; that is, he is to subvert the whole system of succession. It is a farce to say, that the Hindus have any law of inheritance, if its most unquestionable injunctions are to subsist upon the breath of individual caprice. The learned judge's reasoning here is wholly irrelevant; he observes:

If it had been established as law, that a man cannot make a gift or an unequal distribution of *ancestorial immoveable* property to the prejudice of any of his *descendants*, it might not have followed that he, being childless, would be held under the same restraint, when giving to his brothers, where the widow is to be prejudiced by the gift.

But it did not signify in this case what the property was, for whatever he might have done with it wholly or in part during life, he *could not control its disposition after his death*.

With regard to the decisions of the Sadr, we have some on both sides of the question. In that of Eshand Chand Rai *v.* Eshorchand Rai, the gift of a whole estate to an eldest son was confirmed chiefly on the doctrine that though the gift was sinful, it was not invalid; whilst in the case of Bhawanicharn Bunhoojea *v.* the heirs of Ramkant Bunhoojeea the gift of the whole of the ancestral property was declared to be invalid. The last decision was most conformable to the spirit of the law, and most consistent with the duty of the Court, empowered as that is both by common sense, and the purport of the Hindu code, to *make* that *valid* which is *legal, moral* and *right*, in the estimation of all the authorities. In our opinion this is a much more dignified course, and one which will do more to prevent litigation than that which the learned judge seems disposed to recommend, when he would wish to recognise the principle of "factum valet." He says, "this principle, whatever we may think of it, we must desire to see in the most active operation where it can be most beneficially applied"; that is, he would connive at immoral acts, if he thought they led to useful results. This is very like 'the end sanctifying the means' a principle, we trust, we shall never see introduced into English morality, nor even into English law.

We have so fully discussed the doctrine of alienation by widows that we need not advert to the cases illustrative of grants made by them. There is clearly a difference between the situation of a widow inheriting, and a father in possession, because the sons and grandsons have a direct lien upon the estate, which remote heirs have not: although, however, the law might be held to permit a widow's alienation of property to which she succeeds as heir, yet the obvious analogy of the case, and the general impression on the subject, operate to prevent her alienation of fixed property and chattels, and therefore the decisions of the Sadr Dewání in the cases of Mahoda *v.* Kalyani and others, and Vijaya Devi *v.* Annapurna Devi, may be admitted as law, the authority of the Court having been interposed, as we have recommended it should be in every case, to *make* that invalid which was considered immoral.

The next chapter treats of wills, and as the doctrine, on which the right of a Hindu to make a will has been recognised in the supreme Court, has been founded in a great measure upon the opinion of Mr. Colebrooke, we shall cite it, as quoted by Sir F. M.

Upon the right of a *Hindoo* to dispose of his property by will, I have seen the opinion of *Mr. Colebrooke*, and I need not add that there is not any man whose opinions may justly command a greater degree of deference.

He says, "According to the authorities of *Hindu* law which prevail in *Bengal*, a member of an undivided family may *give* away or *otherwise aliene* property to the extent of his *own share* of the joint wealth, and I conceive his disposal of property by will would be here maintained (I. e. within the limits of that province,) in conformity with *Jimúta Váhana's* doctrine, that the *gift or other alienation*, by an *unseparated co-heir*, may be an *immoral* act, but it is not an *invalid* one. — *Dáyabhága, Chapt. 2, Sect. 28.* — *Jagannátha's Digest. vol. 2, Pages 57 and 290.* It would be otherwise in the rest of the provinces."

Again *Mr. Colebrooke* says, "When writing a few days ago, I stated that I thought a *Hindoo's will* must be governed and controlled by the general rules concerning *gifts.* It will hold good, I think, for the same things for which a *gift* made in his life time would do so, and not otherwise. I should have added, however, that his *legacies to his family must be controlled by the rules regarding partition made by the father of* the family. The principle I would lay down is, that a man cannot confer either on a stranger, or on one of his family, *by will* (which I consider to be a donation in contemplation of death) what he could not bestow, either by deed of gift, or partition of patrimony during his life time. The utmost that can be said is, that he may do that by *will* which he could have done by *partition* or *donation* between living persons."

He proceeds, "Upon the principle which I have stated, a *Hindoo* in *Bengal* may leave by will *all his own acquisitions;* but is restricted, if he have sons, from distributing *ancestral property according to his own pleasure.* In countries, in which the doctrines of the *Mitákshará* prevail, he is restrained from giving away *immoveables,* and from making any other partition of his possessions among his male descendants, but such as the law has sanctioned; consequently, on the principle before explained, he would be restricted from distributing *immoveables* in a mode not sanctioned by law, but may dispose of *moveables,* of which the law permits him to make gifts on account of affection; not however to the amount of the whole property. If there be no *sons* or *male* descendants, and the property be not shared by a co-heir, *the whole of his pos-*

sessions, being his separate and distinct property, may be disposed of by will as he pleases." *

It would be presumption in us to say we concur with Mr. Colebrooke, and still more to dispute his doctrine, but we confess, we demur to the last clause of the above, as it might operate to the exclusion of the widow, the daughter, the daughter's son, and all the heirs who by the positive laws of inheritance succeed in default of male descendants. It may be said indeed that the question of a man's being master of his property has never been agitated, except where there are sons or grandsons, who have a part right of ownership, and that during his life he may give, or otherwise aliene it without control. In what he does, during his life, however, it may be supposed a wife exercises some influence, and may by expostulation or endearments, or by the interference of friends, escape being deprived of all share in her husband's wealth. But when he is dead, the operation of a will would be final, and in proportion as the provisions of that will are unfavourable to her acknowledged claims, so far must the deceased have exercised a power not altogether analogous to that which he enjoyed whilst alive. In addition therefore to the clause laid down by Mr. Colebrooke, that his legacies to his family *must be controlled by the rules regarding partition made by the father of the family,* we would add, *and by the estab-*

---

* [Sir T. Strange, L. l., II, p. 431. 435 ff.]

lished course of inheritance after his death. These provisions might be thought to obviate the necessity for any bequests at all, and we do not see any objection to this contingency; for the practice is an innovation in the law, a very frequent violation of it, and a constant channel for the dissipation of the greater part of the bequests in interminable and demoralizing litigation.

The Supreme Court, Sir F. M. observes, will support the devise or bequest of a Hindu, if it be made of such property as the testator could lawfully have disposed of by gift in his life time, but many considerations may influence bequests which would not have any effect upon a person, during his life, in making donations. He adds, the court never professed to go further than to permit that to be effected by will, which might have been done "inter vivos." But can a man alter during his life time the course of succession to his property after his decease? If he is allowed to do this by will; if he is allowed to bequeath to a remote kinsman that which ought after his death to go to his widow, his daughter, or his brother, he does what he could not have done during life; he defrauds them of their just rights, and the court in supporting such a will makes itself a party to the violation of the law, and infringement of the rights of individuals. We are at a loss to reconcile this confident announcement of the practice of the court with a variety of sententious positions laid down by the learned judge in various parts of his book. "I do not recommend innovation, far from it. I desire to adhere to the law in its substance, and to give to every body that which he is entitled to claim" (p. 36). "If one be entitled to the immediate, and the other to the ultimate enjoyment of property, it is reasonable and just, that they should have equal protection, according to their several rights" (p. 90). The interest of him in remainder is as well worthy of the law's protection, as the interests of him in possession (p. 97). In opposition to these texts, we have every where the greatest innovation ever made in Hindu law strenuously advocated, and the rights of heirs completely kept out of view, by the support of a power to leave away from them, what every Hindu lawgiver declares they shall inherit. It does appear to us, that there is nothing so contradictory in the Hindu code, or so inconsistent in the opinions of the Pandits, as may be found in the learned judge's notions of the rights of heirs, when a widow succeeds to the property, and when the deceased owner leaves a will.

Again, we have the following statement of the practice relating to the administration of the law by the Supreme Court.

In many instances the wills of *Hindoos* have been recognised and established in the Supreme Court.

It is *Mr. Colebrooke's* opinion that their right to dispose of their property by will is maintainable in the province of *Bengal*, in conformity with *Jimúta Váhana's* doctrine, that the gift or other alienation of property by a *Hindoo* is *not an invalid*, although it may be an *immoral*, act. In the words *"other alienation" Mr. Colebrooke* supposes alienation by *Will* to be included.

However this may be, it is certain that the Supreme Court grants probate of the wills of *Hindoos*, and administration to the next kin, when it is applied for in the case of an intestate.

We presume the learned judge prefaced this citation with the following passage for the sake of contrast, or to shew that the Supreme Court pays as much respect to acts of Parliament as to the Institutes of Manu.

The Stat. 21st, Geo. 3d, Ch. 70, provides, "That their *Inheritance* and *succession to lands, rents and goods*, and all matters of contract and dealing, between party and party, shall be determined in the case of *Mahomedans* by the laws and usages of *Mahomedans*, and in the case of *Gentoos* by the laws and usages of *Gentoos*.

The determination of the Supreme Court to uphold the wills of the Hindus is, we observe from the acts of the court, very oddly evinced, and the disposition, if not to set them aside, to tamper with them, and re-model them, is singularly conspicuous. Now the Hindus are to make wills, or they are not. If they are to exercise this power, their bequests are to be fulfilled. If they are not, why deceive a dying man with an erroneous impression? for how their wills have been fulfilled, the following cases will shew.

Goculchunder Corformah left all his property, with the exception of a bequest to his step-mother, to the family idol. The will, with that exception, was declared *wholly inoperative*.

Goculchunder Mitter devised that his heirs should succeed conjointly to his estate, and should never have the power to divide, and share the same.

Partition was decreed by the court.

In the will of Nemychurn Mullick it was directed, that the bulk of the family property should remain joint undivided family property under the management of the two elder brothers.

On an appeal to the King in Council, it was ordered, that partition should be made, and the property held in severalty.

In the will of Luckinarain Tagore, as we have seen, the deceased made the concurrence of two of his widows essential to the choice of an adopted son.

The court committed that election to *one* of the widows, and because, they inferred, *she had been her husband's favorite.*

The will of Raja Nobkissen was set aside in favour of an agreement *previously* granted by him, relating to the same purpose, the share of his adopted son, which the will professed to render less than the agreement.

In his will Jugut Adio directed his property to be equally divided, in absolute ownership, between his widow and his son.

The court ordered that the widow's right to her moiety should be that of *a life interest only.*

Now in some of these revisals we do not mean to question the wisdom, or the benevolence of the court; but it is obvious, that such intermeddling with the intentions of the testator is far from compatible with the spirit of the English law, which provides that "the construction be favourable, and as near the minds and apparent intents of the parties as the rules of the law will admit", and that when "the words offer no ambiguity there shall "be no interpretation contrary to their literal import." As to Hindu law, the whole proceeding is an anomaly. The learned Judge would seem to infer the legality of wills in the estimation of Hindus themselves, because very frequently the right of the testator to make particular bequests is not disputed; but we think, this is a very unsatisfactory proof of the legality of the document in Hindu law, although it exhibits a sensible acquiescence in the decisions of the court in which the cause is to be adjudged. The parties forbear to dispute the force of the will, because they know it will be in vain: they are informed, that the court is determined to uphold wills, whatever it may do with their clauses, and therefore very prudently submit to what they cannot help. But let it be understood that the court will receive arguments against the validity of wills, and there will be no lack of objectors nor objections. That they are often gross violations of Hindu law, the learned judge is compelled to admit: thus he says of the will of Sonatun Mullik, "*if it had not been for that will*, it is clear that Bidyamani (his widow) would have been entitled to the whole of his estate for her life, and that after her death it would have gone to her daughters" (p .366), and he observes of another case, "From this state of the family, if Joogul Kishore had died intestate, it is quite clear that his son Nundololl would have succeeded him", instead of which an only son, the undisputed heir of his father's whole property, was restricted to half. As to the intricate and unreasonable enravelments to which the wills of Hindus lead, we have abundant proofs of them in the two cases of Hura Sundari and Lukhinarain Thagore, which we have cited from the pages of the learned judge: and under a conviction, that wills are in the present constitution of Hindu society a mischievous innovation, we rather lament the determination of the Supreme Court to uphold the practice: at any rate, if still permitted, we think, that clear and positive rules should be laid down for their construction, and that none should be capable of being proved which are manifestly incompatible with the provisions of the Hindu law.

The next chapter treats of *contracts* and is made up almost entirely of the reprint of the texts collected in Jagannátha's Digest, translated by Mr. Colebrooke. We shall transcribe the concluding remarks as explanatory of the learned judge's object, and as vindicatory of a part of the Hindu code, at least, from the reproaches of absurdity and inconsistency so abundantly charged against it in other parts of the volume.

> Although it is declared by statute, that all matters of contract and dealing, between parties, shall be determined in the case of *Hindoos* by the laws and usages of *Hindoos*, I never knew, or heard of, an instance in which the Supreme Court was called upon in a case of contract to decide by such laws and usages. I did not, therefore, consider a chapter upon contracts to be *necessary* in this work, but I conceive that the texts which I have collected, and brought together, will be thought interesting and curious.

Those who may take the trouble of reading *Jagannátha's* commentaries upon this particular subject, will wonder perhaps, at the indefatigable industry with which he has endeavoured to make simplicity complex, and to render that which is obvious *unintelligible*.

I have merely given some of the leading texts which relate to the law of contracts, and to my mind the system (generally speaking) appears to be rational and moral. No less moral, and possibly more rational, because it is, in a great degree, abstracted from the *Hindoo* religion, and dependent upon ethics alone; upon principles which are universally admitted, which are immutable in themselves, and which cannot but be eternal in their duration.

Whatever may be said by metaphysicians of the moral sense, it is plain that good faith and fair dealing are required by the Institutes of all civilized people; and although there are offices, the performance of which must depend upon the feelings and the consciences of individuals—although duties must still be distinguished by those of perfect, and those of imperfect, obligation; honesty and rectitude are enforced in all civil politics, if they can be enforced by a legislative sanction.

The merit of having been founders of their jurisprudence cannot be denied to this people; and those, who are at all conversant with the decisions of our own Courts, will acknowledge the analogy which exists between some of their doctrines, and some of the texts which I have cited from the *Hindoo* law. Where this is not to be found, a comparison may, in several instances, be made without disadvantage to the *Hindoos*.

But I must restrain myself, for it is not my purpose to run into a dissertation.

There are certainly extravagancies, although I have not brought them forward, even in this part of the system; but if a prevalence of common sense is to be discovered in the laws of the Hindoos, it must be sought for in that portion of them, containing the precepts by which dealings between one man and another are to be regulated.

The next two chapters on *judicial proceedings* and *evidence* are translations, by Mr. W. H. Macnaghten, of the two first sections of the Mitákshará. That they are highly valuable, the merits of the original and learning of the translator are sufficient guarantees: they are rather however part of the text than considerations on the law. We should wish to see the rest of the Vyavahára portion of the Mitákshará translated by the same hand and published entire, for as given by Sir F. M. it has lost much of its value by compression. It is unnecessary for us to offer any detailed comments upon this part of the publication, as the law there laid down is not reduced to practice, and is so far matter rather of curiosity than use; at the same time, the Hindu System is to be regarded as a whole to be properly appreciated, and the laws of inheritance can scarcely be thoroughly understood without acquaintance with other and, in appearance, remotely connected branches of law. For this reason the institutes of Manu are particularly valuable, and the chapter of the Mitákshará on the Áchára or daily rites, and usages, would equally contribute to the illustration of the parts by conveying a view of the whole. We think the work of the learned judge has been less satisfactory than it might have been, in consequence of his enquiries having confined him to a partial investigation of the subject. There are two topics also, upon which we regret the learned judge should have abstained from offering any opinion, particularly as there is no doubt that they have a practical bearing; these are, title from possession, and the rules of evidence, at least as far as the administration of an oath is concerned: this latter we know to be a daily question of painful interest, and the other we observe from a case recorded by the learned judge has been made the subject of discussion in the Sadr Dewání. In the absence of any remarks from the learned judge we shall offer a few observations on what we conceive of the law as it appears in the translated chapters of the Mitákshará, and other authorities.

In the case of Bhawanicharn Banerjea, and the heirs of Ramkant Bunhojea (p. 283), a deed of partition was declared by the judge to be invalid, because possession was not actually taken; the elder son having instituted a suit to disprove the legality of the apportionment.

The deed was invalid on other grounds, as we have had occasion to observe; but the two Pańdits Chaturbhuj, and Śubha Śástrí, two of the ablest Pańdits we have encountered, disagreed with regard to the effects of actual possession. The former stated that the Hissanáma could not be available without possession, and Śubha Śástrí urged much more rationally that the gift was valid though possession was not taken, as that, being obstructed by the suit instituted by the plaintiff, argued no neglect nor relinquishment of right on the part of the defendants. We have no doubt of the correctness of his conclusion according to Hindu law.

Possession is in Hindu law, as well as in English, a very substantial title, no doubt; but Chaturbhuj himself admits that, to become a valid one, it must be in sight of the adverse party, and without molestation on his part, and that even possession for three generations is not sufficient, if not in sight of the adverse party, and with his acquiescence. Upon his own shewing, therefore, mere possession does not constitute right. One would think the converse of this must naturally follow, and that the absence of possession could not invalidate what its presence could not bestow. No, this would not have answered his object, and therefore he proceeds, "a title-deed *unaccompanied by possession* must be disallowed as evidence of right." Where did he find this to be the law?

In Mr. Macnaghten's translation from the Mitákshará we find "Loss accrues to him, who for twenty years observes his land enjoyed by another *without interfering*, and in the case of moveable property for ten years."* In such a case it would be reasonable, certainly, to infer relinquishment of right or defect of title; but this is very different from the delay of possession arising out of a *disputed claim*. Even in such case, however, it would appear that, if right could be ultimately established, it might be claimed; for no length of enjoyment, without title, can constitute property, as "He who *enjoys without right*,"** even for many hundred years, the ruler of the earth should inflict on that sinner the punishment of a thief" (p. 424).

At the same time it may be admitted, as the Mitákshará argues, that there may be some difficulty in

---

* [ad Yájn. II, 27.]
** [अन्यायेन Mit. l. 1.]

reconciling these texts, and although in the latter case a right is not created, yet it is forfeited by long protracted neglect, unless adequate cause be shewn; as, supposing the parties to be minors or incapable of acting for themselves, or to have been absent from the country, then the property is open to recovery, otherwise a certain period, that of three uninterrupted descents, for example, is sufficient to confirm the right of a fourth, although he have no better title to produce. This applies to fixed property; in the case of moveables the term will be limited by their nature, the difficulty of their recovery, and their liability to decay.

The main arguments in favour of the necessity of possession are the following:

"What is obtained by partition, purchase, or inheritance, or what is received from a king, is secured by possession, and lost by neglect." *Vrihaspati.*— "Ownership lost by neglect is not resumable at will." —*Dáyatattwa.* "Possession without a deed, and not a deed without possession, but proof is firmly established by the union of both."—*Brahma Sanhitá.* "A title to land *may be* established by possession alone, or by an incontrovertible deed, if it is established by the concurrence of both, no otherwise."—*Vrihaspati Sanhitá.* All this, however, only proves, that *wilful neglect* may forfeit right, and that title-deeds and actual possession confirm each other.

The strongest text, however, is that of Náruda: "Though there be a writing, though there be living witnesses, yet in the matter of immoveables especially, such as is not possessed is not confirmed."* Not *Sthira* stable, firm. The purport of this law turns very much on the meaning of the word *Sthira*, and in its most obvious acceptation is does not mean that the right is lost; but that it is less secure, writings and witnesses being proofs of an inferior description to possession. That the latter does not convey right, the same authority positively declares, "Nárada has said, possession with a clear title, affords evidence, but possession constitutes no evidence if unaccompanied by a clear title"** (p. 430): this must be understood, it is true, of the first acquirer of property; but it leaves no doubt of the real intentions of the lawgiver.

Again we have a text from Yájnavalkya:*** "A deed is not strong where there is not a little possession"; but what does this imply? The title requires one of its conditions to be rendered indisputable. This being wanting, it is so far weak. Mr. Macnaghten translates this "where there is not the least possession, "there a title is not sufficient"; but this *might* be understood to signify what the law does not propose, the text being literally as we have given it, and being

---

* [Viramitr., 65 r., 4.]
** [Mitáksh. ad Yájn. II. 27. Viramitr., 63 r., 3. Vyav. May. II, 2, 1.]
*** [जानमे ऽपि मवत् नैव भुमि: कोकाऽपि यत्र नो । Yájn. II, 27. "acquisition by title is of no avail without possession for a short time." Dr. Röer's translation.]

explained by the commentator that "the strength in the deed is not entire." The same indeed with its context explains clearly its purport; the author states that "deeds, witnesses, and possession are the three kinds of proof; that deeds are of more weight than possession, except where possession has been hereditary; and that deeds are weak where there is no possession whatever." That is, the commentator observes, of three persons the first may plead the deed of gift, and the last may urge possession; the second may plead the gift, and the 'little' possession, the family has had of it. The term 'little' here, although literal, is therefore to be understood in the sense of 'limited' and as applied to individuals, or to time, not to a portion of the thing possessed. The Vyavahára Mátriká, however, argues upon the literal sense, and concludes that, "as the law declares the occupation of a part of a field &c. granted by a royal edict to be the virtual occupation of the whole, so the possession of no part is the relinquishment of the whole", founding this on one of the above cited texts, that the neglect of fixed property is its relinquishment. This conclusion, however, implies voluntary indifference or abandonment, and does not regard the delay of possession occasioned by adequate cause.

It is, therefore, in our estimation quite clear, that the Hindu law and common sense go hand in hand. A man may forego his rights, if he pleases, and any capricious abandonment of them for an unreasonable time is to be punished by their forfeiture. But he is not to be deprived of what is really his, because legal proceedings, interested opposition, accident, distance or disease, debar him from taking possession of it when it first becomes his due.

The other question which calls for a few observations is the practice observed in the courts, of taking evidence upon oath: the usual form is that of placing a copper vessel of Ganges water with a leaf of the *Tulasí* plant in it in one hand, whilst the witness touches the water with the other, and utters the following or similar declarations.

"Having touched Gangá water, copper, and Tulasí, I swear that I will truly answer the questions put to me: if I utter untruth, may I perish in a future life", or "may I perish both in this world and the next."

Popular feeling in Bengal is decidedly hostile to this practice, and it is considered highly disreputable to have taken such an oath. The disgrace attaches to a man through life, and is made a serious subject of reproach, even by his friends and connexions. Accordingly, no man who has any regard for his character will enter a court of Justice, if he can possibly avoid it, and few decent individuals will subpœna respectable witnesses, however essential to their cause; they will rather pay high and multiply the false testimony, that is to be had for hire. When subpœnaed, a man of any reputation is painfully distressed, and he secretes himself or flies beyond the jurisdiction of the court, until the suit is decided. These circumstances are too notorious to be questioned, and it can be as little doubted that they are unfavourable to the ends of Justice, as they banish from the court the only individuals from whom veracity might be expected.

The objections of the people are so far well founded, that the practice does not appear to be authorised by any of the works *on law*, ancient or modern; the provisions of which in the first stage of investigation at least are summed up in the following translation from the Mitákshará (p. 447):*

Manu has propounded a rule to be observed in taking the depositions of *Brahmins* and others. "Let the Judge imprecate a priest by his veracity; a soldier by his horse, elephant, and weapons; a merchant by his kine, grain, and gold; a mechanic, or servile man, by imprecating on his own head, if he speaks falsely, all possible crimes." The meaning is, he shall adjure the *Brahmin* by saying, if you speak falsely, your truth will be destroyed; a *Kshatriya* by saying, your horse, elephant, weapons, will become useless; a *Vaisya*, your cattle, seeds, and gold, will be unproductive; a *Súdra*, if you speak falsely, all sins will be on your head.

"Regenerate men, who tend herds of cattle, who trade, who practise mechanical arts, who profess dancing and singing, who are hired servants, or usurers, let the Judge exhort and examine, as if they were Súdras."

The Vyavahára Mayúkha** adds this text from *Vrihaspati:* "Truth, carriage, arms, kine, seed, and gold, the feet of gods, and Brahmans, the head of a wife or of a child, these are declared to be oaths of efficacy in matters of minor concern, but in oaths of

---

* [Man., VIII, 113. 102.]
** [III, 3. Vyavahára Tattwa, 57. Víramitr. 68, v., 12.]

the highest importance the truth must be established by ordeal." The Ordeal is of five kinds,—scales, water, fire, poison and sacred libation. An interesting account of each is to be found in the Asiatic Researches (vol. I.),* but in no stage of the evidence is touching the Ganges water or any other sacred object made a test of the truth of evidence by any legal authorities.

As however the practice was introduced throughout all the courts, both civil and military, under the British Government, it is impossible to suppose that the measure was adopted without due enquiry, or that it was an innovation unwarranted by the code or customs of the country: accordingly it may be defended by the practice of the act, as alluded to in the Puránas and Tantras, and by local usages.

In the villages of Bengal, in the case of private disputes or arbitrations, the feet of a Brahman or the head of a child are the most usual attestations of assertion; the same are commonly referred to in the western provinces. But the sacred poems, the Tulasí leaf, Sálagrám stone, Gangá water, and even spirituous liquors, are in more extensive use, and they are not unusual though less frequent in Bengal; the practice is therefore perfectly consistent with the customs of the country.

In the Tantras, *Siva* appeals to the Gangá, which is supposed to flow from his head in proof of his asser-

---

* [See also Stenzler, "die indischen Gottesurtheile", in Zeitschrift der d. morgenl. Ges., IX, 661-82.]

tion. Thus he observes: "How is it possible to doubt the truth of my words when uttered in contact with the Ganges, the Snake, and the Bull?"

The chief authority for the practice is, however, the Brahma Vaivartta Purāña, and this declares various hells to be the portion of those who utter untruth after touching the Sálagrám, the Tulasí, or the Gangá.

"Whoever, having taken the Tulasí leaf in his hand, "does not adhere to his engagement, is punished in "the hell *Kálasútra*, as long as the Sun and Moon "endure. Whoever takes a false oath by the Tulasí "leaf, is sentenced to the *Kumbhipáka* hell for the "reigns of fourteen Indras. Whoever, holding the "Sálagrám stone, utters a lie, suffers in the *Kúrma-*"*danshtra* hell for the life of Brahma. Whoever touch-"ing the Sálagrám stone breaks his promise, is con-"signed to the *Asipatra* hell for a hundred thousand "Manvantaras."

"Having heard the words of Brahma, the lord of " wisdom, the chief of the wise took the water of the "Gangá in his hand, and pledged his faith: if any one, "having touched the water of the Ganges, utters a "false assertion, he is punished in the Kálasútra hell "during the existence of Brahma."

These texts therefore shew that the practice was no innovation, and their authority, although not law, will scarcely be denied by any class of Hindus. At the same time, they are really very worthless, and apply to a state of things wholly foreign to the primitive systems both of religion and law. The Tantras are the authorities of the worshippers of Śiva and Śakti; the Brahma Vaivartta is a decided Vaishṅava work. Most of the Tantras are modern, and the Brahma Vaivartta is of very recent date, being a collection of absurd legends relating to Krishña and Rádhá, objects of veneration as conjoined not more than four or five centuries old. Under any circumstances, the Tantras and Puráṅas cannot be received in opposition to the Śruti and Smṛiti, the religious and legal codes, and in this instance the individual works appealed to are of the worst description. Although, therefore, there is authority for the form of oath administered by the English courts to Hindu witnesses, it is still unquestionably foreign to the spirit of the law, neither does it derive any weight from being a rite of popular practice, for its observance chiefly prevails amongst the inferior castes, and rather loses than gains respectability from its popular adoption. We should therefore wish to see some other system introduced, and are confident that, wherever the form was objected to, a simple affirmation subject to the penalty of perjury would be much more conducive to the ends of public justice than the existing usage.

The importance of the subject must plead our excuse for devoting so large a portion of our pages to the examination of this work: we now take leave of it. Upon the whole we cannot deny the general utility of the Considerations on Hindu Law, and in the information it unfolds of the objects and practice of the Supreme Court it will be a most serviceable record:

at the same time it will not answer the purpose of its publication, as the conclusions are too loose, and, as we have presumed to argue, are in many instances too inaccurate to entitle it to become a safe and sure guide in matters of Hindu law. The utility of the work is also much impaired by the utter want of arrangement which prevails throughout, and for which the learned judge pleads in extenuation the haste with which the work was put together, as we have cited his apologies to prove. But what occasion was there for so much precipitancy? Why could not the materials have been taken home, and digested by the learned Judge in the *otium cum dignitate*, he is about to enjoy? We might then have had a work worthy of his known powers and long experience, and which would have entitled Sir F. Macnaghten to the permanent gratitude of the profession, and of the public.

XII.

REVIEW
of
BHAGAVAD GITA,
id est
ΘΕΣΠΕΣΙΟΝ ΜΕΛΟΣ,

sive Almi Krishnæ et Arjunæ Colloquium de Rebus divinis Bharatæ Episodium. Textum recensuit et interpretationem latinam adjecit AUGUSTUS GUILIELMUS SCHLEGEL.

BONN (1823), 1 vol. 8vo.

From the Oriental Quarterly Review. Calc. 1825. Vol. III, p. 1-51.

THE cultivation of Sanskrit by the Scholars of the Continent is no pretended nor unprofitable pursuit: they have not engaged in it merely to acquire the repute of mastering a venerable and difficult language, or to familiarise themselves with a new branch of literature for their private gratification, but they have come forward to exhibit public proofs of their proficiency, and have enriched the community of letters with the spoils of individual research. Amongst the foremost is AUGUSTUS WILLIAM SCHLEGEL, a name long known in the highest departments of literature, and one particularly dear to Englishmen, as that of the enthusiastic and able commentator of Shakespeare.

To an almost universal conversancy with the languages of ancient and modern Europe, Schlegel has superadded a very extensive knowledge of the Sanskrit language, proofs of which attainment have been for some time before the public, in his Indische Bibliothek, particularly in his elaborate and masterly review of Wilson's Sanskrit Dictionary. He has however now adduced one still more convincing in his edition of the text of the Bhagavad Gítá with a Latin translation and critical annotations, and he is about to furnish still more ample testimony in the text and translation of the Rámáyaña. How far he is equal to this latter undertaking may be inferred from the success of the present, of which we shall proceed to offer some account. The learned translator has a right to demand this at our hands, as the worthy rival of our countrymen in a path they have hitherto almost monopolised: the monopoly is theirs no longer, and Frank, Bopp, Chezy, and Schlegel have all preferred respectable claims to participation in the walk of Sanskrit literature; claims which it is to be hoped will only serve to animate our zeal, and urge us to prove that we have not been indebted for distinction only to the absence of competitors.

The first object of Schlegel, in publishing the Bhagavad Gítá, was the wish to employ in a becoming manner the fount of Nágarí types presented by the King of Prussia to the university of Bonn. This fount was executed at Paris under the professor's inspection, and is a creditable specimen of typographic art. We are not disposed, however, to admire exceedingly the forms of the letters: the vowels, which occur above and below the lines, are inelegantly engraved and clumsily connected, many of the conjunct consonants are much too slight, and the heads of the letters are too square. Such as they are however, the characters are neatly executed, and, with the advantage of Europe ink and printing, make the handsomest book, except the Nalus of Bopp, which has yet been published in the sacred language of the Hindus.

The text of the Gítá has been printed from a copy made by Schlegel himself from four Manuscripts in the Royal Library at Paris; three of these were described by Hamilton in his catalogue, the fourth is a recent addition from the collection of Col. Polier. Schlegel's copy was also compared with the Calcutta Edition of 1808, which it appears is no longer procurable even in England, and which Schlegel obtained from a friend. The text now printed, it must be admitted, is singularly correct, much more so than that of the Calcutta edition: a circumstance not very surprising, however, as the latter was the work of Native Editors without any assistance from European superintendance.

Of the translation we shall speak in detail, and shall particularise such passages, as seem to be erroneously rendered. In doing this, however, we must observe that particular exceptions are not to be regarded as detracting from the merits of the whole: on the contrary, as the objections are almost entirely verbal, and few mistakes or misconceptions of any moment occur, the necessity of seeking for blemishes in matters of so little moment is the highest compliment that can be paid to the accuracy and knowledge of the translator.

That the translation made by Mr. Wilkins in 1787 was of essential service to the present translator is fully acknowledged by him. "In interpretatione Bhagavad Gitæ elaboranda interpretationem v. cl. Caroli Wilkins magno mihi adjumento fuisse, non modo non diffiteor, sed ultro gratoque animo id agnosco:" he adds however, what is correct, that he has occasionally deviated from the steps of his predecessor, and that, if the original translator were now to revise his performance, he would no doubt authorise such deviations. In this we are disposed to concur with him, as there are several passages in Wilkins's translation, which might be amended; on the whole however it is very correctly executed, and with reference to the early period of Sanskrit study, at which it was accomplished, and the absence of all assistance from Grammars and Dictionaries, a publication of singular merit. Some of Schlegel's variations are very justifiable, and he might have made them more numerous still, as we think in some places he has been misled by the English version. Occasionally, however, his variations are not warranted by the text, as we shall have occasion to observe.

The Bhagavad Gítá, as is well known, is a treatise on theology, communicated by Krishńa to his friend and pupil Arjuna during a short suspension of the engagement between the Pándava and Kuru armies. It is a section of the Mahábhárata and, as observed by Schlegel, is proved by the concurrence of the Parisian manuscripts, the printed text of Calcutta, and the translation of Wilkins, to be a genuine and unadulterated work. Schlegel and Wilkins both regard it as a composition of high antiquity; but this requires proof. We may admit with the former, that the origin of philosophy amongst the Hindus is remote, "sine dubio valde antiqua fuit apud Indos philosophiæ origo", and that the Brahmans of India investigated subjects of theological philosophy long before Plato or Pythagoras; but, upon examining the doctrines of the Bhagavad Gítá, we shall find many as foreign to the theology of the Vedas as to philosophical speculation, and indicative of a deviation from the primitive system, which we shrewdly suspect is the work of a comparatively recent date.

The original Hindu system comprised a two-fold division, and inculcated the worship of the minor deities by works, or sacrifice, gifts, and penance, and the knowledge of the great universal spirit by abstract and secluded meditation. These two divisions were not incompatible: works were proper for men engaged in active life, and who had to discharge the positive duties of their caste and condition. But when they arrived at an age, at which they could no longer take a useful share in social pursuits, it was enjoined them to leave the world, and in the silence and solitude of the hermitage to devote themselves to the cultivation of divine knowledge, performing in the first stage of this course the essential ceremonies, but finally depositing, as it is quaintly expressed, the holy fires in the mind, or discarding further attention to the ceremonial offices of religion. With the natural tendency of enthusiasm it soon happened, that the period of seclusion was accelerated, and men adopting the notion, that works were altogether unworthy of human attention, deserted their active duties for ascetic contemplation. It may be doubted, however, whether this was the spirit of the Vedas,* and it may be most probably referred to a period subsequent to those works, prior however to the Grecian invasion; for at that time a number of sects were already in existence, as the Gymnosophists, Sarmanes or Germanes, and Hylobii, all of the ascetic class.

---

* Manu permits the householder to become a Sannyási at once, or to pass over the intermediate stage of the hermit with attention to ceremonies. His commentator adds, a Brahman may proceed from the *first order*, or the student, to the state of a Sannyási, but this is quite at variance with the text, which declares that, if a Brahman have not read the Vedas, begotten a Son, and performed sacrifices, and yet aim at final beatitude, he shall sink to a place of degradation. These are called the three debts—to the sages, the manes, and the gods; and it is repeatedly declared that the man who has not acquitted himself of those obligations shall not pretend to supreme felicity, or to divine wisdom derived from contemplative devotion. The text is therefore entirely consistent with the old system: the comment interpolates more modern ideas.—Manu, Ch. vi, v. 25. 35. 38; also 94. 95. [Lassen, I, 580.]

In compliance with the purport of the Vedas, the Vedánta philosophy, though it did not prohibit works, countenanced them only so far as they prepared the soul for that state, in which it should be capable of acquiring divine knowledge, and when purified from all mundane illusion it might be fit to recognise its identity with the Supreme. The union with the supreme spirit resulting from this identification, and the consequent exemption from returning to any human form, are, according to the Vedánta, attainable by divine knowledge alone, and at all events, such knowledge being attained, the performance of rites and the observance of ceremonies became objects of comparative indifference, as*—"If purificatory rites be considered essential, (it may be said) they are indifferent, for if Janaka and others observed rites and ceremonies, yet wise men have offered no sacrifice with fire", *Brahma Sútra* 3, 4, 9. And the doctrine was further extended to the neglect of all instituted observances whatever: "If it be said, the attainment of (divine) knowledge cannot be without the observance of the stated orders, (as student &c. and the ceremonies incident to caste,) that is not the case—it may be attained in them, that is obvious: but it may be attained out of them, as well as in them, as was seen with Raikka and others, and it is also confirmed by the law, for

---

* आचारद्धर्ममादिति वैमुख्यं तु दर्शनं जनकादेर्वचा कर्मीचारद्धर्म कम् । विद्ववितःयमिवितं न तु हवाविश्विरे. [The author has omitted to mention, which of the many commentaries on the Brahma Sútras he follows in these quotations. It is not Śankara's.]

the sacred codes relate that Samwartta and others, belonging to no instituted order, attained perfection." Ibid. 3, 4, 36.* Passages from the Upanishads also may be adduced, undervaluing the ritual. "Nothing obtained through perishable means can be eternal, hence what use of rites?" "Neither can he (the Supreme) be conceived by the help of austerities or religious rites." "All votaries who repose on God alone their firm belief, originating from a knowledge of the Vedánta, and who by forsaking religious rites obtain purification, being continually occupied in divine reflections during life, are at the time of death entirely freed from ignorance, and absorbed into God. "*Muńdaka Upanishad,*** *translated by Rammohun Roy.*"

In permitting however the practice of the ritual, even after divine knowledge is obtained, the Vedánta makes a wide distinction between its ceremonies, and positively interdicts all those performed for any particular objects, as sacrifices supposed to be the means of obtaining power, wealth, progeny, and other worldly goods: the only works authorized are the Nitya and Naimittika, the constant and occasional rites incumbent on every order of Hindus, as the daily Sandhyas, oblations with fire, and libations to the manes. In these also the performer must propose to himself no

---

* यथानाअभिवां सर्वथा विद्यानधिकार इति वेद । वजरा-
द्यापि तु तनूहे: । शावमनन्तराद्विनाथि च ज्ञानं जात । ऐकान्तिकदुर्ब-
नादूपि च अर्बति । अज्ञानन्ने ब्रह्मसंकादीनां विचिन्तुनो कर्बति ।
** [III, 1, 8. 2, 6.]

benefit, and must observe them merely in conformity to the directions of the Sástras. With such a reservation, recommendation of the observance of certain ceremonies is not unfrequently urged. "Those rites, the prescription of which wise men found in the Vedas, are truly the means of producing good consequences." *Muṇḍaka Upan.* "All acts are to be regarded, before knowledge is obtained, for the purification of the intellect, as a steed to convey a traveller to his home." *Brahma Sútra.**

"The duties of the order are to be discharged, according to the text: that is, it is said in the Kaushárava—Beholding this as himself, let him perform rites without hesitation,"** meaning that the individual, possessed of divine knowledge, shall discharge the duties of his order, not those which do not appertain to his caste." *Ibid.*—The work we are about to examine also admits, though rather reluctantly, the superiority of divine knowledge and contemplative exercise over works and faith. Thus Arjuna is directed to fix his mind on Kŕishńa: if he cannot do that at once, he must endeavour to effect it by practice; if that is above his strength, he is to perform works, abandoning their fruit; and if that is still too great an effort, he is to put his trust in Kŕishńa. The subsequent

---

* सर्वापेक्षा च यज्ञादिश्रुतेरश्ववत्. [III, 4, 26.]

** विहितत्वाच्चाश्रमकर्मापि । ३२ । पक्षाश्रमसामान्यं पुर्व्वात्कर्म्मीति शिवारमयुक्ता विहितत्वाद्वाश्रमकर्म्म अपि नामर्ष्यक्त च कर्म्म त्यागी कुर्व्वात ।

passage in a great manner disarranges this series, but the scope of the section corroborates its tenor, and it harmonises with the general spirit of Hindu theology.

It may therefore be concluded, that the Vedánta philosophy, although it places the ritual as subordinate to divine knowledge, rather inclines to the performance of disinterested acts of devotion, and recommends those ceremonies, which propose no particular fruit to the performer. This is not the case with some other philosophical divisions of the Hindus, and as observed in the Gítá, "some learned men have taught that acts should be shunned as faulty." *Lect.* 18, 8.*
This, as *Sankara* and *Srídhara Swámí* observe, refers particularly to the Sánhhyas, who object to all the sacrificial ceremonial of the Vedas, and declare that all acts are to be relinquished: although, however condemning the ritual of the Vedas as sanguinary and futile, the Sánkhyas do not exclude all attention to outward observances, and they enjoin particular postures, modes of breathing, and looking, which they profess contribute to constrain the wanderings of the spirit, and force it into a conjunction with its primitive source.

These practices are properly the invention of a different School, the Pátanjala, in which in like manner they are substitutes for the ceremonies of the Vedas. They effect the *Yoga*, or Union of the individualised with the universal spirit, and hence the system by

---

* ताज्व हेयमदिशेषे कर्म प्राज्ञमनीषिण: ।

which they are inculcated is called the Yoga Śástra. The like identification, however, or consequent exemption from transmigration, is the great object of all the philosophical sects, and the term is, therefore, familiar to them, as well as to that to which it is particularly applied. They have also adopted more or less extensively the ceremonial of the yoga, or the contrivances by which intellectual aberration is to be restrained, and the mind forced into exclusive meditation on spirit. In this light the Bhagavad Gítá is a Yoga work, and the different divisions treat of various kinds of *Yoga*, or the various means by which union with the supreme spirit is to be attained.

Whether the ritual of the Vedas be observed or not, there is no reason to conclude, that either the Sánkhya or the Vedánta School admits the compatibility of divine knowledge with the discharge of active social duties. Up to the period of seclusion, the student or the householder may be preparing himself by a tranquillised mind, and indifference to the objects of human solicitude, for that perfect calm in which knowledge is alone attainable, but it is not possible that a man engaged in worldly occupations should accomplish the requisite condition of quiescence. Hence the institution of the different degrees or áśramas, and particularly those of the Vánaprastha and Bhikshuka, or Hermit and Beggar, as indispensable stages in the scale of perfection.

In the course of time it was probably found, either that the encouragement given to ascetic devotion was injurious to social happiness, or that it was considered an unfair monopoly of emancipation, and a kind of compromise was admitted, by which the acquisition of divine knowledge should be placed within the reach of all whom it was worth while to conciliate. Hence the practice of mortification and penance came to be discountenanced,* and the discharge of social duties according to station and caste of the individual to be insisted on, at the same time that emancipation was pursued. Indifference to the result was all that was stipulated for: men were to adore, as Epicurus worshipped, nulla spe, nullo pretio inductus: the doctrine of the Vedas, that those works especially which propose some benefit should be abandoned, was strained into the position that no works should be abandoned, but that the fruit or consequence of all should be disregarded, and that this disregard of consequences was alone the real abandonment of works.** This principle

---

* In the Gítá the practisers of austere penance and mortifications are denounced as followers of a demoniac faith.
अशास्त्रविहितं घोरं तप्यन्ते ये तपो जनाः। दम्भाहंकारसंयुक्ताः कामरागबलान्विताः॥ कर्षयन्तः शरीरस्थं भूतग्राममचेतसः। मां चैवान्तःशरीरस्थं तान् विद्ध्यासुरनिश्चयान्॥
Those men who, filled with pride and hypocrisy, perform horrid penance, undirected by the ritual, and characterised by violence, passion and desire, are fools who torment the aggregated elementary essence of the body, and me who am present in it; know them to put their faith in fiends. 17, 5. 6.

** सर्वकर्मफलत्यागं प्राहुस्त्यागं विचक्षणाः: 18, 2. The wise declare the abandonment of fruits to be abandonment. यज्ञार्थात् कर्मणोऽन्यत्र कर्म करोति यः। स संन्यासी च योगी च न निरग्निर्न

was applied not only to the ceremonial of religion, but to the duties of origin and profession, and even to the faculties and organs of the body.* In this enlarged interpretation of the doctrine of the Vedas the Puránas were chiefly instrumental, and amongst the principal agents was the Mahúbhárata or at least the Bhagavad Gítá.

The doctrine thus promulgated might be considered to deviate from the original faith only as far as the interpretation was questionable. It was still founded on the text of the Vedas, and might be held by some interpreters to be no more than what was fully warranted by those works. The Puráńas, however, did not stop here: they superadded a dogma wholly at variance with the spirit and letter of the Vedas when they made Faith—implicit reliance on any one deity —sufficient for emancipation. In this new sentiment the Bhagavad Gítá stands pre-eminent, and it is re-

---

वाचिन्न: 6, 1. He who performs proper acts without regard to the consequences of acts, is the real Sannyási and Yogí, not he who is without a sacred fire or abstains from acts.

* यज्ञदानतप:कर्म न त्याज्यं कार्यमेव तत् Sacrifice, alms and penance are acts never to be relinquished, but to be performed. 18, 5.

ते ते कर्मन्यभिरत: संसिद्धिं लभते नर: A man attains perfection by the diligent discharge of his peculiar duty. [18, 45.]

बाधैन मनसा शुद्धा चैवमेरिन्दियैरपि । योगिन: कर्म कुर्वन्ति सङ्गं त्यक्का त्मशुद्धये ॥

The adepts perform acts in body, heart, and mind, and with the simple organs, for the purification of the spirit, abandoning desire. 5, 11.

peatedly declared in it that trust in Kŕishńa is of itself exemption from all return to worldly existence." Such assertions are a clear proof that the work which maintains them is the production of a more modern and degenerate Hinduism.**

According to all the systems of Philosophy derived from the Vedas, the most assiduous worship of the Gods of the Hindu Pantheon can only elevate the worshipper to equal rank with them. "Those observers of ceremonies who perform the adoration of celestial Gods as well as the worship of the sacred fire and oblation to sages, ancestors, men and other creatures,

---

* सर्वधर्मान्परित्यज्य मामेकं शरणं व्रज Abandoning all duties take refuge with me alone, 18, 66. मय्यावेश्य मनो ये मां नित्ययुक्ता उपासते । श्रद्धया परयोपेतास्ते मे युक्ततमा मताः ॥ Those who have imbued their minds with me, and worship me constantly, being endowed with firm faith, are held most perfect by me [XII. 2].

मत्तः परतरं नान्यत्किंचिदस्ति धनंजय । जानुं द्रुष्टुं च तत्त्वेन प्रवेष्टुं च परंतप ॥ I am such, oh Arjuna, that by faith placed in me, and in no other, alone may men know, behold, and be absorbed in me, subduer of thy foes. 11, 54.

** The worship of particular deities for particular purposes is the main purport of the practical portion of all the Vedas, but no one divinity occupies more than his share or swallows up the rest: neither is mere faith, trust without worship, enjoined: formulæ are however produced from the Atharvańa or fourth Veda, which differ very essentially in this respect from the hymns and prayers of the other three. The authenticity of these is rather questionable, and even if proved establishes but little, as the history and character of this Veda are far from being ascertained: the style of the fragments is much more modern than that of the other Vedas.

will by means of the latter surmount the obstacles presented by natural temptations, and will attain the state of the celestial Gods through the practice of the former." *Isopanishad, translated by Rammohun Roy.** The Bhagavad Gítá admits this of all the Gods except Krishńa, conforming to the sectarial character which is peculiar to the Puráńas. "Those who worship the Gods go to the Gods,—those who worship the Progenitors go to the Progenitors,—those who sacrifice to the Ghosts go to the Ghosts,—those who worship me go to me." [IX, 25.] And again, "Those born of sinful wombs who diligently depend on me, Women, Vaiśyas and Śúdras, obtain supreme felicity." 9, 32. The doctrine is carried *ad absurdum*, but precisely in the spirit of the Puráńas. "Whosoever worships me exclusively, although addicted to unholy practices, he shall be held sanctified and well addressed: he quickly becomes of a virtuous spirit and attains eternal rest, for be assured, Kaunteya, no one who trusteth in me perisheth." 9, 30, 31,** and this is called union (with the supreme) by the *royal* knowledge, the *royal mystery*.***

---

* [Śankara ad Iśop. 11.]

** अपि चेत्सुदुराचारो भजते मामनन्यभाक् । साधुरेव स मन्तव्यः सम्यग्व्यवसितो हि सः ॥ क्षिप्रं भवति धर्मात्मा शश्वच्छान्तिं निगच्छति । कौन्तेय प्रतिजानीहि न मे भक्तः प्रणश्यति ॥ ९, ३०, ३१. The mischievous tendency of the doctrine is evident, and that no doubt of it might be left, the popular works represent, in legendary adventures, the commission of various crimes as matters that are easily expiated, by firm belief in Krishńa, Bhagavad or Mahádeva.

*** Śankara Swámi, indeed, asserts that the Gítá teaches eman-

From these observations the character of the Bhagavad Gítá will now be understood, and it was the more necessary to offer some such preliminary view, as the learned translator has abstained from commenting upon the philosophy of his text. He pleads want of leisure for the undertaking, having been anxious to publish the book without delay. He urges also in further excuse the absence of the best commentaries. We doubt whether he would have received that aid from the commentators he seems to have anticipated: —they are far from explicit, and make extensive use of previous and collateral knowledge, the references to which they rarely explain. In addition to their glosses, therefore, it would be necessary to enter more deeply, than perhaps the means attainable in Europe permit, into the systems of Hindu theology, to do full justice to the speculations of the Gítá. We do not think, indeed, that they deserve the labour, as they are of too popular and spurious an origin, and we should rather see such acquirements and acumen as Schlegel's exercised upon some of the more abstruse and unadulterated performances of the Vedánta and Sánkhya schools.

cipation from knowledge only, and not from works nor faith, availing himself of Krishna's injunctions to take refuge with him alone, and identifying Krishna with the Supreme: he labours very assiduously to prove also that works are only recommended as the means of obtaining knowledge, but his arguments are more subtle than satisfactory, and he is evidently influenced by the popularity of the Gítá in the attempt to derive from it that support to his own doctrines which it does not afford.

Having thus taken a general view of the doctrine of the Bhagavad Gítá, we shall now enter upon an examination of the work in detail, with accompanying reference to the Translation. The work is divided into eighteen adhyáyas or lectures, each in the original described by its appropriate denomination. These Wilkins has translated—Schlegel has left them untouched, in consequence of entertaining some doubts of their being the work of the author of the text. We do not see any reason for the doubt, as the titles invariably occur in the manuscripts, and are sufficiently applicable to the subject of each section.

The Bhagavad Gítá opens with the report made to Dhritaráshtra, the father of the Kurus, by Sanjaya, his charioteer, of what has recently occurred at Kurukshetra, where the hostile hosts of the Pándavas and Kauravas are assembled. Previous to the engagement, Arjuna, observing kinsmen and connexions in either army, expresses to Krishńa, his friend and charioteer, great reluctance to engage in a contest so unnatural. Krishńa, to overcome this feeling, enters upon a dissertation on the nature of spirit, his own divinity, the merit of various kinds of worship, and the propriety of discharging religious and moral obligations; in consequence of which Arjuna consents to fight. This is the business of the episode. Arjuna's regret, *Arjuna-vishada*, forms the subject of the first *adhyáya*, rendered lecture by Wilkins, and lectio by Schlegel.

It has been the avowed object of the translator to be as literal as possible, and he has therefore translated most of the epithets,—thus he renders *Mahára-tha*, the common title of the leaders, signifying one fighting in a chariot, magno curru vectus; and *sarva-mahárathák* omnes æque magnis curribus vecti: although *mahá* does mean great, it does not bear that acceptation only in these places, and might have been omitted or modified without any violation of fidelity.

V. 10. Schlegel has substituted non satis idoneus [impar, 2nd ed.] and idoneus, for Wilkins's translation of *Aparyáptam* and *Paryáptam*, innumerable and numerable. The commentators differ in their explanation of these terms. Śrídhara Swámí explains them by *Asamartha* and *Samartha*, which authorises Schlegel's translation. Nílakańtha however prefers *Bahu* and *Alpa*, which agree with Wilkins. The sense of the passage renders Wilkins's translation preferable in our opinion, as it would be rather inconsistent in Sanjaya to detract from his own friends, of whom he is actually speaking, by asserting that they were unable to face the enemy. The readings may be reconciled by considering the expression elliptical, as suggested by the second named commentator; *Aparyáptam* meaning, not capable of being surrounded or opposed by the enemy, and not, unfit to contend with them.

V. 13. *Pañava* and *Ánaka* are here translated cymbala et cornua; for the sake of variety, we presume, as they signify no such things; but merely differently formed drums. Wilkins has avoided all dispute here by grouping them as warlike instruments.

V. 15. The conch shell is the favorite instrument of the Hindus, both in war and sacrifice. In the Mahábhárata, we find every hero provided with his conch, and in general it bears a distinct appellation:—in this place several are enumerated, and we mention it to show how well the Latin Language translates these denominations, and how dexterously Schlegel has adapted the terms: thus *Pánchajanya*, once the shell of Panchajanya a giant, he renders Gigantea: *Devadatta*, Theodotes: *Paundra*, from its being of the colour of sugar cane, Arundinea: *Anantavijaya*, Triumphatrix: and *Sughosha* and *Manipushpaka*, literally Dulcisona and Jemmiflorea.

V. 30. *Bhramatíva cha me manas* is rendered mens mea quasi titubat. This translation is scarcely correct, for titubo does not signify to wander or whirl round, the sense of *bhramati*: perhaps torquet or vagatur would have been preferable, or perturbatur would have been closer to the purport, if not to the letter of the expression.

V. 38. *Lobha* is rendered libido, but we think cupiditas would have been less ambiguous: Arjuna's remark is that the minds of the opposite party are distracted by the desire of supremacy and wealth, or, as Wilkins expresses it, by the lust of power.

V. 40. Some indistinctness pervades the translation in this and the following verses with regard to the term *Kuladharmáh*, rendered by sacra gentilitia, and *Játidharmáh*, by *familiarum* [ordinum] sacra. *Dharma* is not merely sacred or religious, but moral and social duty," the obligation contracted by birth, and station: in this sense *Kuladharmáh*, should be rather familiarum munera or officia. Wilkins renders these terms "family virtue, and virtue of a tribe", but virtue is too general a term. The service of Brahmans is the *Dharma*, the duty, of Śúdras, for instance, but it could scarcely be called either piety or virtue. The sense of the original would be tolerably well conveyed by the ritus familiæ patruumque of the old Roman Law.

In the same passage the term *kulastriyah* is rendered feminae nobiles by Schlegel, women of a family by Wilkins; neither is quite correct, as *kulastrí* means a woman of character, a chaste and respectable woman, one who preserves a family, attends to its duties, and adds to its reputation; being explained कुलरिका, कुलव-कुलधर्मी and कुलकीर्तिकरी by different commentators on the Amara Kosha, where the term occurs synonymous with कुलपालिका, the preserver of a race.

V. 47. *Sankhye*, in acie, is more acccurately rendered by Wilkins, "in the war."

In the second Lecture Krishńa undertakes to prove the unreasonableness of Arjuna's reluctance to combat with his relations in the Kuru ranks, and draws his arguments chiefly from the *Sánkhya* philosophy, hence the section is denominated *Sánkhya Yoga*, Spiritual union according to the Sánkhya doctrines. Wilkins has translated it, "Of the nature of the soul, and spe-

---

* भारद्वाजधर्मः, Dharma is so named from upholding, preserving mankind, and the universe.—Haradatta on Gautama's aphorisms.

culative doctrines"; but the principles of the Sánkhya
are no more speculative than those of any other school.
Schlegel, as observed, avoids translating these titles,
but in the body of the text, when the term Sánkhya
occurs, he renders it Ratiocinium, and Scientia rationalis,—terms as little applicable as specific designations, as speculative, and founded probably upon the
previous employment of that word. It is true that it
is not easy to render the meaning of the original. Srídhara Swámí defines it etymologically* as the real
nature of spirit made manifest by perfect knowledge.
Sankara explains it discrimination between matter and
spirit, or Prakriti and Purusha: and it is elsewhere
defined as the doctrine of enumeration, or in which
the sage proceeds by regularly enumerated steps to
perfection: *sankhyá* meaning number, enumeration.**
It had better therefore we think, have been left un-
translated, in the same way as we use the denominations of the Greek schools, Stoic, Platonic, &c. with
little or no modification. As employed in the Gítá,
the followers of the Sánkhya doctrines mean those
who disclaim works, as opposed to those who observe
them, who are called Yogís, a term which is likewise
calculated to create some perplexity: thus Sankara

---

* व्यक्तव्यापी प्रकाशते वस्तुतत्त्वमर्घेति संज्ञा समन्वर्थं
तस्मिन्नभ्यानुभावनात्मकं सांख्यं ॥ [v. 39.]

** सम्यगावेति वस्तिब्रह्माश्रे तत्त्वार्थ ॥ [See Professor Goldstücker's
"Pánini". London: 1861, p. 151, and Professor F. E. Hall's
Preface to his edition of the Sánkhyapravachanabháshya. Calc.
1856, p. 1-6.]

says the Sánkhyas are those who are possessed of knowledge, arising from discrimination between that which is spirit and that which is not; who, abandoning works from the period of studentship, have acquired certainty in the understanding of the Vedánta; who are known as mendicants and hermits, and stand firm in Brahma. The Yogís, as mentioned in the text of the Gítá, he contents himself with calling *Karmís*, those performing karma or acts. It might have been preferable, therefore, when speaking of the disciples of these systems, to have distinguished them as Contemplationem colentes, und Ritus asservantes, instead of Scientiæ rationalis and Operum devoti.

V. 5. *Bhunjíya bhogán* is translated much too literally, 'vescar dapibus', as it implies, 'I should enjoy enjoyments'. The preferable reading attaches the epithet *Arthakámán* to *Bhogán*, signifying the enjoyments arising from pleasure and wealth; hence Wilkins renders it, "I should partake of possessions, wealth and pleasures." Schlegel has added the epithet to *Gurún*, the elders of the Kurus, desirous of wealth, Magistris opum avidis, and this is allowable.

V. 7. *Dharma-sammúdha-chetáh*: Arjuna says of himself, his mind is bewildered as to his duty; that is whether as a warrior he ought to fight the enemy, or whether as of kin to them he ought to avoid the combat. This idea is far from being correctly conveyed by the expression 'religione mentem attonitus'. Wilkins has preserved the thought, though he has not expressed it very happily, "my understanding is confounded by the dictates of my duty:" the note he adds, however, shews that he perfectly understood it.

V. 14. *Mátrásparśáh*, elementorum contactus, is a palpable mistake, committed too in the face of the more correct translation of Wilkins, "sensibility of the faculties", at least with regard to the first of the two terms: *Mátrá* is explained by both Śankara and Śrídhara, as he renders it, Faculties: the *Mátrás* they say are those, by which the objects of sense are measured or perceived;* they constitute the *Vritti*, the peculiar practice or faculty of the organs of perception. *Sparśa* again, though literally touch or contact, has not that limited sense here: it is the exercise of the faculties or their being acted upon** by the objects of their exercise. So far Wilkins's translation of the word by sensibility is objectionable, as it is not ability, but action, that is intended.

V. 39. Kŕishńa, having exposed the folly of Arjuna's regret by arguments drawn from the Sánkhya doctrine of the eternity and imperishableness of both matter and spirit, now proceeds to combat his sentiments with the doctrines of the Yoga School. "This knowledge thus expounded to you is derived from the Sánkhya,—now hear what the Yoga declares, being possessed of which knowledge you shall laugh at the bonds of action." Yoga in the Gítá most usually implies the performance of works, as subsequently ex-

---

* मात्रा आभिर्मीयन्ते शब्दादय: Śankara Bhashya.
** मात्राणां स्पर्शा: शब्दादिभि: संयोगा: ॥

plained, being only so far modified that the absence of all desire of benefit is indispensable.* Śankara asserts that the *Samádhi Yoga*, or performance of certain meditative acts, is also comprised. *Sánkhya*, as already noticed, is explained by Schlegel Ratiocinium, in our estimation much too loosely, and in like manner we object to his rendering *Yoga*, Devotio; although he follows Wilkins, who renders it Devotion. As we however understand devotion, we can scarcely conceive it to be identifiable with the performance of religious ceremonies, pro forma, with an utter disregard of consequences. Ritibus Assensus would perhaps better convey the sense of the term, and A ritibus Dissentio, the opposed purport of the Sánkhya; but as these phrases would still only convey a partial impression

---

* विद्धसिद्ध्यो: समो भूला समलं योग उच्चते Being alike indifferent to the attainment or non-attainment (of the object of the act), that equality (or indifference) is termed Yoga, v. 48.
Yoga is also said to be the absence of pain दु:खसंयोगवियोगं योगसंज्ञितं 6, 23. Sejunctionem a doloris conjugio scint devotionis nomine designari. Again Śankara calls Yoga कारणानां चटनं योगै-र्वर्यसामर्ध्यं सर्ववलं योगबलं योग उच्चते "Restraint of spirit; faculties derived from the accession of superhuman power; omniscience derived from abstract exercises: that is called Yoga", and again he describes it as the exercise by which the intellect is delivered up to the supreme deity for the purpose of union, इश्वरार्पयुद्गुद्धीयमान योगार्चलायीन उच्चते. In the Linga Purána, Yoga is considered *Nirodha*, final emancipation, or identification with Śiva; it is there said also that it cannot be expounded by the learned, but the knowledge of it is easily obtained by discipline, or the practice of those personal and mental restraints which coerce the senses, and purify the spirit.

of the purport of the terms, we should prefer, as we have before observed, the use of themselves to any translation.

In the same stanza also we object to the translation of *Buddhi* by Sententia: it is not merely the doctrine or opinion of either school that is communicated to Arjuna, but the result, the knowledge of the divine nature of spirit and matter. *Buddhi* therefore is in this place considered by Śankara as synonymous with *Jnána*, a word we should rather have translated by Sapientia, than Scientia, usually preferred by Schlegel, and which, though literally correct, is exceptionable from its extended and in a manner indefinite application: on the contrary Sapientia, as a term of the schools, is precisely equivalent to *Jnána*: 'Sapientia autem est, ut a veteribus philosophis definitum est, rerum divinarum et humanarum caussarumque, quibus hæ continentur, scientia.' Cic. de officiis, 6. 2.

V. 42. *Vedavádaratáḥ, Pártha, nányad astíti vádinaḥ,* "Librorum sacrorum dictis gaudentes, nec ultra quidquam dari affirmantes." We are rather at a loss to understand what the translator intends in this place. The original contains not a word about 'giving'. The passage is simply, "Those who are attached to the doctrines of the Vedas assert, that there is nothing else:" that is, they maintain, that the Vedas offer the only path to salvation; sacrifice and prayer are all; there is no other path to heaven. There is considerable obscurity in the rest of this stanza, and some faulty translation. *Swargapará* is not "sedem apud superos finem bonorum prædicantes", but sedem apud superos summam felicitatem existimantes, those who hold the paradise of Indra to be the supreme happiness. The translator is also so far wrong, in rendering *Janmakarmaphalapradām* insignes natales tanquam operum præmium pollicentem, that the phrase is general, not restrictive, and "lofty birth" and "reward" are not the simple senses of *Janma*, and *Phala*, which signify only 'birth' and 'fruit or consequence'. The dogma alluded to is said to be one, "assigning birth as the consequence of acts:" that is, according to the act of an individual in a previous existence, he is born again either to misery or happiness.

V. 45. The Hindu system arranges all the attributes of spirit in action under three heads or qualities—the *Sattwa*, *Rajas*, and *Tamas*: the first comprises the presence of all good and absence of all evil; the last the presence of all evil and absence of all good: and the middle one is a mixed quality, in which the operation of the affections and passions is strongest, and gives occasional predominance to good and ill. In this verse Kŕishńa recommends to Arjuna to eschew the two latter qualities, and to cultivate the first alone; to be *Nirdwandwa*, exempt from the double alternatives of existence, as pleasure or pain &c. and to be *Nityasattwastha*, always firm in *Sattwa*, the quality of Sattwa, which is perhaps best rendered purity or excellence. Schlegel however translates it essentia, a sense the word bears as derived from *Sat, ens*, being, but certainly not applicable to it as one of the three *guṇas.* That the quality is intended, is obvious from the context, as Śankara explains the term accordingly, तदा सत्त्वगुणबाहितो भव. What the *Sattwaguṇa* is, is equally indisputable, as we may learn from the following definition, सत्त्वं निर्मलत्वात्प्रकाशकमनामयं, the Sattwa from its purity is light and tranquillity, 14, 6. Śrīdhara and Nīlakaṅtha, it is true, interpret *Sattwa* by *Dhairya*, firmness, fortitude, but they intend the same thing in fact with the Sattwa quality, or the mens solida of the upright man who is unmoved by ignorance and passion. It appears to be the same as the Temperantia or Tranquillitas of the Stoics, whilst the *Rajas* might be expressed by Perturbatio, and *Tamas* by Intemperantia.

In the same stanza, *Niryogakshemo bhava* is rendered, expers sollicitudinum esto, following no doubt Wilkins's "Be void of care." The compound admits of such a translation, it is true, but it is not very precise. *Yoga* means here acquisition, and *Kshema* preservation, and Kṛishṇa recommends to Arjuna to be neither desirous of obtaining what he does not possess, nor of preserving what he possesses.*

V. 48. The word *Sanga* is we think rather injudiciouly interpreted by ambitio: as well observed by the translator, it signifies the attachment of the French, "studium vel affectus quo animus vehementer tenetur",

---

* [चन्नुपात्तस्योपार्जनं योगः । उपात्तस्य रक्षणं क्षेमः ।] See Śankara and Śrīdhara ad 9, 22. Benfey's Sáma Veda Gl. p. 155. Colebrooke's transl. of Mitáksharà I, 4, 23.]

the eagerness evinced in the attainment of any object, or the close and intense connexion that subsists between the individual and the thing affected. It is accordingly rendered in the Trikáúḍa Śesha *Gŕidhnutá*, cupidity, greediness. In the note attached to this passage, Schlegel objects to the etymology of *Sanga*, as given in Wilson's Dictionary, सम्, with, and गम्, to go, with the affix घ; and the etymology there is so far defective, that it applies only to the leading sense of the word, i. e. "meeting, encountering", and to the two last, "union, joining, and the confluence of rivers" —in the remaining sense, "desire, cupidity", it would have been as well if the root सञ्ज्, to be attached to, had been also inserted. Schlegel however mistakes when he concludes, that *Sanga* so formed must necessarily be an adjective, for it is given by Amara[*] as a synonyme of सङ्गम or, as explained by Krishńa Swámí, सङ्गति, both of which are substantives, and nouns, of the act or action, not names of the agent. Again Schlegel proposes to derive *Sanga* from सज्ज्; in preference to *Shanja*, on the principle that the latter root occasionally drops the nasal;—that is true, but whence does सज्ज् ever derive a nasal? for, unfortunately for his theory, all the lists of roots, and the Siddhánta Kaumudí, explain सज्ज् by सङ्गे 'embrace, association', and सञ्ज् by गतौ 'going, motion'. He has taxed the author of the Dictionary with confounding

---

[* (Bhánudikshita ad Amarakosha III, 3, 29, and Lassen's note on the passage in question.)]

these two roots, but we suspect the charge is urged against the wrong quarter: the Kaumudí, the first grammatical authority current, confirms precisely what is there stated, and वश् वडे makes खवनि in the 3d person present, while वस्र मनी in the same tense and person makes खश्नी and खकनि. We are unable to see any perplexity here, or any deviation from indisputable guides.

V. 52. A wide difference occurs here in the reading of the two translators, and Wilkins calls *Nirveda* 'knowledge', whilst Schlegel makes it 'ignorantia (neglectus'). It is clear that they cannot both be right, and to a certain extent both are wrong. We apprehend, however, that, although Wilkins's translation of the whole passage is no doubt faulty, yet *nirveda* is rather knowledge than ignorance. Schlegel's error arises partly out of a spirit of system to which the learned of Europe are too ready to incline:—a Paṇḍit however eminent is content to follow established authorities, and admits the law that they have laid down; a European scholar is suspicious of authorities, and carries this so far as not unfrequently to question them without cause. Now Amara, Maheśwara, Hemachandra, Medinikára, and every other Lexicographer of note, have explained the particle *Nir*, (निर् निश्चयनिषेधयोः) 'certainty, and negation', it being sometimes an affirmative, and sometimes a privative particle. We think this might satisfy the most scrupulous, as, although the senses are opposed, the interpretation is positive. Schlegel however endeavours sometimes to explain away the sense of affirmation, as we shall have occasion hereafter to notice, and at others, as in the present case, alters the sense. Now all the commentators* agree to interpret *Nirveda* by निर्वेद, the absence of passion properly, but here, indifference. But of what nature is this indifference? it is the result of ascertained knowledge (from *Nir*, certainty, and *Veda*, knowing) of the futility of the dogmas of the Vedas; Krishńa telling Arjuna, that, when his understanding shall overpass the glooms of infatuation, he will have attained independence, or the knowledge, which will make him independent of all that he has heard, or may have to hear."" To say that he shall have attained ignorance of what he has heard or has yet to hear, would be a strange step towards perfection. *Srotarya* and *Sruta* imply the lessons of the Vedas: that which is to be heard, or is heard. Schlegel has made a rather unwarranted addition in explaining it by "disputable doctrine." "Pervenies ad ignorantiam omnium quæ de doctrina sacra disputari possunt vel disputata sunt." He must know that the Vedas collectively are called *Sruti*, the knowledge heard, in opposition to *Smriti*, Law, the knowledge remembered—the one being preserved by traditional communication, from sage to sage, the other being the recollection of previously divulged codes: there is no allusion therefore to dis-

---

* [See also Śankara ad Muṇḍaka Up. 1, 2, 12.]
** यदा ते मोहकलिलं बुद्धिर्व्यतितरिष्यति । तदा गन्तासि निर्वेदं श्रोतव्यस्य श्रुतस्य च ।

putatious matters. The whole of Kŕishńa's arguments have been directed against the assertors of the sacrificial injunctions of the Vedas, and in the same spirit he assures his friend, that, when he becomes wholly indifferent to the consequences of acts, he will possess a knowledge to which the wisdom of the Vedas will be foolishness.

V. 89. This stanza is at best rather obscure: Wilkins has by far the best notion of it, but has rendered it too literally. Schlegel has mistaken the whole purport of the passage, the verse is— विषया विनिवर्तंते निराहारस्य देहिनः । रसवर्जं रसोऽप्यस्य परं दृष्ट्वा निवर्तते ॥

"The hungry man loseth every other object but the gratification of his appetite, and when he is become acquainted with the supreme, he loseth even that."—*Wilkins.*

"Res sensibus obviæ recedunt a mortali abstinente, temperantia ejus insigni animadversa ipse appetitus recedit." *Schlegel.* The first half of this version might be allowed to pass unquestioned, but abstinens should be taken in its widest acceptation, as implying one who is engaged in self-denial, and refraining from every kind of gratification. The latter portion however is altogether erroneous, and not very intelligible: temperantia occurs nowhere in the original, and so far from its leading to the supreme, ascetic practices are said in the text, and in the commentary, to be characteristic of a fool or a fiend. The translator has here lost sight of the spirit of his original apparently, or he would have adhered closer to his English guide, who errs only in making that special which is general, being misled by the double sense of *Nirāhāra*, which means *without food*, or *without seizure or possession*, that is, of the objects of sense. The doctrine laid down is, that, however much a person may restrain his inclination towards the natural tendency of the senses, the attractive quality of sensual objects still exists; they continue to be temptations still, successfully a man may resist them: but let him once obtain a knowledge of supreme spirit, a correct view of his own nature, and that of the divinity, and he is not only able to resist temptations, but in fact he is exposed to none, every thing that made them seductive wholly disappearing. Křishńa accordingly says in this stanza —"The objects of sense recede from the incorporated spirit, which refrains from their enjoyment, the taste for them excepted (i. e. it remains); but this taste or flavour, (affecting the) individual ceases altogether, when he has seen the supreme."*

There are several other passages in this Lecture to which we might take exception, but not to be too minute in our comments, we shall allow them to escape animadversion, and not to confine our remarks to blemishes, shall cite the following passage** in this book as one specimen of many that might be adduced of accurate and spirited interpretation: many of the

---

* [This construction, proposed by Śridhara Swāmí, is against the diction of the Bhag. Gítā.]
** [II, 17–25.]

ideas forcibly recall the language of Scipio's dream. "Indelebile autem, hoc scias, est illud, a quo Universum hoc expansum: deletionem inexhausti istius nemini efficere licet. Caduca hæc corpora dicuntur, immutabili spiritu animata, indelebili atque immenso: quare pugna, o Bhárata! Qui eum arbitratur occisorem, quive eundem censet occisum, hi ambo non recte intelligunt; neque occidit ille, neque occiditur. Non nascitur moriturve unquam; non ille exstitit, exsistitve, non exstiturus: innatus, immutabilis, æternus ille, priscus, non occiditur occiso corpore. Qui novit indelebilem, æternum illum, innatum, inexhaustum, quomodo is homo quempiam occidendum curet, vel ipse occidat? Perinde ac obsoletis vestibus abiectis, novas sumit homo alias, sic abiectis corporibus obsoletis, alia ingreditur nova spiritus. Non illum penetrant tela, non illum comburit flamma, neque illum perfundunt aquæ, nec ventus exsiccat. Impenetrabilis ille, incombustibilis ille, imperfusibilis ille, nec non inexsiccabilis, perpetuus, omnivagus, stabilis, inconcussus ille atque aeternus, invisibilis ille, inenarrabilis ille, immutabilis ille declaratur. Quare, quum talem cognoveris, non luctu eum prosequi te oportet."

Lecture 3. If knowledge is superior to works, or the active discharge of moral and religious obligations, then Arjuna very pertinently enquires why Kŕishńa should urge him to a deed so horrible as the slaughter of his relations. Kŕishńa replies to his question in this chapter, and shews from positive precept, the impulses of nature and other arguments, that man must necessarily discharge active duties, taking care only to hold himself indifferent as to their results, and endeavouring, with more subtilty than truth, to establish, that such indifference is the only real abstinence from these actions; a doctrine which, as we have already observed, it is one of the two great objects of the Gítá to promulgate. We shall not enter so minutely into the questionable passages of the translation of this and the following chapters as we have done in the preceding, as we should otherwise make a very disproportionate claim upon the attention of our readers: indeed the celebrity of the translator is our only excuse for devoting so great a portion of our pages to the analysis of this translation.

V. 15 is explained very differently from the acceptation, in which the commentators concur: *Karma Brahmodbhavam* is rendered by Schlegel opus e numine ortum, but *Brahma** does not mean here *numen*, but the *Veda*: works originate with the Veda. Again, *Brahmáksharasamudbhavam* is not numen e simplici et individuo ortum, a translation the purport of which is not very intelligible, any more than the grounds on which it rests, but "the Veda originates with the Imperishable". The line thus expresses a clear and connected sense which is quite lost in the translation.

V. 16. *Iha* does not mean in hoc sæculo, but in hoc mundo, and *Agháyuh*, leading a sinful life, is strangely rendered by 'incaste ævo transacto'.

---

* [According to Śankara and Śrídhara.]

V. 18. *Arthavyapáśraya* is not so much ullius commodi expectatio as 'the object on which he may place dependence' of Wilkins: *Vyapáśraya* is the means or aid, the commodum itself, not the expectation of it.

V. 35. *Śreyán swadharmo viguńah paradharmát swanushthitát* is rendered, satius est suo officio, etsi deficientibus viribus, fungi, quam alienum officium accurate implere. The translation is not correct: *Viguńah* is an epithet of *Dharma*, implying void of *Guńa*, quality or merit; *Swanushthitát* is also an attributive of *Dharma*, implying well or excellently regulated: the passage therefore conveys the doctrine, that a man's own duty, although inferior in degree, is, with respect to himself, superior to another of a more lofty description: as, for instance, the servitude of a Śúdra is preferable for a Śúdra to study, which is the peculiar province of the Brahman.

In a note on the 10th verse of this section Schlegel has very justly called in question the accuracy of the form *Prasavishyadhwam*, propagabimini, as such an inflexion is unknown to the verb: at the same time all the manuscripts concur in the reading, and it is therefore considered as a poetical license, the word being properly *Prásavishyadhwam*, the first long vowel being made arbitrarily short for the adaptation of the metre.*

---

* [Schlegel, in the second edition, calls it "formam, quam definire possis terminationem et vim imperativi ad futurum secundum

Lecture 4. In this discourse Krĭshṅa enters upon further explanation of the union of spirit by means of divine knowledge, and endeavours to prove, that it is but that indifference to the consequence of actions, of which he had before treated. The performance and non-performance of works, intending in this section social duties, is therefore the same, and disregard of their results is virtually their relinquishment; as in the 20th verse: "He who, having abandoned every desire of fruit, is always satisfied and independent, although he may be engaged in action, verily doeth nothing."

V. 10. *Manmayá* is better rendered by Wilkins "filled with my spirit", than by Schlegel 'mei similes', the affix मयट् implying made or consisting of, so that *Manmaya* literally means consisting of me, or one with me: it is explained by Śaṅkara, those who see no difference in Íswara, or supreme spirit, ईश्वरभेददर्शिनः.

V. 17. and 18, profess to explain what *Karma* or action, and what *Akarma* or inaction are, and which have, as Krĭshṅa declares in the stanza preceding, puzzled the wisest. His definitions, however, are calculated to fasten rather than untie the knot, and are good specimens of the style, in which the Gítá throughout evades the question between social and ascetic practices, the merits of sacrifice, or the claims of ab-

---

translatam." The commentators on this passage and on Rámáy. I, 29, 25 explain it by the Imperative. Modern languages, e. g. Bengali and Hindi, present similar formations.]

straction. The passage is somewhat obscure, and it is not wonderful therefore that the translation is not very distinct: it is rendered however less clear than it might be by one or two mistakes. Schlegel renders the first verse 'ad ipsum opus est attendendum, attendendum quoque ad secessionem ab opere,[*] attendendum tandem ad otium; obscura est operis ratio.' Now in the first place, the *Karma* here discussed refers to active occupation, the duties of social life or of caste; actio would therefore, we think, have been preferable to opus. In the next place *Bodhavyam* is not attendendum, it is intelligendum rather, and refers to a noun understood, *Tattwam*, the real nature or character of action, inaction &c. Again *Vikarma* is erroneously rendered by secessio ab opere, as it means, as Wilkins correctly translates it, 'improper works', deeds that are prohibited by the Śástras; *Akarma* is secessio ab opere or inactio. Otium is a rather equivocal word. The second of these two stanzas is thus rendered: 'Qui in opere otium cernit, et in otio opus, is sapit inter mortales; is devotus, cunctis operibus peragendis aptus est.' Otium and opus are both very objectionable here, as they do not convey the spirit of the original, and therefore heighten the obscurity. There is but one position in both assertions, and the doctrine implied is, that, as there is no such thing as individual spirit, those who think they are performing deeds of which they must singly reap the fruit, or those who

---

[*] [2nd ed. ad opus haud rite impensum.]

in like manner think they abstain from works in their individual capacities, are both mistaken. The actions of the first lead to nothing, and the expectations of the latter put them on a level with the former: both are blinded by terrestrial illusion.

V. 23. *Yajnáyácharataḥ karma samagram pravilíyate*, Hominis sacrificii gratia sese accingentis opus integrum quasi evanescit. The translation is literal enough, but it is rather too close to convey the sense of the original, which states that, when a man freed from all desire performs sacrifices, merely to *promote their observation by others*, or preserve them in the world, then those acts are annihilated together with their fruits, that is to say they are not to be considered as acts at all.

V. 25. Divorum porro alii devoti religionem colunt, in theologiæ igne alii religionem ipsa religione denuo sacrificant. The translation here by no means conveys the sense of the original: we doubt indeed whether in this as in many of the doctrinal passages, particularly where verbal subtleties occur, the translator has entertained a precise idea of what he would express. In this passage he has further contributed to the obscurity of the original by rendering *Yajna*, Religio. It is, as he has frequently translated it in other places, sacrifice, and although it may be extended to every ceremonial rite of religion, it cannot be applied in the widest sense of that term. The translator has also lost sight of the antitheses of the two lines, the one of which alludes to the performers of rites for specific purposes, and the other to the cultivators of divine knowledge who observe rites only as the *means* of its acquirement. The sense of the stanza in this point of view is, 'Some observers of acts address sacrifice to the Gods, whilst others* offer up sacrifice with sacrifice in the fire that is identical with spirit,'—that is to say, in the performance of ceremonies they seek only the means of acquiring divine knowledge, and *that* being obtained, they yield or relinquish to it the benefit of all ceremonies, to be consumed by it, as it were by fire.

Lect. 5. Arjuna, and he is not singular perhaps, is now completely puzzled, and begs Krishńa to inform him which is really the best, the performance or abandonment of works. Krishńa replies to his question by stating that there is no real difference between them, according to the predominant doctrine of the whole treatise: that the abandonment of consequences is the real abandonment of works, and that, although the bodily or intellectual functions may be discharged, yet as long as no interest is felt in them the spirit is wholly inactive.

V. 2. On the word *Niśreyas*, final emancipation, Schlegel has a note in support of his theory of the meaning of the particle *Nir*, in opposition to the etymology in Wilson's Dictionary (निः for निर्) implying eternity or certainty, and श्रेयस् best, च added. He

---

* [Srídhara: अपरे तु ज्ञानयोगिनो ब्रह्मरूपेऽपौ वशैश्वरीपादेन महार्षमित्राकुत्समकारैव यज्ञमुपजुह्वति यज्ञादिसर्वकर्माणि अभिसायपरीक्षर्थं: ।]

maintains that श्रेयस् is not the superlative, but the comparative, and that *Nir* prefixed has a negative sense: the compound implying "*That*, than which nothing is better". We should have no great objection to this explanation in this place, although it is probably more ingenious than just. *Sreyas* is constantly used in the superlative sense, and in the very passage of Amara[*] referred to in the Dictionary *Śreyas* occurs, uncompounded, as one synonyme of final beatitude. It cannot there be regarded as possessing only the force of the comparative degree. Again, of the commentators on Amara, Rámáśrama explains *Nir* in *Niśreyas* by *Nitarám*, perpetually, eternally, and Ráya Mukuta by *Niśchitam*, certain, ascertained, whilst Kshíra Swámí[**] explains *Śreyas* by *atiśayena praśastam*, or most excellent. We must confess a disposition to lean to authorities like these in preference to the theory of a novice, however plausible it may appear, or however dexterously it may be maintained.

The sixth Lecture continues to explain the identity of the relinquishment of works with their performance independent of desire. It also recommends the exercise of those practices which constitute the technical Yoga, or postures and gestures by which attention to outward objects is restrained, and the mind devoted to the undisturbed consideration of its own nature. Some indication of the other chief doctrines of the

---

[*] (Amarak. I, 1, 4, 15. See also Śank. ad Kaushít. Up. II, 14.]
[**] [ad Am. K. III, 58.]

Gítá are also introduced, establishing the importance of faith in Krishńa, and making him one with the Supreme Universal Spirit. Krishńa observes:[*]

'Qui me cernit ubique et universum in me cernit, ex eo ego non evanesco, neque is ex me evanescit: omnibus animantibus immorantem qui me colit, unitati intentus, quocunque tandem modo versetur, devotus ille mecum versatur.' There is nothing in this section of the translation, that calls for particular remark,—we might contest some verbal translation, and we are disposed to think the explanation of *Niráta* in the note[**] a little too refined; but the extent of our comments must compel us to waive any more particular notice in this place. The section prosecutes the doctrine of Krishńa's identity with the Supreme spirit, and the union of those who worship him with him, eventually, whilst those who worship the Divinities reap only the inferior kind of fruition which their respective degrees in the regions above the earth are calculated to afford, and which besides being of a sensual description, involve the necessity of a return to life, and future transmigrations in a mortal frame.

[VII,] v. 11. contains in the translation a misconception of one term, and ambiguous equivalent for another. Krishńa says, "He is the strength of the strong and that desire in beings which is not contrary to the

---

[*] यो मां पश्यति सर्वत्र सर्वं च मयि पश्यति । तस्याहं न प्रणश्यामि स च मे न प्रणश्यति । सर्वभूतस्थितं यो मां भजत्येकत्वमास्थितः । सर्वथा वर्तमानोऽपि स योगी मयि वर्तते ॥ [VI, 30f.]

[**] [ad v. 19.]

laws;" *Dharmáviruddhañ kámo'smi.* The first Schlegel renders by Robur robustorum, but this does not convey the idea of moral strength which the epithet attached to it, 'void of passion or desire', implies. The next is however more important, as the sense has the appearance of being the reverse of that which the original intends. Nulla lege refrenata* in animantibus Libido sum: the desire restrained by no law may indeed be admitted to signify that which there is no law to restrain, but the first impression is that it is desire which does not acknowledge moral control. Wilkins renders the passage with tolerable correctness, "I am desire regulated by moral fitness"; it is however rather desire not opposed to moral fitness than regulated by it. Śankara explains it as the natural desire by which the body is preserved, the natural wants, as hunger, thirst and the like: Śridhara gives us in illustration of it the procreation of legitimate offspring.**

The close of this section furnishes the subject of the next. Krishńa states that those who put their whole trust in him, and seek for liberation from infirmity and death, are acquainted with the *Brahma*, the *Adhyátmam, karma, adhibhútam, adhidaivam,* and the *adhiyajnah*: and Arjuna asks for an explanation of these terms. The explanation is brief, but as they all resolve themselves into Krishńa as the *Paramah*

---

* [Lego non impedita, 2nd ed.]

** [Śank.: देहाद्वारम्भकानाम् दक्षनयानादिविषयः कामो ऽस्मि ।
Śridhara: सदारेषु पुत्रोत्पादनमात्रोपयोगी कामो ऽहम् ।]

Purushah, he proceeds to explain the meaning of that expression, which forms the subject of the 8th Lecture.

The explanation of these terms is of importance, as conveying a summary of the whole system: the literal translation of *Brahma* is the imperishable and supreme: *adhyátmam* is the innate disposition, the individuated portion of the soul: *karma* is that letting go of the divine particles, which produced the substance of the elements: *adhibhútam* is the property of dissolution: *adhidaivatam* is Purusha, the embodied male supreme being who occupied the universe before creation: and *adhiyajnaí* is declared by Kŕishńa to be himself; that is, he as one with all the gods is the object of all adoration. We do not think the following translation very accurately conveys these ideas: "Essentia simplex ac individua est summum numen. Indoles supra spiritum dicitur; animantium geniturae efficax emanatio operis nomine significatur; super animantia est natura dividua; Geniusque supra divos; supra religiones ego ipse sum."* The attempt at closeness is injurious not only to perspicuity but accuracy; for though *adhi* in all the compounds means supra, *adhyátmá* does not mean supra spiritum; it is rather spiritus qui præest, or corpori individuo præsidens.

---

* [2nd ed.: "Indoles intimus spiritus dicitur; animantium geniturae efficax emanatio operis nomine significatur; anima animantium est natura dividua, Geniusque numen deorum; auctor religionum ego ipse sum". See on these terms Goldstücker's Sanskrit Dictionary s. vv. *adhibhúta* and *adhyátma*; Johaentgen, "Ueber das Gesetzbuch des Manu", Berlin: 1863, p. 57 ff.]

The translation of *Purusha* by Genius, we look upon as happy, although it is not perhaps exactly the sense. It conveys however the spirit of the term, and we prefer that in all cases to the letter.

Lect. 9. contains the pith of the whole doctrine, the royal knowledge, and prince of mysteries, or in other words, as we have already observed, the superior efficacy of faith in Kṛishṅa over every other system of worship, or tenor of belief. Śankara admits that this is the scope of the section, or that the sum of the argument is *Vásudevaḱi sarvam*, Kṛishṅa is all. Kṛishṅa, however, he per force renders *Iśwara*, the supreme, or *átmá*, spirit, and then asserts that the Gítá harmonises with the text of the Vedas, *Idam sarvam eva adwitiyam*, 'Spirit was this universe without a second.' There is nothing in the translation to call for any particular remark.

The tenth chapter continues the subject of Kṛishṅa's supremacy, or the pre-eminent conditions in which he is to be contemplated, in association with existing objects, as the sun amongst the planets, Kṛishṅa amongst the gods, Meru amongst mountains, Gangá amongst rivers, the soul of all beings, and the beginning, middle, and end of all things. These identifications are called *Vibhútayaḱ*, varieties of supreme being, or as Wilkins translates it, "the diversities of the divine nature". Schlegel seems to have been undecided in his choice of an equivalent, and calls *vibhúti* sometimes majestas, sometimes virtus, and at others miraculum, neither of which is precisely applicable.

V. 7. presents the terms *Vibhúti* and *Yoga*, both rather stumbling blocks, but particularly the latter. However in this place it has clearly no reference to connexion with works, and is confined to the mysterious relation between supreme and individuated spirit. Krishńa says, एतां विभूतिं योगं च यो वेत्ति तत्त्वत: । सोऽवि-कम्पेन योगेन युज्यते नात्र संशय: । which Schlegel translates, Qui hanc meam majestatem et facultatem mysticam novit penitus, is indefessa devotione sese devovet* sine ullo dubio. This is by no means the purpose of the stanza; the sense of which is that, whoever knows the various conditions of spirit and its connexion with that of the universe, becomes united with mystic powers which identify him with the deity. The *Yoga* of the first stanza, being the power resulting from the possession of union, may be called the mystic faculty, but in the second place it implies the same thing, and is therefore very inaccurately expressed by devotio.

The 11th Section prosecutes the same subject in a manner singular enough. Krishńa desires Arjuna to look into his mouth, which having done the latter beholds there the whole of creation. The metre changes here to the *Upajáti* species of the *Trishtubh* verse, a more stately measure, and whatever may be thought of the ideas, there is no disputing the magnificence of the style, the majestic, and at the same time exquisite melodiousness of the verse. In general the translation is close and correct.

---

* [2nd edit.: inconcussa devotione imbuitur.]

Lecture 12th is introduced with a question from Arjuna, pertinent enough, 'which class of worshippers is preferable, those who adore Krishṅa in his visible or invisible form?' The reply which occupies the whole section is after all evasive: however, it appears that there are four modes of attaining final emancipation, absolute knowledge, the exercise of contemplation, the practice of works independent of desire, and simple faith; the latter is placed the lowest in the scale, but the gradation is regulated by the ability of the mortal, for as the result is but one, they are of course equally efficacious. The section is short and the translation calls for no remark.

Lecture 13th is chiefly occupied with the explanation of the distinction between matter and spirit as intended by the terms *Kshetra*, (क्षेत्र) the body, *Kshetrajna*, (क्षेत्रज्ञः) that which knows its nature, *Jneya*, (ज्ञेय) the object to be known, *Jnána*, (ज्ञान) true knowledge, and *Purusha*, (पुरुषः) the active, and *Prakriti*, (प्रकृतिः) the passive principle of creation. There is in this section much that is very indistinct and equivocal, and it has given Śankara no small trouble to reconcile the doctrines it obscurely expresses with the pure Adwaita theology, in which one only object is admitted. Thus in the 13th verse, *Prakriti* and *Purusha*, matter and spirit, are declared to be both without beginning, a doctrine involving the eternity of matter, as maintained by the Sánkhyas and Naiyáyikas. To get rid of this, Śankara asserts that their eternity is understood of them only as attributes or manifestations of

Íswara, the supreme eternal being, as parts of whose nature, without beginning or end, they may also be called interminable and from the first: an explanation which is clearly an evasion, not a solution, of the difficulty.

Kshetra, which implies properly a field, expresses the bodily aggregate, rather than the body, or the site of the elementary matter, the senses, the feelings, the passions, and the understanding: it is not badly rendered therefore by Terrenum. *Kshetrajna* is literally Terreni gnarus, spirit being understood.*

V. 4. We doubt if *Hetumadbhir vinischitaih* is correctly rendered by 'circa principia rerum versantibus, clare demonstratis': the expression is of a more technical character, and refers to the logical predicates of the texts inculcating divine wisdom, which comprehend motives and proofs. Wilkins is more near this sense of the original in his "including arguments and proofs".

In V. 5. an exception may be taken to the translation of *Avyaktam* by invisibile, although it is literal; but the order of the series in the original leaves no ambiguity, whilst the unfamiliarity of the subject in the translation involves considerable uncertainty. Kŕishńa enumerates the eight parts that compose bodily substance, or the five elements, individuality, divine intellect, and the invisible portion. This invisible portion we should naturally infer to be spirit,

---

* [See Johaentgen, l. l., p. 30.]

but then an obvious perplexity arises in considering as one predicate of the *Kshetra* or body that, which is declared to be the faculty by which it is known; the Terreni gnarus as separate from the Terrenum. In fact no such confusion is made in the original: the *Avyaktam* is not divine spirit, it is the *Múlaprakṛiti*, the primeval delusion by which terrestrial substances and acts appear to be real, the illusory or passive principle which we may call nature, and which before creation was, and in fact still is, an attribute or portion of the supreme. Schlegel has elsewhere termed this principium naturæ, and had he employed the same in this place, all uncertainty would have been avoided.

V. 6. Amongst the properties or constituent parts of the *Kshetra* here enumerated are *Sanghāta* (सङ्घातः), *Chetaná* (चेतना), and *Dhṛiti* (धृतिः). These are rendered, multiplex conditio, cogitatio, pertinacia; but these are by no means close interpretations, *Sanghāta* meaning aggregation, *Chetaná* sensation, the collection of the organs and faculties or susceptibility of impressions, and *Dhṛiti* is the principle by which the whole are preserved from decay, the vis conservatrix naturæ. In the long list of terms that ensues, several others might be questioned.

We doubt whether the translator has understood the definition V. 20. of *Prakṛiti* or nature by *Kárya-káraṇa-kartṛitwe hetuḥ*, which he renders In actu ministerii rerum agendarum principium.* The literal

---

* [2nd edit.: in actione ministerii corporalis principium.]

translation would be, the principle that operates in the agency of the instrumental causes of action: but this would be scarcely more intelligible, and the sentence required to have been analytically or paraphrastically rendered: the purport being that *prakriti*, nature, is the principle, or rather the cause, by which the combination of passions and feelings with the elementary particles of matter was effected, and the universal frame independent of spirit was evolved: the passions and perceptions incident to the human being would however be inert without the presence of spirit; they therefore still constitute the passive principle which requires association with the active principle before their influences are felt or exerted; this active spirit is the *Purusha*, the male or genius, the subsequent description of which is very well rendered in the following passages.*

Genius in doloris ac voluptatis perceptione principium declaratur. Genius naturae infusus nimirum particeps fit naturalium qualitatum: propensio erga qualitates causa est generationum ejus e bono vel malo utero. Spectator monitorque, sustentator, perceptor, magnus dominus, summus spiritus quoque dicitur in hoc corpore Genius ille eximius.

The 14th Section treats of the three *Gunas* or properties of nature, the *Sattwa*, *Rajas*, and *Tamas*,

---

* पुरुष: सुखदुःखानां भोक्तृत्वे हेतुरुच्यते । पुरुष: प्रकृतिस्थो हि भुङ्क्ते प्रकृतिजान्गुणान् । कार्यं कृकरणकर्तृत्वे ऽस्मिन् सद्सद्योनिजन्मसु । उपद्रष्टानुमन्ता च भर्ता भोक्ता महेश्वर: । परमात्मेति चाप्युक्तो देहे ऽस्मिन्पुरुष: पर: ॥

translated by Schlegel Essentia, Impetus, and Caligo, on which we have already had occasion to comment.*

In the 6th verse *Nirmalatwam* as the predicate of the *Sattwa Guña* is rendered sinceritas, but *nirmala* means exempt from stain or soil, and the property is illustrated by that of transparent crystal.** Again *Anâmayam* is translated Sana, which is the literal sense, it is true, but as applicable to the *Sattwa Guña* it means gentle, dispassionate, being explained by *nirupadrava* and *śánta*.

V. 14. *Dehabhŕit* is very loosely rendered mortalis; it is that which cherishes or upholds the body or, in other words, spirit: a mortal body is too well disposed of after dissolution, to obtain the region of purity, and spirit under all circumstances is immortal.

The 15th Section discriminates the different kinds of *Purusha*, or active spirit, according to its various conditions of being, as special, or general, or supreme: the first exists in all bodies from Brahma to a stone; the second exists detached from body; and the third is paramount, thence denominated *Purushottama*. This Purushottama is of course Kŕishńa or Vishńu, of whom it is one of the most familiar appellations in a popular and less mystic sense.

This book opens with the expansion of an idea derived from the Vedas, that the world is a fig tree whose roots grow above and the branches below,

---

* [See also Johaentgen, "Ueber das Gesetzbuch des Manu", p. 89 ff.]   ** [Śridhara: सकलानर्थाविजमविरित्व.]

whose leaves are the Vedas, &c. Wilkins has mistaken the object of the comparison, and has substituted the "incorruptible being" for 'the world': he was probably misled by the term *Avyayam*, unexpended, perpetual, which however is only an epithet of the tree, as meaning the *Sansára* or world. Schlegel has assigned the adjective to its proper substantive, but his translation affords no clue to the purport or object of the simile; he calls the tree Ficum religiosam *quandam*, the last condition being an accessory to his text, and shewing that he was not quite certain what the resemblance referred to: besides this, there is considerable mysticism in the whole section, and though rendered literally enough, and with a few exceptions accurately enough, by the translator, it is still very unintelligible from the want of annotations.*

The 16th Section is upon the difference between good and evil natures, and an attack upon the professors of an adverse creed rather than any further elucidation of the doctrine of the Gítá. It is entitled *Daivásura-sampad-vibhága-yoga*, the doctrine of the apportionment of divine and demoniac condition. Wilkins renders it good and evil destiny, and Schlegel, following him most probably, explains it divina et dæmoniaca sors. The latter term is no doubt preferable, for it may be questionable how far destiny is properly in-

---

* [These have been amply supplied in the 2nd edition. See also A. Kuhn, "Die Herabkunft des Feuers". Berlin: 1859, p. 198 ff. W. Mannhardt, "Germanische Mythen". Berlin: 1858, p. 553 ff.]

tended, as the good or evil consequences resulting from these different designations are necessarily the result of the characteristics of good and evil creations, which, as (V. 6.) Kṛishṅa observes, divide the world.

V. 2. *Alolatwam*[*] should have been interpreted 'indifference to objects of sense', rather than alienus a lascivia animus.

V. 6. *Sarga* is rendered *natura*[**], but it is properly creation or class of creatures.

V. 7. *Pravṛittim cha nivṛittim cha janá na vidur ásurát́í,* neque agendi nec cessandi rationem norunt homines dæmonii; but what is the ratio of acting or desisting? In giving the literal meaning of the terms, the translator has here, as in many places, lost sight of the conventional sense they bear. *Pravṛitti* means the discharge of active duties, *nivṛitti* their abandonment at the proper season: the first implies the discharge of the obligations of caste and station, the performance of rites and observance of ceremonies, whilst the second expresses addiction to contemplative meditation alone. The man of the demoniac creation, it is said, regards neither the one nor the other of these duties, or, in other words, is neither a follower of the Vedas nor a worshipper of Vishṅu. It is clear from the subsequent passage that the Bauddhas are especi-

---

[*] [See also Lassen's note in 2nd ed. Śrīdhara's reading च-लोजुपर्त्, which he considers as an archaistic form for चलोजुपर्त् (चवर्जनोपस्तार्व:), is also expressed by Galanos' translation ni ταQuita.]

[**] [indoles, 2nd ed.]

ally intended as the beings of the demoniacal order. Śankara states them to be the members of the Lokáyatika sect, a sect which was a division of the Bauddhas.*

The 17th Section is upon the three kinds of faith, or faith as influenced by the prevalence of the three Guńas severally; and all acts, whether of the ceremonial or abstractive class, performed without faith, are declared to be *Asat*, non existent and null.

The question put by Arjuna which leads to this exposition is, what is the condition or classification of those who worship in faith without regard to the rules of the Śástras? *Nishthá*, rendered Statio by Schlegel, and guide by Wilkins, is rather *Avasthá*, or *Áśraya*, manner or place of being, and the 'Legis scriptæ præceptis neglectis' conveys perhaps more than is intended by the text, as it is the inattention to forms or ceremonial rites, rather than to legal or moral precept, that is alluded to.

In V. 10 we think the term *Yátayáma* is imperfectly rendered by vapidum: it is literally that of which the time is past, but is described as signifying food ill-dressed, or that which has been suffered to get half cold before it is eaten. *Paryushitam*, stale, is omitted altogether, and it is similarly left out, or at least misplaced, in the English translation.

V. 19. *Múdhágraheńa* is the person, not the thing;

---

* [? Comp. Colebrooke's Essays, p. 259, and Zeitschrift der Deutschen morgenl. Ges., XIV, 520.]

it is he who assents to a foolish doctrine, and not ex inepto commento only.

In V. 26 we are disposed to question the translation of the explanation given of the term *Sat*, which is there said to signify the properties of what is real and righteous and all excellent acts. It is not therefore merely said or used 'de veritate ac honestate', but it actually imports the abstract properties of being and excellence, and the term essentia, which has been rather exceptionally applied to the *Sattwa Guña*, would have been very correctly substituted in this place for veritas: whilst, in lieu of honestas, præstantia would have been more apposite. Again, *praśaste karmañi* should be 'in', not 'de', laudabili opere, for in the marriage ceremony and other rites the formula '*Om tat sat*' is repeated, and it is the repetition of *Sat* on such occasions that is here especially alluded to, conformably to the tenor of the two preceding stanzas. In the following stanza *Karma tadarthiyam* is of disputable translation: the word *tat*, that, being applicable either to what has gone before, sacrifice, &c., or to *Brahma* or supreme spirit. Schlegel follows the first, Wilkins the second interpretation: we are rather disposed to prefer the latter.

The eighteenth and concluding section is a summary of the doctrines of the Gítá, and explains particularly what is intended by the abandonment of works. This is, as before, resolved into relinquishment of consequences, and it is declared, that acts of worship, mortification, and charity are not to be forsaken, neither are the duties of caste and condition to be neglected: it is only indispensable, that all hope of benefit from the discharge of these obligations shall be utterly discarded, and this, with trust in Krishńa as the supreme, secures emancipation from corporal existence.

V. 13. The word *Kritánta* has not been understood by the translator. He has rendered *Sánkhye kritánte proktáni* by 'rationali demonstrationi explicata'; but *Kritánte* is not an epithet of *Sánkhye*: it is the denomination of a different school of philosophy, or as Wilkins accurately translates the passage, 'declared in the Sánkhya and Vedánta Sástras', *Kritánta* meaning literally the end of works, or the Philosophy which crowns the previous observances enjoined by the Veda.

In the following stanza again *adhishthánam* has been misunderstood: it does not mean regimen,* but site, receptacle, or in other words the body as the seat of the elements and faculties: five instrumental causes being necessary, it is said, to the accomplishment of all acts, viz. place, agent, instrument, active effort, and the will of God, not as Schlegel writes, fatum.

In the specification of the different kinds of knowledge in verse 21 and 22, the translation is far from distinct or correct. Knowledge is affected by the three guńas: in conjunction with the *sattwa guńa* it recognises the universality and identity of spirit in all states; this is the doctrine of the Vedánta and of the Gítá. When influenced by the *rajo guńa*, it contemplates

---

* [2nd ed. "dirio".]

spirit as individualised by eternal impressions; and when associated with the *tamo guña*, it limits spirit by its connexion with matter, and gives it only local and temporary existence: the stanzas conveying these notions relatively to the two last qualities run thus. "That knowledge which by the individuality of bodies conceives distinct properties and forms (of spirit) in all being, that is knowledge influenced by passion. But that knowledge which attaches itself to a single object as to the whole, which springs from no cause, which possesses not the truth, and is contemptible, that is considered as the knowledge that is affected by darkness." The passage is thus rendered in the Latin translation: Singulatim autem quæ cognitio varios existendi modos peculiares novit in omnibus quæ existunt, hanc cognitionem scias esse impetuosam. Quæ vero ad singulum negotium applicata est, quasi sit universitas rerum, principiis carens, veri summæ haud consentanea atque angusta, ea cognitio caliginosa nuncupatur.

An emendation is made in the last stanza of the poem, and Schlegel reads the second line *Tatra trir vijayo bhútir dhruváñiti matir mama*, hic faustitas, victoria, principatus; cuncta ea stabilia. Sic stat sententia. The last phrase would at any rate be so far incorrect that it omits 'men'. Sanjaya, the speaker, giving it only as *his* conviction that all the blessings enumerated result from Krishńa's presence. Instead of *dhruváñiti*, stabilia, however, the common and no doubt correct reading is *dhruvá*, Fortitudo, and *nítir*,

Consilium; *niti* being detached by all the commentators, and explained by its cognate synonyme *naya,* royal leading, state policy or the wisdom of administration. Although, therefore, the emendation is plausible, and according to European taste might be an improvement in the construction of the sentence, it cannot be admitted in the face of all concurrent testimony against its necessity.

We have now completed our survey of Schlegel's translation of the Bhagavad Gítá. It will be seen that we have been able to point out many questionable and defective passages in the translation, and we might, if so disposed, have extended their number. With very few exceptions however the criticisms are merely verbal, and the instances in which the sense of a passage is materially misapprehended are by no means frequent: that this should be the case, is we think highly creditable to the translator. The subject is abstruse, and the manner of treating it not always perspicuous, and that the translation should have been so generally correct, is therefore matter of more surprise, than that it should have been occasionally erroneous. Schlegel also mentions that he was, as we have noticed, not possessed of any commentaries on the work, and this is evident, for many of the faulty passages would no doubt have been given correctly if he could have had the advantage of the light thrown upon their purport by the observations of the annotators. In some of the latter books we can trace a partial reference to Śrídhara Swámí, the circumstances of which are explained in the preface to the translation, but the references are not frequent and leave to the translator the merit of independent interpretation. On the whole therefore we are of opinion, that the translation of the Bhagavad Gítá is not unworthy of Schlegel's reputation, and that he is entitled to that rank amongst oriental scholars, which he has long enjoyed amongst the scholars of the west.

In entering so largely as we have done upon the analysis of the doctrines of the Gítá, we have not had in view only the necessity of their being understood in order that the character of the work might be duly appreciated, but we have wished to direct the attention of our readers to those suggestions which the Hindu dogmas are calculated to inspire. It is impossible to avoid noticing in the double doctrine of the Gítá an analogy to the double doctrine of the early Christian church, and the same question as to the merits of contemplative and practical religion engendered many differences of opinion and observance in the first ages of Christianity. These discussions, it is true, grew out of the admixture of the platonic philosophical notions with the lessons of Christianity, and had long pervaded the east, before the commencement of our era: it would not follow, therefore, that the divisions of the Christian Church originated the doctrine of the Hindus, and there is no reason to doubt that in all essential respects the Hindu schools are of a much earlier date: at the same time, it is not at all unlikely that the speculations of those schools were re-agitated and re-modified in the general stimulus which Christianity seems to have given to metaphysical enquiry, and it is not impossible that the attempts to model the ancient systems into a popular form, by engrafting on them, in particular, the vital importance of faith, were indirectly influenced by the diffusion of the Christian religion. It is highly desirable that this subject should be further investigated, as besides the illustration of the history of the Hindu religion and literature to be derived from it, it is of some importance to the early annals of our Church, and still more to the history of philosophy.

XIII.

PREFACE
TO THE
SANSKRIT DICTIONARY
(1st edition. Calcutta: 1810).

The cultivation of the Sanskrit language by European scholars has been hitherto much impeded by the absence of such assistance as that which is now proffered them. The elements of the language have been fully and distinctly developed and explained, and they have been studied, in a few instances, with a zeal proportioned to the difficulty of the task, and a success that could scarcely have been anticipated from the arduousness of the attempt and inadequacy of the means: in general, however, the want of a Dictionary has tended to deter application, and retard advancement, and has proved a serious obstacle to the intimate and extended acquirement of a language, which holds a most important place in literary history, and should be an object of primary interest to all who are charged with the government and happiness of Hindus.

To supply a deficiency as fatal to nascent curiosity, as embarrassing to study more advanced, the present translation of an extensive original compilation has been prepared. The original work was commenced shortly after the institution of the College of Fort William, for the use of which it was designed, being evidently connected with the objects and interests of that excellent establishment. Having been necessarily entrusted to native scholars, and being a task not very familiar to their literary habits, it is not surprising that much time should have been expended upon its execution, and that a delay more than commensurate with the extent and value of the work should have occurred: it was not finished till the year 1809, under the final superintendence of the late Raghumaṇi Bhaṭṭáchárya; and then constituted, although far from complete, the only compilation in the Sanskrit language to which the name of Dictionary could with propriety be applied.

The Koshas of the Sanskrit Lexicographers, of which the best, the Amara Kosha, has been published with a translation by Mr. Colebrooke, are with a few exceptions mere vocabularies: their contents are classed according to analogy of import, and distributed into sections or chapters, according to the judgment or fancy of the author, and the synonymes of each signification are then strung together in a metrical combination, in which they take the situation that rhythm and quantity prescribe. The inconvenience of this arrangement is obvious: it is not always easy in the first instance to know in what division of the work the word we are in quest of is to be found; when this is ascertained, the discovery of the stanza or line in which it occurs is an occupation of some time and trouble, and when in imagination we have reached the goal, and attained the situation where the object of our search should be, the amalgamation of Sanskrit vocables by the laws of Sandhi, or the euphonous combination of letters, frequently renders the extraction of the individual term a task that requires more skill and experience than a student, nay even a Pańdit, is found to possess. This last difficulty is of invariable occurrence, but in some Koshas, and in the *Nánártha* chapters of all, or those chapters which treat of words possessing various senses, an approach is made to an alphabetical arrangement and the form of a Dictionary. The alphabetical arrangement, however, is in some cases only partial, as in the Amara Kosha, where words terminating with the same final letter are contiguously placed, but they are then disposed at random: in others, as in Ajayapála, the initial letter is the connective characteristic, but there, as in the former case, the arrangement goes no farther. In the Medini again, which is exclusively appropriated to homonymous terms, a methodical system is adopted, perplexing from its fastidious exactness. The vocables are in that compilation arranged first according to their final letters; they are then classed agreeably to the number of syllables they contain, and they are then placed in an order, which is in general strictly alphabetical. The method adopted in the Medini, of arranging words according to their final letters and syllabic extent, is the prevailing plan of the Nánártha Koshas, but that work, and the last chapter of Hemachandra, are the only ones in which much attention is paid to their subsequent disposition, and these vocabularies therefore, although consulted with more facility than those which are described above, still present many difficulties to the practised scholar, and are of little value or advantage to the early student.

The Sanskrit vocabularies still in use are in considerable number: they repeat each other of course, but each has in general made some additions to the labours of its predecessors, and is consequently deserving of reference: the words of the language are thus scattered through a variety of authorities, none of which can be readily consulted or understood with ease.

To collect these different authorities into one compilation, and arrange their united contents in an accessible shape, were the objects of the work undertaken for the use of the College; and to these were added the citation of the authority, and the synonymes there given, the specification of the genders of nouns, and the etymological analysis. It was written in the Bengálí character, and occupied four large folio volumes.

A copy of the Dictionary thus described came into my possession shortly after I commenced my Sanskrit studies, and I anticipated the most valuable assistance to them from such a source. I found, however, that it comprehended in its etymological details, and lengthened quotations of synonymes, much more than I then required, and that from its unwieldy size it was inconvenient and embarrassing in use. I therefore effected its conversion into a more commodious form, and prepared a translation of its abbreviated contents for my private reference. I state these circumstances to obviate the charge of presumption in engaging at so early a period, and with such inadequate powers, in a task of this nature, and for undertaking which at all this explanation will account.—I may further add, that even at this time I was encouraged in the attempt by the approbation of the late zealous and accomplished Orientalist Doctor John Leyden, whose own unwearied ardour in the prosecution of Asiatic literature delighted to cherish in others the faintest dawn of a congenial spirit.

Upon the completion of my task, circumstances led to the communication of its results to Mr. Colebrooke, a name which in Hindu literature and science carries with it a weight and authority that all must bow to, and by his advice I was induced to revise my labours, and to hope that they might be rendered serviceable to the study of Sanskrit lore. How far that hope is likely to be realized, depends now upon the opinion of the Public, but it may be necessary to the accuracy of its decision to be apprised of the intentions I proposed to effect, and the means I had of executing them; so that I may not be unjustly censured for failing in a project I never entertained, or imperfectly accomplishing a task that my materials were incompetent to perform.

The preparation of the Dictionary as it now appears rendered my first work of no practical utility, especially as in the course of the first translation it had not occurred to me to question or verify the correctness of my original. I had therefore to recommence my labours, and carefully to collate the compilation of Raghumaṅi with the authorities on which it rested, and it soon appeared that accuracy was no part of the Compiler's merits: the mistakes were innumerable, and of every kind; words incorrectly written and erroneously interpreted, fanciful etymologies covering and sanctioning those errors, passages wrongly cited, and the names of the original vocabularies constantly confounded, met me in every page, and the adjustment of these inaccuracies, added to the difficulty inseparable from a reference to such unmethodical guides as the Sanskrit Koshas, has rendered the business of collation the most laborious and harrassing portion of my task. Fortunately it was a duty in which my native assistants were best employed, and they have been especially so occupied. To those who are acquainted with the character of these assistants it is needless to expatiate upon the necessity of vigilantly superintending and revising whatever they do, and it would be difficult to convey to a person not acquainted with them any conception of their carelessness and indolence, and of the limited dependance to be placed upon native research, when not sedulously and unremittingly controlled. I have had in the course of my labours the aid of many Paṅdits of high credit and respectable acquirements, and regret much, that

I cannot associate the name of any one of them with my own, as a partner in the little credit I may hope to derive from the present publication.

The plan of the original compilation, including the contents of the vocabularies alone, left the work exceedingly defective: the Roots of the language are all excluded from those collections, as are most technical terms and words of common occurrence, and none of these accordingly were comprised in Raghumaṇi's Dictionary. I am disposed, indeed, to question the expedience of the primary plan, and to conceive that a more useful Lexicon might have been drawn up from the classical compositions of the best Hindu writers, instead of deriving it from the Koshas only. At the same time, as these last are the received authorities of all India, and as the interpretations resting on general writings may be contested; as they are also perpetually cited in the ablest commentaries, and their omission might have given undue importance to their supposed contents, it was absolutely necessary to comprehend within the scope of the work as many of them as were procurable. To have added to these authorities the general body of Hindu compositions would have involved an amount of labour, cost and time, and a voluminous extent of preparation, which the state of Sanskrit study does not yet require, and perhaps does not permit, and it is therefore with some hesitation that I suggest any objections to the original plan. To remedy its deficiencies at all was obviously not incumbent upon one who appeared in the humble character of Translator only, and I should have been justified therefore in confining the limits of my Translation to those of the original. As some of its omissions were however of importance, I felt myself bound to supply them, and I have made very considerable additions to the original work. These additions were such as were most obviously useful, and particularly include the whole number of the *Radicals* of the language. But I shall not pause here, to offer a more detailed notice of them, as their specification will more consistently occur under the description I shall now proceed to give of the sources whence not only they, but the contents of the entire work, are derived. The authorities cited in the original compilation, and collated in the course of translation, are for the greater part the same as those enumerated in the preface to Mr. Colebrooke's translation of the Amara Kosha. The text of that work employed on the present occasion is that of his very accurate edition, and I have been indebted to him for the copies of the different commentaries consulted by him in his translation, and which were handed over to me, with the ready liberality which has always characterised that distinguished scholar. To his account, therefore, of these works I might be contented to refer; but, as I hope to add something to the limited knowledge we possess of the author of the Amara Kosha, and as I have to notice several works not adverted to by Mr. Colebrooke, I have thought it advisable to include the whole in the enumeration of my authorities, and thus bring into one view all the information we possess at present of those writers who are celebrated as lexicographers by the Hindus.

The *Amara Kosha*, or vocabulary of Amara Sinha, is a compilation too well known in Europe to need any particular description. It is in India the vocabulary most generally celebrated, and of the widest circulation, being a work of unquestionable authority in all the schools, and with every sect. The author, by his appellation *Sinha*, would seem to have belonged to the *Kshatriya* or military tribe, but it may merely designate his eminence, in which sense it is often conjoined to words: in like manner, though in Amara Deva, another appellation by which he is known, the latter term is a Brahmanical surname, yet it may be merely an epithet alluding to his superior or divine merit. He is generally, and apparently with reason, considered to have been a follower of *Buddha*, although this is denied by one of his late commentators, Rámáśrama, and all tradition concurs in enumerating him amongst the learned men who, in metaphorical phraseology of the Hindus, are denominated the "*nine gems*" of the court of Vikramáditya.

The era at which the author of the Amara Kosha flourished, connected as it is by these long and universally current traditions with a period of peculiar splendour in the literary annals of India, is an object of profound interest: to ascertain it within any reasonable bounds would fix the date of a number of celebrated compositions, whose age is involved at present in utter obscurity, and would determine the time and existence of a monarch, of whom, notwithstanding he furnishes an epoch by which Hindu dates are still regulated, the accounts are contradictory and perplexed. How far it is practicable to effect this object, will best appear from the following considerations, the extent of which will find a sufficient excuse in the important associations which are involved in the result. Authorities which assert the contemporary existence of Amara and Vikramáditya might be indefinitely multiplied, and those are equally numerous which class him amongst the "*nine gems*". The specification of these worthies, including the name of Amara Sinha, occurs however in a verse which appears in a great measure traditionary only, as I have not been able to trace it to any authentic source, although it is in the mouth of every Pańḍit, when interrogated on the subject. It has been published by Mr. Bentley, in his Essay on the Hindu systems of Astronomy, in the 8th volume of the Asiatic Researches, and as it is sufficient for the purposes of the present enquiry I shall here insert it.*

धन्वन्तरिक्षपणकामरसिंहशङ्कु-
वेतालभट्टघटकर्परकालिदासाः ।

---

* Asiatic Researches VIII, 242. It may be observed that in this verse, as printed in the Researches, the name of Ghaṭakarpara is misspelt, Ghaṭakarpúra: the name is itself a poetical one, and the meaning of it with the passage in which it originally occurs are given in Mr. Colebrooke's Essay on Sanskrit and Prákrit Poetry, Asiatic Researches X, 402. [Misc. Essays, II, 75.]

धन्वन्तरिक्षपणकामरसिंहशङ्कु
वेतालभट्टघटखर्परकालिदासाः ।
ख्यातो वराहमिहिरो नृपतेः सभायां
रत्नानि वै वररुचिर्नव विक्रमस्य ॥

"Dhanwantari, Kshapaṅaka, Amara Sinha, Śanku, Vetála Bhaṭṭa, Ghaṭakarpara, Kálidása, the celebrated Varáhamihira, and Vararuchi, were the nine gems in the court of the Monarch Vikrama."

From the identity of some of the names, contained in the above stanza, with some which occur in a work entitled the *Bhoja Prabandha*, a collection of literary anecdotes relating to the prince of Dhárá named *Bhoja*, and from its being undoubtedly true that the term Vikrama is a title rather than a proper name, and applied in Indian history to many different princes, it has been inferred that the Vikrama mentioned in the stanza is either Bhoja himself, or his immediate successor whose name is said to have been Vikrama, and that the "*nine gems*" flourished during the reigns of these two princes, being first in the council of Rájá Bhoja, and afterwards in that of Vikramáditya, his successor.* The reign of Bhoja is placed by Mr. Bentley at the end of the tenth, and beginning of the eleventh century, or from 982 to 1082;† and by Major Wilford Bhoja's death is placed in the year 977 or 982 at latest.‡ In either case, if Amara, and the other writers enumerated in the verse, were contemporary with Bhoja, the golden age of Hindu literature will be transferred from the century preceding the

---

* Asiatic Researches VIII, 243. † Asiatic Res. VIII, 243.
‡ Asiatic Researches IX, 157.

Christian era to which it is usually referred, or the commencement of the era of Vikramáditya, to a comparatively modern period, and be not much more than eight centuries remote.

The accuracy of this conclusion, opposed as it is by the concurring and consistent traditions of the country, and by a belief that has existed, unaltered and unassailed, for many centuries, cannot be unhesitatingly admitted, especially when upon investigation it appears to have been advanced upon grounds of a slight and frail texture in themselves, and loosely or partially examined.

The first subject of doubt is the authenticity and weight of the stanza, which is given to us, as the authority for the contemporary existence of the individuals it particularises; no mention is made of the work whence it is extracted, nor the writer to whom it is ascribed, nor are we furnished with any data by which to judge of the claims it possesses on our credit.* In truth, it appears to be little more than traditionary, as although familiar to every Paṅdit, I never met with one who could tell me its origin or author. It is attributed by some to the *Vikrama Charitra*, but they have only asserted this upon report, and I have not been able to procure a copy of that work in order to

---

* [Prof. F. E. Hall was the first to assign the verses in question to the author of the Jyotirvidábharaṅa, a modern composition. See his edition of Wilson's Vishṅupuráṅa, I, p. VII-IX; comp. also Bháu Dájí in Journal As. Soc. Bombay, Vol. VI, p. 23 ff.]

verify the assertion; it may be doubted indeed whether the entire work exists, as Major Wilford at Benares could not meet with it, and was indebted to extracts supplied by Colonel Mackenzie from an imperfect manuscript procured in the Peninsula.* If the statement be correct, however, it adds but little strength to the argument, as the *Vikrama Charitra*, like the *Sinhásana Dwátrinśati*, and *Vetála Panchavinśati*, is a collection of mere fables, and of no historical weight. As a composition of apparently modern date, it is probably a mere transcript of some popular tradition in the list of Vikramáditya's *"nine gems"*; and we are therefore obliged to assail this tradition with the instruments itself supplies, and derive from traditionary evidence our only proof, that all such evidence is unworthy of belief. If the verse under discussion be a proof that Amara was the contemporary of any of the literary characters there named, it proves also that he was contemporary with *Rájá Vikrama*, and in order to be consistent in the argument which reduces Amara's antiquity, it becomes necessary to affix the name of the monarch to some other than the original Vikramáditya to whom it is usually assigned. That the enumeration is not entirely accurate, may be inferred from its comprising Vararuchi as well as Amara; as the former is considered by the commentators as one of Amara's authorities, and necessarily

---

* Asiatic Researches X, 30. [Mackenzie Collection I, 343 ff. Journal Asiatique, IVme Série, VI, 288 ff. Lassen, Ind. Alt., II, 759.]

therefore his predecessor, but as it is consistent with general belief, we need not place any stress on this exception. That by Vikrama however is intended either *Rájá Bhoja* or his successor, may confidently be denied.

The principal argument for placing the nine writers in the court of Bhoja is supposed to be furnished by the *Bhoja Prabandha*, a work in which it is said, that the "*nine gems*" are stated to have flourished under that prince, and that they are specified as the very persons named in the list above cited: assertions of which the first is untrue, and the second but partially correct.

The *Bhoja Prabandha* is a work of no estimation nor authority: its purport is the commemoration of the liberal patronage which men of letters experienced from Bhoja, the sovereign of Dhárá or Dhar in Málwá, and it introduces a number of the most celebrated writers in India as interlocutors in short dialogues with each other, or with the prince, in which they are supposed to display peculiar readiness of wit, brilliancy of imagination, or beauty of expression.* It might have been conceived to hold the character of a Sanskrit Anthology, or a collection of 'Elegant Extracts', had not the author neglected the variety of characteristic selection for the sameness of original

---

* [Prof. F. E. Hall justly observes: "It is high time to give up speaking of this prince as a great patron of literature. His pretensions to be so considered rest on the frailest foundation possible." Bengal Journal for 1862, p. 13.]

composition. According to Mr. Bentley it was written by *Vallála Sena*,* a prince who lived in the twelfth century.† Mr. Ward says, it was written by Bhoja himself, which is an evident inaccuracy.‡ One copy in my possession agrees so far with the first of these statements, as to term the writer *Vallála Pańdita;* but another, and a more correct copy denominates him *Vallabha Pańdita*. The last is a name of no note, nor are any data given for conjecturing his age; but from the names of authors contained in the work, whose dates are ascertained, it is clear that Vallabha Pańdita, if a correct appellation of the writer, could not have composed it earlier than the age of *Vallála Sena*, and neither of these authors therefore can be supposed peculiarly well qualified to report conversations, which they describe as having been held some centuries before; and the whole is a fiction of no historical value. If any weight can be attached to it, it can only be supposed as intended to give an account of the writers who were distinguished in the three or four centuries preceding the Author's own time, and cannot be admitted as an accurate notice of those of any particular age or reign. We have proofs of this indeed in the contemporary association of individuals, who we know lived at distant intervals; and Maheśwara whose date is A. D. 1111, and Mádhava who

---

* Asiatic Researches VIII, 244.   † Ibid. V, 64.
‡ Ward on the History, Religion, and Literature of the Hindus, I, 516.

wrote about A. D. 1340, are both present in the court of Bhoja, who himself died at the latest in 1082: such being the consistency and the accuracy of a record, which has been supposed to establish for the works of "Varáha, Amara Sinha, Kálidása, and Vararuchi an antiquity of little more than seven hundred years."*

The general unfitness of the Bhoja Prabandha to be regarded as an authority, which has thus been pointed out, might be sufficient to show, that no inference of Amara's existing at Bhoja's court as drawn from the Bhoja Prabandha is entitled to our attention; but as an object of literary discussion, and to shew the spirit in which some part of this enquiry has been conducted, I must be permitted to dwell a little longer on the subject.

The most correct copy of the work I have been able to procure, and which was brought by my friend Captain Price from Benares, I have perused with the closest attention. In no part of it is it asserted that there were "nine gems" at Bhoja's court, nor do the names of more than two of those *nine gems* occur in it. Individually and successively introduced as interlocutors in the dialogue, the different writers are very

---

* [See Journal As. Soc. Bombay, VI, 23; Prof. Hall in the preface to his edition of the Vásavadattá, p. 7, who calls the author of the Bhoja Prabandha *Ballála Misra*; Lassen, Ind. Alt., III, 836 ff. Prof. Aufrecht (Catal. Sanscr. MSS. I, 151) places the Bhojaprabandha at the end of the 16th century, which is more probable than the 13th to which M. Pavie (Journal Asiatique, Vme Série, IV, 429) assigns it.]

numerous, but amongst them the only name that occurs in the stanza above given is that of *Kálidása*: we have however in the following enumeration of Bhoja's learned men one other appellative which may be identified with one in the verse:

अथ धारानगरे न कोऽपि मूर्खौ निवसति । अमैव पञ्च-
शतानि देवली विदुषां श्रीभोजम् । वररुचिसुबन्धुमायूरमयू-
ररामदेवहरिवंशशङ्करकलिङ्गकर्पूरविनायकमदनविद्यावि-
नोदकोकिलतारेन्द्रमुखाः ।*

"Then there was no blockhead in the city Dhárá, but five hundred learned men severally attended on Śrí Bhoja, as Vararuchi, Subandhu, Váńa, Mayúra, Rámadeva, Harivanśa, Śankara, Kalinga, Karpúra, Vináyaku, Madana, Vidyávinoda, Kokila, Tárendra, and others,"—a very different series of names, and authors, from the 'nine gems' we have enumerated, with the single apparent exception of Vararuchi.

It is now perfectly well understood, that in India identity of name is by no means identity of person, and that the celebrity of any particular denomination is the cause of its being assumed by many besides its original possessor. In the history of the Mogul empire in Hindustan many Vikramádityas or Bickermajits are found amongst their tributary Rájás, and at this moment many *Kálidásas* are to be met with in India as poets at the courts of men of opulence and rank, as if they expected to inherit with these attributes of their

---

* [In M. T. Pavie's edition p. 21 and v. l. p. 131. Journal Asiatique, l. l., p. 396.]

illustrious prototype some spark of his divine spirit. That there were at least *two* eminent bards of this name, is the general opinion of Hindu scholars, and the belief is borne out by the internal evidence of the compositions ascribed to Kálidása, which have every mark of having been written at different periods, both of time and taste. The existence of a Kálidása at the court of Bhoja is therefore no argument against Amara's being contemporary with another bard of that name, or to their both having flourished long anterior to the reign of that prince.*

That the name of *Vararuchi* has in like manner been applied to different individuals, might fairly be inferred from the practice thus described; but we have in this case a remarkable confirmation of our conjectures, and find, from the varying statements of several writers, that two, if not three, persons of this denomination are celebrated in the literary history of the Hindus.

In the *Kathá Sarit Ságara*, the same work in substance as the Vṛihat Kathá, and by the same author Somadeva, who declares that his abridgement has omitted no essential part of his own original, the ancient Grammarian *Kátyáyana* is said to be the same person as Vararuchi, and to be called indiscriminately by either name. The opening of this work, in the usual style of Hindu story-telling, introduces us to

---

* [See Journal Bombay As. Soc. Vol. VI, 19 ff.; 207 ff. Lassen, Ind. Alt., II, 1157 ff. Weber's "Málaviká und Agnimitra". Berlin: 1856, Introduction.]

superhuman agency: a demi-god named Pushpadanta, an attendant upon Śiva, has incurred the displeasure of his irascible mistress Durgá, and is condemned to expiate his offence by wearing for a certain time the human form; in obedience to this sentence, he appears upon earth as a learned Brahman, named indifferently Kátyáyana or Vararuchi, तत: स सर्वमुखा पुष्पदन्त: परि-
भ्रमन् । नाम्ना वररुचि: शिष्य कात्यायन इति श्रुत: ॥*

Proceeding a few pages, we find Kátyáyana narrating his story to the Brahmans Vyádi and Indradatta, and he tells them that his birth was proclaimed by a voice from heaven, in the following stanza:

एकश्रुतधरो बालो विद्यां वर्षाद्वाप्स्यति ।
शिष्य वार्षस्य कोपि प्रतिष्ठां प्रापयिष्यति ॥
नाम्ना वररुचिर्लोके तत्सदृशो हि रोचते ।
वररुचि रवेतिक्रिर्द्धिङ्गुक्का भगुधारयत् ॥†

"A Śrutadhara is born who shall acquire knowledge from Varsha (a foolish Brahman so named), and shall give perfection to grammatical science amongst men: something of whatever is excellent (varam) shines (rochate) in him, and therefore he shall be known in the world by the name Vararuchi. Having thus spoken the voice ceased."

That Vararuchi, alias Kátyáyana, was a different person from the Vararuchi of Bhoja's court, will scarcely be disputed: the latter is regarded as the Purohita, or family priest, of the monarch, and is little known as an author. He is said to have written the

---

* [Tar. II, 1.]   † [Tar. II, 69. 70.]

Bhoja Champú in conjunction with his royal master, and to have completed the work after that prince's death. He is also known as the maternal uncle of *Subandhu*, the author of the Vásavadattá, a tale which that author appears to have modernised, and which in its older form, and with different names, is told in the Vṛihat Kathá, and is also alluded to by Kálidása* and Bhavabhúti, who consequently are prior to Subandhu, and who might have been contemporary or nearly so with his uncle. This Vararuchi must therefore be a very different character from Vararuchi or Kátyáyana, the grammarian, one of Páṇini's earliest commentators, the author of the Várttika, of the Prákṛita Manorama, and possibly of the work which is enumerated by the commentators on Amara amongst the authorities of that vocabulary. *They* indeed reckon amongst those authorities Kátyáyana also, and consequently make a distinction between these two writers. It is possible that they are correct, but the discrepancy that thus occurs between the two accounts is favourable to the present enquiry, as it renders it possible that we have *three* Vararuchis instead of one, and at least furnishes a positive proof, that the name is far from being the exclusive property of the person noticed in the Bhoja Prabandha.

It may indeed be asserted, that the Kathá Sarit Sá-

---

* Megha Dúta with translation, 36 and note [p. 341 in Vol. II of this division of Prof. Wilson's works]: also Asiatic Researches X, 151. [Colebrooke's Misc. Essays, II, 134.]

gara, or rather Vṛihat Kathá, is not a much better guide than the Bhoja Prabandha, and that a collection of idle stories is bad historical evidence. It must be remembered, however, that those tales are not of Somadeva's invention: he has only the merit of telling them in his own way, and of having collected them together from various quarters. Thus we have most of the legends relating to Vikrama, which constitute the Sinhásana Dwátriṅśati, and Vetála Panchaviṅśati, and we have also a very considerable portion of the Hitopadeśa, or Panchatantra, comprised in this selection: such as the tales are, therefore, they are of remote origin and existence, and are at least faithful records of the state of popular belief many ages ago. The compilation itself is of some antiquity. Major Wilford states that it is to be considered to be between 6 and 700 years old, and this antiquity is corroborated by the mention* of the work made by Govarddhana, the author of the Sapta Satí, who flourished probably in the twelfth century. Now seven centuries would bring the Vṛihat Kathá very near to the reign

---

* Catalogue of oriental works presented to the Royal Society by Lady Jones, No. 15. Sir William Jones' works XIII, 409. The original verse is:

श्रीरामायणभारतवृहत्कथानां कवीन्प्रमन्ये:
विजीता एव सरखा सरखती खुरति त्रिविधा ॥

thus rendered by Sir William Jones, "we do homage to the poets who composed the Rámáyaṅa, the Mahábhárata, and the Vṛihatkathá, by whom delightful eloquence blazes forth divided like the river with three streams." [F. E. Hall in the Preface to his edition of the Vásavadattá, p. 22.]

of Bhoja himself, and if the date of that reign has been ascertained with any correctness, the prince and his minister must have been characters familiar to the recollection of the author; that they were so, and consequently not yet objects of traditionary fiction, may be inferred from no notice being taken of them in any of the fables contained in the collection. At all events, if there had been a Vararuchi in Bhoja's court, it is not likely that at so recent a period he should have been confounded with the ancient grammarian Kátyáyana: nor would Somadeva, or any of the old fablers, have asserted, what all their contemporaries could contradict, that Bhoja's Vararuchi lived prior to the birth of Sátaváhana or Sáliváhana, the founder of the Śáka era, an antiquity which is assigned to him in one of the early chapters of the Vrihat Kathá. Whatever therefore we may think of Vararuchi and Kátyáyana being identified, it is very clear that a writer of the former name did precede the Vararuchi, who appears to have flourished in the reign of Bhoja, and the earlier of the two is most probably intended by the tradition which makes him the contemporary of Vikrama and Amara Sinha.[*]

I have thus shewn that the supposed coincidence

---

[*] [Lassen, Ind. Alt., II, 1156; IV, 805; Müller's Ancient Sanskrit Lit., 239 ff.; Cowell's edition of the Prákrita Prakáśa, Preface; Goldstücker's 'Páṇini'. London: 1861, p. 81 ff.; Weber's 'Indische Studien', V, 93 ff.; James d'Alwis, 'Introduction to Kachcháyana's grammar of the Páli language'. Colombo: 1863, p. XXXVI ff.]

of the persons in the verse which assigns the '*nine gems*' to Vikrama, and those enumerated in the Bhoja Prabandha, has no satisfactory existence, and that, except in the two doubtful cases I have specified, it has no existence at all: as far therefore as depends upon the Bhoja Prabandha, we have no reason to consider its hero as the same prince with the Vikrama of the verse, nor that Amara Sinha lived at so comparatively recent a period as his reign. That the latter was not the case, however, we have other and more probable testimony.

An inscription found by Mr. Wilkins at Buddha Gayá, of which he published a translation in the Asiatic Researches,[*] and which was written to commemorate the foundation of a temple of Buddha by Amara Sinha, bears the date 1005 of the era of Vikramáditya, answering to the Christian year 949: the authenticity of this inscription we have no reason to question, as it professes no object to which suspicion of fraud or interest can be attached, and it is perfectly consistent with the character and traditions of the place in which it was found: the identity of the person is also indisputable, as all ancient authorities concur in representing Amara as a worshipper of Buddha, and he is designated in the inscription in the usual manner as one of the nine gems of Vikramáditya's court.

Admitting therefore the testimony of this record, it follows that Amara Sinha was a person of some ce-

---

[*] Asiatic Researches, I, 284.

lebrity prior to the date given in it, or A.D. 949, and it is not likely therefore that he should be contemporary with Bhoja, who had scarcely commenced his reign according to Major Wilford's theory, or who did not ascend the throne till 30 years subsequent, according to Mr. Bentley's view of the subject. In fact however the tenor of the inscription renders either equally impossible, since that absolutely authorises our placing Amara long anterior to the period of its composition.

The author states his having derived his knowledge of Amara's being the founder of the temple from its records, or as it is translated "from the authority of the place", an authority which no doubt existed, as most celebrated shrines are furnished with a legend, a lying one it may be granted, which professes to give their history: and it matters not here, of what description was the record of the temple of Buddha, as, if in the middle of the tenth century it had converted Amara Sinha into the hero of a holy fable, it at least proves his prior and remote existence.

To return to the inscription: the writer states that "Amara was the favourite and minister of Vikramáditya, who was certainly a king renowned in the world", and whom he intends by Vikramáditya, can scarcely be doubted, as he dates from that prince's era: it is therefore perfectly clear that at so distant a period as A.D. 949, if the inscription is to be trusted, the same traditionary account of Amara's date prevailed, which is still received, and however accurate or incorrect this tradition may have been, its existence is fatal to the supposition that the subject of it was alive at the period when such a belief was current, and still more so to the opinion we have noticed of his flourishing at some subsequent date.

That the inscription is worthy of credit,* I see no reason to doubt, and it is assuredly an authority of more weight than the notions of nameless Paṅdits,† the sole impugners of the belief it sanctions.

The certainty that Amara Sinha lived before the time of Bhoja, and the inference fairly deducible from the only positive record we possess of his living *long before* that period, leave us still in doubt as to the precise time at which he flourished.

Tradition, uniform and consistent, and as we see by the inscription, and as we know from other testimonies, of unvarying tenor for seven or eight centuries, places him in the court of Vikramáditya, in the origin of the Samvat era, or 56 years before Christ; an antiquity far from unreasonable or improbable, although deemed by modern scepticism too remote. The only grounds on which this belief could ever have rested, the authority of the Bhoja Prabandha, I have shewn to be untenable, and I cannot therefore conceive the argument by which it can further be supported. The dispute, to use the words of *Harris* on a similar topic,

---

* [Comp. also Col. A. Cunningham's Report in As. J. of Bengal, Vol. XXXII, No. 13 ff.]

† Asiatic Researches, VIII, 243.

appears to arise from the 'disputants running into the opposite vice of incredulity, in order to avoid being thought credulous': for even in his day there was occasion to notice a defect, which is outrageously conspicuous in the writers of the present, when ancient India is their theme, "and whose opposition to the many claims of the Hindus is not so much founded in greater learning or superior talents, as in strong prejudices in favour of their own countries, and in high conceit of their own abilities."

The real date of Vikramáditya's reign is however still a desideratum in Indian History,* and in spite of the learned labours of that profound and patient investigator Major Wilford† we have yet to ascertain whether the voice of tradition be that of truth. The circumstances of Amara's being contemporary with him depends upon no positive proof, and there is some inconsistency in making the Buddha philologist the favourite and minister of a monarch, who is always described in the legends recorded of him as a pious worshipper of the orthodox divinities: and the liberal

---

* [Lassen, Ind. Alt., II, 800 ff. Weber, Ind. Stud., II, 416. Ind. Literaturgeschichte, p. 188. Bombay Asiatic Soc. Journal, VI, 27 ff.]

† Asiatic Researches, IX. Essay on Vikramáditya and Sáliváhana. [See Prinsep's Essays, ed. 2. Thomas, II, 249.]

‡ The Jains, I am informed, consider Vikramáditya to have been of their persuasion; in the Vrihatkathá, Sinhásana Dwátrinśati, and Vetála Panchavinśati, he always appears as the worshipper of Durgá or Devi especially.

patron of the regular priesthood. The age of the Amara Kosha can scarcely be fixed within any narrow limits, and we can only feel satisfied of its composition at some period long anterior to the tenth century,* an opinion further warranted by the grammarian Vopadeva, who is generally assigned to the twelfth century,† and who enumerates Amara amongst the eight *old* grammarians,‡ an epithet he would no more have attached to a writer but two or three centuries anterior to himself than any grammarian of the present day would think of giving to Bhattoji Dikshita, who compiled the Kaumudí about 200 years ago. Amara Sinha may therefore be left agreeably to tradition to the beginning of the Christian era, or, as connected with other traditionary notices of names and events which I shall proceed to describe, he may be brought down to a later date, and placed about the middle or end of the fifth century after Christ.

In the verse which specifies the names of the *nine gems*, and which I have inserted above, we find the name of the astronomer Varáha Mihira who, according to this authority, is therefore contemporary with

---

* [Lassen, Ind. Alt., IV, 633 f., now places Amarasinha before Varáhamihira, about 200 years later than he had done before, II, 1155. See also Goldstücker's Sanskrit Dictionary s. v. Amarasinha.]

† Asiatic Researches, VIII, 467; [to the second half of the thirteenth. See Burnouf, Bhág. Pur., I, CI, and Lassen, Ind. Alt., IV, 599.]

‡ Preface to Colebrooke's Sanskrit Grammar. [Misc. Ess., II, 89.]

Amara Sinha; this astronomer, upon grounds similar to those on which Mr. Bentley reduced the antiquity of Amara, has accordingly been placed by him* in the twelfth century, an opinion contrary to the general belief, and one which there is every reason to conclude is far from correct.

From astronomical data derived from the work of *Varáha Mihira*,† the Vṛihat Sanhitá, it appears that an antiquity must be assigned to this author of either 1216 or 1440 years, reckoning from A.D. 1800; the mean of this is assumed by Mr. Colebrooke, or A.D. 472, as being the probable era of his existence, and as agreeing sufficiently with the date usually given him, or A.D. 499, and not far from that contained in a list of astronomical writers prepared at Oujein, or A.D. 505-6. According to the same authority: he is

---

* Asiatic Researches, VIII, 243.

† Colebrooke on the age of Varáha Mihira, introduction to Indian Algebra &c. [Miscell. Essays, II, 466 ff. Lassen, Ind. Alt., IV, 841 ff.]

‡ See also introduction to Colebrooke's edition of the Hitopadeśa, p. II. The notice occurs in the first Tantra or chapter [v. 238] in the same story but somewhat differently told, which is in the Hitopadeśa, (Sir William Jones's works, Vol. XIII, 177) of a Vaka killed by a crab. The astronomer is thus introduced: the Vaka tells the crab that by the position of the planets a twelve years' drought may be expected, as it is said by Varáha Mihira "when the son of Súrya (Saturn) divides the car of Rohiṇí, then in the world Mádhava will shed no rain upon the earth for twelve years."

यथा वराहमिहिरेण ।

also named in the Pancha Tantra, the original of the Hitopadesa, and which was translated into Persian in the reign of Nushirván, in the latter part of the sixth and beginning of the seventh century, and this early notice is a decisive confirmation of the accuracy of the above date. It seems therefore to be ascertained, with as much precision as the subject admits, that an astronomical writer denominated Varáha Mihira did flourish at Oujein in the course of the fifth century of our era: and it is farther possible that he was cotemporary with a prince named Vikramáditya, and the subject of our Researches.

Major Wilford, in his elaborate Essay on Vikramáditya* and Sálivahana, has succeeded in disentangling from the perplexity occasioned by the repetition of names, and the confusion of dates, *three* princes of great power and celebrity, who were all known under the former appellation: the first of these is the sovereign from whom the era in use is denominated, and whose claims to be the patron of the *nine gems* we are contented to leave undetermined; the second Vikrama† is the same with Śrí Karńa Deva, called also Śúdraka and Śúraka and Áditya;‡ he began his reign A.D. 191, and this date agrees with the age of an elder Varáha Mihira, placed by the astronomers of Oujein in the

---

यदा भिंगी सूर्यंयुगी रोहिचा: यकटनिए लोबे ।
द्वादशवर्षाणि तदा न हि वर्षति माघवो भूवी ॥
[See on this quotation Henfey's "Pantschatantra", II, 302 f.]

* Asiatic Researches, IX.   † Ibid. 146.   ‡ Ibid. 139.

year of Christ 200;* his capital is called Charchitá or Charchitu Nagara,† the city of investigation, as the struggle between the original Hindu system, and the innovation of the Bauddhas and others is supposed to have commenced there and at this time. As Śrí Karńa Deva, however, was the sovereign of Magadha or Behar, and resided at a place now called Jangira,‡ half way between Mongir and Bhágalpore, it is impossible that Charchita Nagara could be the same as Ujjayiní or Oujein, in which city alone we are to look for the patron of the *nine gems*, and this prince consequently cannot be the Vikramáditya in question. The third Vikramáditya has better claims;§ he is not designated by any other name or title; his capital was Oujein, and his reign began in 441; a date that accords with the existence of Amara, as the cotemporary of Varáha Mihira in the fifth century, and with his being implicated in the changes which the temporary ascendancy of the Brahmans apparently began about that time to effect in Hindustan.

The persecution of the followers of Buddha by the Brahmanical order is a subject on which both sects are agreed; one of the earliest and most harmless effects of it, it is generally believed, was the anathematising of the Bauddha works, and amongst

---

* Colebrooke's Indian Algebra, introduction, dissertation E. [Misc. Essays, II, 467. Lassen, Ind. Alt., II, 1133.]

† Asiatic Researches, X, 91.

‡ Asiatic Researches, IX, 103.   § Ibid. 139. [E. Thomas' edition of Prinsep's Useful Tables, p. 249 f. Lassen, I. L, II, 759.]

them, of the compositions of Amara, all which consequently perished, with the exception of his Vocabulary.* As the persecution is thus restricted to Amara's literary existence, we may infer his personal exemption from its fury by his existence prior to that event, and by ascertaining therefore the time of its commencement we may be able to add another conjecture to those we have formed of our author's age. Celebrated as is the persecution and temporary suppression of the Bauddha heresy, it is an occurrence of which the date is as uncertain as of any other event in Hindu history: its institution is generally attributed to Sankara Áchárya,† and with his age therefore must originate our enquiry.

The birth of Śankara presents the same discordance of opinion as every other remarkable incident amongst the Hindus.

The Kadáll Brahmans, who form an establishment following and teaching his system, assert his appearance about 2000 years† since; some accounts place him about the beginning of the Christian era,‡ others in the third or fourth century § after; a manuscript history of the kings of Konga, in Colonel Makenzie's collection," makes him cotemporary with Tiru Vikrama Deva Chakravartí, sovereign of Skandapura in the

---

* Asiatic Researches, VII, 214.
† Buchanan's Mysore, III, 301.
‡ Wilks's History of Mysore, I, Appendix No. V.
§ Buchanan's Mysore, II, 74.
[Madras Lit. Soc. Journal, Vol. XIV, pp. 6 and 65.]

Dekhan, A.D. 178; at Śriṅgagiri, on the edge of the Western Ghauts, and now in the Mysore territory, at which place he is said to have founded a College that still exists, and assumes the supreme control of the Smártal Brahmans of the Peninsula, an antiquity of 1600 years is attributed to him, and common tradition makes him about 1200 years old. The Bhoja Prabandha enumerates Śankara amongst its worthies, and as contemporary with that prince; his antiquity will then be between eight and nine centuries. The followers of Madhwáchárya in Tuluva seem to have attempted to reconcile these contradictory accounts by supposing him to have been born three times; first at Sivuli in Tuluva about 1500 years ago, again in Malabar some centuries later, and finally at Pádukachaytra in Tuluva* no more than 600 years since; the latter assertion being intended evidently to do honour to their own founder, whose date that was, by enabling him to triumph over Śankara in a supposititious controversy. The Vaishńava Brahmans of Madura say that Śankara appeared in the ninth century of Sáliváhana or tenth of our era;† Dr. Taylor thinks that, if we allow him about 900 years, we shall not be far from the truth,‡ and Mr. Colebrooke is inclined to give him an antiquity of about 1000 years.§ This last is the age which my friend Rammohun Roy, a diligent

---

* Buchanan's Mysore, III, 91.   † Ibid. I, 143.
‡ Dedication to the translation of the Prabodha Chandrodaya.
§ Preface to the translation of the Dáya Bhága, [p. XI].

student of Śankara's works, and philosophical teacher of his doctrines, is disposed to concur in, and he infers that, "from a calculation of the spiritual generations of the followers of Śankara Swámí from his time up to this date, he seems to have lived between the seventh and eighth centuries of the Christian era,"— a distance of time agreeing with the statements made to Dr. Buchanan in his journey through Śankara's native country, Malabar,* and in union with the assertion of the Kerala Utpatti, a work giving an historical and statistical account of the same province, and which, according to Mr. Duncan's citation of it, mentions the regulations of the castes of Malabar by this philosopher to have been effected about 1000 years before 1798.† At the same time it must be observed that a manuscript translation of this same work, in Colonel Makenzie's possession, states Śankara Áchárya to have been born about the middle of the fifth century, or between thirteen and fourteen hundred years ago, differing in this respect from Mr. Duncan's statement,‡ — a difference of the less importance, as

---

* Buchanan's Mysore, II, 424.
† Asiatic Researches, V, 5.
‡ [See Mackenzie, Collection, II, p. 73 ff.] The manuscript agrees however with Mr. Duncan's statement in one important particular; the admission of Śankara's living in the time of the Malabar prince Cheruman Perumal, a prince who, from his connection with the Malabar Christian Church, has been long an object of attention to the scholars of the West. [Lassen, I. I., IV, 254 f.] According to Scaliger (De emendatione temporum, 525)

the manuscript in question, either from defects in the original or translation, presents many palpable errors, and cannot consequently be depended upon. The weight of authority therefore is altogether in favour of an antiquity of about ten centuries, and I am disposed to adopt this estimate of Śankara's date, and to place him in the end of the eighth and beginning of the ninth century of the Christian era.*

Although the popular belief attributes the origin of the Bauddha persecution to Śankara Ácháryu, yet in this case we have some reason to distrust its accuracy. Opposed to it we have the mild character of the reformer, who is described as uniformly gentle and tolerant, and speaking from my own limited reading in Vedánta works, and the more satisfactory testimony of Rámmohun Roy, which he permits me to adduce, it does not appear that any traces of his being instrumental to any persecution are to be found in his own writings, all which are extant, and the object of which is by no means the correction of the Bauddha or any

---

Calicut was founded in 907, and this event is ascribed to that prince by Assemannus (Bibl. Orient., Tom. 3, Part 2nd, 341 et seq.), but who observes that, according to Vischerus, it took place much earlier, or in 825. Cheruman Perumal is said to have granted many privileges to the Christians, inscribed on plates of copper, of which Du Perron procured copies, (Zend Avesta, Dis. Prel. clxxviii, and note) and which according to him corroborate the account of this transaction derived from Assemannus. This date will therefore nearly confirm the above view of Śankara's age and give us about ten centuries for his antiquity.

* [Lassen, Ind. Alt., IV, 618 ff.; 833 ff.]

other schism, but the refutation of all other doctrines besides his own, and the reformation or re-establishment of the fourth religious order. It is therefore probable that the Brahmans enjoyed the ascendancy in his times, and that the violent suppression of any powerful sect had considerably preceded the appearance of his peaceable system of worldly privation and abstract devotion.

Many works in celebration of this distinguished character, and in commemoration of his triumph over the errors of all other systems of theology, have been composed, entitled *Sankara-vijaya*,* or *Sankara-jaya*: they profess to narrate the most remarkable incidents of the reformer's life, and the different disputes held by him with his principal opponents. One of these I have examined: it is the work of Mádhava, a commentator on the Vedas agreeably to the Vedánta notions, and a writer of great celebrity. He is known to have lived about the year 1300,† by his making mention of Sangama, the father of Bukka Ráya and Harihara,‡ the founders of Vijayanagara. According to his

---

* [See on the Sankaradigvijaya and other accounts of Sankara's life 'Hindu Sects', new edition, p. 197 ff.]

† [1350.]

‡ Asiatic Researches, IX, 414; in addition to the instances there specified it may be observed, that *Sáyaña*, the author of the Mádhavíya-dhátu-vritti, calls himself the uterine brother of Mádhava and the son of Máyaña (?), the prime minister of Sangama, the son of Kampa, monarch of the eastern, southern, and western seas, or in fact of the Peninsula of India. इति पूर्वदिग्विजयविज-यसुद्रधीरक्षम्यराजयुतसङ्गमरायमहामन्त्रिणा माबयुवेद मा-

own statement, his work is but the substance of a much older performance, माधीयप्रदूरवये सारसंमुद्धमै कुरम् । and he speaks of Śankara as being celebrated by all the ancient writers, सूनो रपि सम्बद्धविभि: पुराबै: । confirming therefore at the least the antiquity I have above assigned to that theologian.

As far as the Śankara-vijaya of Mádhava can be admitted as an authority, and it is much too poetical and legendary to be so acknowledged without very great limitation, we may draw the same conclusion that is to be inferred from Śankara's own compositions, that it is a popular error to ascribe to him the work of persecution: he does not appear at all occupied in that odious task, nor is he engaged in particular controversy with any of the Bauddhas: the more prominent objects of his opposition are the Mímánsakas as represented by Mandana Miśra, with whom he holds a long and rather acrimonious discussion, and the Naiyáyikas and Sánkhyas, and the vulgar sects of Vaishṇavas and Śaivas are alike the object of his opposition; he is especially hostile to the latter, and particularly to the Kápálikas,* a class of Śiva's worshippers, who again are his most active enemies, and on one occasion assail his existence.

He comes in personal contact with the Bauddhas,

भवच्चोद्रेव सायवाचार्येव विरचिता माधवीया शानुभूति: ष
[See Westergaard, Rad. Sanscr., pref. p. II; A. Weber, 'Die Sanskrit-Handschriften', No. 789; Th. Aufrecht, Catal. Codd. Sanskr., I, 167.]

* [Hindu Sects, p. 21; 204. Lassen, Ind. Alt., III, 881; IV, 629.]

indeed, according to our authority, in but two instances: the first is a short conference with an Árhata, who advocates the Mádhyamika* doctrines, or those of a Bauddha sect, and which is held in the Bahlika country, a region identified by name and geographical position with the modern Balkh,† and the second happens in Kashmir, where amongst the many sects who oppose Sankara's access to the temple of Saraswatí, a short time before his death, the Bauddhas make their appearance. Besides the positive conclusion presented by these circumstances that Sankara was not engaged actively in any personal conflict with the followers of the Bauddha schism, we derive from them a very probable conjecture as to the situation of the Bauddhas in the time at which Mádhava flourished, and as he places them no nearer than in Kashmir and Khorasan, it appears likely that some period prior to his date was the epoch at which Bauddha faith was compelled to retire from its native seats towards those northern regions in which it still prevails.

The persecution of the Bauddhas is ascribed by Mádhava to another reformer, *Kumárila Bhatta*, the predecessor of Sankara. According to our author Kumárila Bhatta was an incarnation of Kártikeya, the object of whose descent was the extirpation of the Saugatas, and in consequence of whose miraculous victory over

---

* [See H. H. Wilson's Essays and Lectures, Vol. II, 363. Colebrooke's Essays, p. 251. Lassen, Ind. Alt., II, 460.]

† [Lassen, l. l., IV, 731 f.]

his heretical antagonists, the prince Sudhanwá issued the fatal orders to that effect:

जघ्नेतोरगुचाराद्विर्विाणां वृद्धबालकान् ।
न हन्ति यः स हन्तव्यो भूव्रानिबन्धशृङ्गवः ॥

"The king thus commanded his attendants, 'let those who slay not be slain, the old man amongst the Bauddhas and the babe, from the bridge of Ráma to the snowy mountains'."

The priority of the Bauddha persecution by Kumárila Bhatta to the age of Sankara is further corroborated by the manuscript account of Malabar, the Kerala Utpatti, which I have already adverted to. According to this authority, the establishment of this teacher in Malabar, local testimonies of which it is said existed when the work was written, took place about a century before the birth of Sankara, and occasioned the entire expulsion of the Bauddhanmár or Bauddhas from that kingdom; and we find on that side of India other accounts confirming this fact, and that the Brahmans of Tuluva who were originally followers of Bhatta Áchárya, the same with Kumárila Bhatta, assert his having had great success against the heretical sects some time before Sankara, who is represented as having disputed with, and converted the followers of Bhatta's particular doctrine.*

As the Bauddha sect, according to Mádhava, was annihilated by Kumárila Bhatta, it would have been a

---

* Buchanan's Mysore, III, 91. [Lassen, I. I., IV, 708. Wilson's Essays and Lectures, II, 366.]

work of supererogation to commit the same task to Śankara, and we have therefore further reason to doubt his ever having engaged in it at all, much more his having been the author and chief agent of the persecution. As, indeed, his reform is rather addressed to the admitted systems of theology, than to those considered heterodox, we must conclude that these latter had really suffered some temporary or partial discomfiture, so long prior to the age of Śankara Áchárya, as to have left time for the introduction and diffusion of various attempts towards the reformation of the orthodox faith, in the same manner as the innovations of Wickliffe and Huss preceded by a considerable interval the more successful efforts of Luther and Calvin.

According to the authority of Mádhava and that of tradition, Kumárila Bhatta committed himself to the flames in the presence of Śankara Áchárya: they would consequently be regarded as contemporary. We need not however lay much stress on these accounts, especially as Vyása and Jaimini, nay even Agastya, are all manifest personally to our reformer, if we are to give credit to our guide, and as, according to other authorities, Kumárila Bhatta was the pupil of Jaimini, the founder of the Mímánsá school of philosophy,* who there is reason to suppose is much more ancient. We can only therefore conclude generally that the triumph

---

* Dr. Taylor's Prabodha Chandrodaya, 119. [Brockhaus' edition, p. 110. Lassen, Ind. Alt., I, 836. Goldstücker, Pániní, p. 150; p. 8 ff.]

of Kumárila Bhaṭṭa and the persecution of the Bauddhas took place at some period anterior to the age of Śankara and before the eighth century; and, agreeably to the inference above deduced, at some period considerably antecedent, in which case the occurrence may be approximated to the date we have thought it probable to be that of Amara, or at least to the time, when his works might have required such celebrity, as to become obnoxious to a hostile and intolerant sect.

We have already had occasion to notice, upon the authority of Major Wilford, that the capital of Śúdraka, whose reign began in 191,[*] was named Charchita Nagara, with reference to its being the seat of the earliest disputes between the orthodox and dissentient classes of the Hindus. The assertion rests upon the authority of the Kumáriká Khaṅḍa, which in the prophetic style of the Puráṇas declares, that 'In the year 3291 of the Kali-yuga (or 191 after Christ) king Śúdraka will reign in the town of Charchita Nagara, and destroy the workers of iniquity;' and this, Major Wilford observes, points out a persecution in religious matters at a very early period. At the same time, we know that the utter extermination of the Bauddha sect in India did not take place till some time between the twelfth and fifteenth centuries, and we must conclude, consequently, that the contending parties were for a long period too equally matched for any permanent and vigorous

---

[*] Asiatic Researches, X, 91. [Wilson's Introd. to the Mrichchhakaṭí.]

persecution of either by the other to have taken place, and especially for some time after the beginning of the conflict. If therefore the contest began in the third century, and the temporary ascendancy of the Brahmans was established some time before the eighth, we may conjecture, with every appearance of conjecturing happily, that the fifth and sixth centuries form the season, in which the Bauddhas were most actively and triumphantly assailed by the interested professors of the orthodox creed.*

The time thus made out for the height of the Bauddha persecution agrees in a very remarkable manner with the date of events recorded in the countries where the faith of Buddha now predominates, and was entirely connected with the condition of his Indian votaries in their native realms. It was early in the sixth century (A.D. 519),† that China received from India the prophet Dharma, who gave a new impulse to the worship of Buddha, then languishing in that country, and fixed it as the national faith. In 530 the religion of Buddha was introduced into Corea;‡ in 540-50 into

---

* [Lassen, Ind. Alt., IV, 709.]

† Kæmpfer's Japan, B. 2, Chap. 4. The first introduction of the Bauddha faith into China took place much earlier; according to De Guignes, A.D. 65; but he adds, "on n'eut alors qu'une idée confuse de la religion de Fo, et ce n'est que dans la suite, qu'elle a été plus en vogue." He also notices 'la protection singulière' which the dynasty of the Liang that reigned from 519 [502] to 557, gave to the Religion of Fo. [Lassen. l. l., IV, 741 ff.; II, Beilage II, p. IX; Köppen, die Rel. Buddha's, I, 587; II, 31.]

‡ [According to Klaproth, 372 in Kao-li, and 384 in Pe-tsi. See Lassen, p. 746 f.]

Japan, and the year 572 was remarkable for the arrival in that kingdom of an immense number of Priests and Idols, who came from countries beyond the sea. We may conclude this branch of our enquiry by citing the opinion of the able historian of Java, Sir Thomas Raffles, that the Bauddha religion was introduced into that island during the sixth and seventh centuries, and that the same period was remarkable for the arrival of numerous Hindu emigrants on Java and the eastern islands.*

The examination I have thus instituted into the age of Amara Sinha has extended itself to limits, no doubt disproportioned to the importance of the enquiry: I had however to correct error, and to controvert prejudice, as well as to contend with the natural difficulties of the subject, and to support my averments by the best authorities within my reach. As to the result of the research, I shall willingly, if convinced by worthy testimony of having erred in my conclusions, submit to correction. Those conclusions, indeed, are only positive within certain limits, and as the sum of the investigation, I have only satisfied myself with the choice of one or two alternatives: either assent to the tradition which places Amara Sinha in the time of the primitive Vikramáditya, 56 years before the *Christian* era, or to the inference deduced from the contiguous position of a number of persons and things connected more or less directly with our author's supposed his-

---

* History of Java, II, 86. [Lassen, IV, 467 ff.]

tory, which designate the early part of the fifth century as the time at which Amara flourished.

Those notions which attribute an extravagant antiquity to the Hindus are fully as absurd as those which deny them any antiquity at all: as I have combated one set of opinions, therefore, it would have been just to expose the other, as epitomised in Fra Bartolomeo's account of Amara Sinha. To do this, however, it will be sufficient to cite his expressions, pausing only to observe that these absurdities are the composition of a man, who lavished every term of abuse upon the Angli Calcuttenses, then engaged under the auspices of Warren Hastings and Sir William Jones in instituting the legitimate enquiries which alone have displayed to European knowledge the true extent and character of Indian learning, and which he arrogantly and abruptly denounced as vain speculations and idle dreams. After most gratuitously and ridiculously converting Amara Sinha into Amara Chhihna and explaining that to signify librum cœli signa continentem, he proceeds: ita certe hujus vocabuli etymologiam et analysim mihi tradidit linguæ Samserdamicæ peritissimus vir, Ciangra Aashan, atque hallucinatos fuisse puto Calcuttenses Anglos, qui Amarasinha philosophum et Vikramaditya regis Indici a consiliis virum fuisse adstruunt, ipsique hunc librum nullo prorsus fundamento innixi adscribunt, cum tamen evidens esse videatur, *librum istum unà cum Idolatria Indica compositum fuisse, ac non solum totius mythologiæ et liturgiæ basim, sed primum librum precatorium esse, quo Brahmanes in ipso suæ* *idolatriæ exordio usi sunt;*[*] elevating in this extraordinary manner a common vocabulary to the distinction of a Ritual and *Liturgy* co-existent with the origin of the Hindu Idolatry, and the basis of the *Brahmanical* superstitions! A blunder of another character, although of an equally absurd description, connected with the Amara Kosha, has been committed by Anquetil Du Perron, and has been adduced by Mr. Mill,[†] with his usual want of knowledge and judgment, as '*a remarkable instance of the disposition of Brahmans to accommodate by falsification even their sacred records to the ideas of Europeans.*' Du Perron says: si je n'avois pas sçu que le commencement de l'Amarkosh contenait la description du Lingam, peut-être m'eut il été impossible de découvrir, que mes Brahmes, qui ne vouloient pas dévoiler le fond de leurs mystères, paraphrasoient et pallioient plutôt qu'ils ne traduisoient: a description of the Lingam in the introduction to the Amara Kosha! Du Perron's Brahmans must have been much astonished at the discovery, and at the perverse spirit and gross ignorance which converted Amara's account of the contents of his vocabulary, comprising the genders (linga) of nouns, into the mystical mention of an object with which his preamble

---

[*] Systema Brahmanicum, 194. [If P. Paul. a S. Bartholomæo ever entertained the notions so severely criticised in the text, he had certainly given them up when he wrote the preface to his "Amarasinha. Sectio prima." Rome: 1798, especially p. XI f. See also his "Vyácarana". Rome: 1804, p. XVII and 329.].

[†] History of India, Vol. I, 410.

has no kind of connection, except the indispensable employment of a grammatical term, that happens also to have the same meaning, but which occurring where and how it does, the merest novice in Sanskrit literature could not possibly misunderstand. We have had too much of mere pretenders to knowledge in oriental literature, and it is high time to weigh accurately the real merit of all authorities on matters of Asiatic learning and history if we wish to gain any real acquaintance with such subjects, or if we retain the slightest veneration for truth.

The vocabulary of Amara Sinha, though perhaps the oldest extant, is not considered as the first work of the kind; the author himself in his introductory lines mentions generally his having consulted other works, and his commentators particularise the Trikáṇḍa and Utpaliní Kosha and the works of Vyádi, Rabhasa, Kátyáyana, and Vararuchi, as the authorities to which he alludes. The text of the work has been some time known in Europe, though imperfectly,[*] and it is now placed within the reach of every scholar by the excellent edition of it with a marginal translation,

---

[*] Du Perron carried two copies to Europe, it was also noticed in the first volume of the *Asiatic Researches* (354): we have seen what Bartolomeo says of the work, and he took home a copy of it. Several copies more or less perfect were presented by Lady Jones to the Royal Society, and Frederick Schlegel in his work 'Ueber die Sprache und Weisheit der Indier', notices a manuscript of it in the Royal Library at Paris with a Latin interpretation [not mentioned by M. L. Deslongchamps in the preface to his edition of the Amarakosha.]

published by Mr. Colebrooke, and printed at Serampore, in 1808: it is to this edition that my references apply. They will be found very numerous, and I am happy to acknowledge it as the guide and basis of my labours, and to bear testimony to its uniform and unrivalled correctness.

The different commentaries on the text of the Amara Kosha, to which I have also made frequent reference, are the same as those employed by its learned translator. I was indebted indeed to his kindness for the copies which were prepared for his use, and which were the best procurable, and I have little or nothing to add to the notices which he has given of their authors.

The commentary which takes precedence of the rest by the earlier date of its composition, is that of *Kshira Swámí:* it is a work of merit, but concise; and the interpretations frequently differ from those given by the other commentators. The age of the author is not known; but he is one of the authorities cited by Mallinátha, the commentator on several of the most celebrated poems, and who probably wrote in the twelfth or thirteenth century.*

The next in the order of antiquity is the work of *Mukuta* or *Ráya Mukuta Mani,* compiled according to the author's own account from sixteen older commentaries to which he frequently refers: they seem however to be in many cases original compositions,

---

* [according to Prof. Aufrecht, (Catal. codd. MSS. Sanscr., I, 113) not before the 14th.]

and not merely glosses on the text of Amara. The list includes the work of *Kshíra Swámí, Subhúti, Hadda Chandra, Kalinga, Konkata, Sarvadhara, Rájadeva, Govardhana, Dravida* and *Bhoja Rája*, and the *Vyákhyámŕita, Tíkásarvasva, Mádhaví, Madhu Mádhaví, Sarvánanda,* and *Abhinanda*. Mukuṭa also cites the names of the principal grammatical writers, and quotes many Koshas of which the titles are of frequent and familiar occurrence, amongst which some, as the Viśva and Medíní, are still in existence. The commentary of Ráya Mukuṭa is full and satisfactory—it is erroneous sometimes in the etymological analysis of grammatical derivatives, but it is in general accurate, and in most of the schools is of high authority. The date of the composition is inferred from dates mentioned by the author, 1352 Śáka or A.D. 1430.[*]

The *Vyákhyá Sudhá*[†] is the ablest commentary on the Amara Kosha, that has yet appeared: the interpretations are full and distinct, and the etymological analysis founded on the most thorough acquaintance with the system of Páṇini: the commentator is also a very industrious corrector of the mistakes of his brethren, and rectifies especially the grammatical errors of his predecessor Mukuṭa. In compliance with the usual practice I have referred to this writer under

---

[*] Asiatic Researches, VII, 216; and Preface to the Amara Kosha. [Misc. Essays, II, 18 ff.; 54 ff.]

[†] [On this and the two preceding comp. Aufrecht, l. l., p. 182 f.]

the appellation of Rámáśrama; but, as is mentioned by Mr. Colebrooke, the name of the author is variously written in different copies and is sometimes the same with that which I have used, and is sometimes termed Bhánu Díkshita. In the copy I have used I find an apparent solution of this difficulty, and Rámáśrama, or more correctly Bhadra Rámáśrama, is a title implying the author's belonging to a particular class of devotees, whilst his real name is Bhánu Díkshita, and he is the son, as he informs us, of Bhattoji Díkshita, the celebrated grammarian. I must add, however, that this is denied by the Pandits, who insist that the two persons are distinct, and that Bhánu Díkshita, the son of Bhattoji, was after his father's death the disciple of the ascetic Rámáśrama, who is the author of other works. The work was written, according to the passage which specifies the author's name, at the desire of Kírttisinha, ruler of Mahídhara, a prince of the Bandhaila* family, and the termination Sinha, we may observe, is attached to the Búndela and Ajmere princes† who make their appearance in the reigns of Shah Jehán and Aurungzebe, in the course of which, or the seventeenth century, a son or pupil of Bhattoji Díkshita must have written.

---

* [*Baghela* in the Benares edition of the Amarakosha. See Sir H. Elliot's Glossary s. v. The Dikshitas were a subdivision of the Kánaujya Brahmans; ib. p. 125.]

† Hidjar Singh, Rájá of Búndelkhand, Dow III, 126. Judger Singh, Rájá of Búndela, ibid. 154.

The *Vyákhyá Pradipa* is a commentary by Achyuta Upádhyáya: it is a work of little merit, being an unacknowledged abridgment of Mukuṭa's work. I have not been able to meet with any account of the author, but he is probably modern.

The preceding commentaries agree in giving the derivation of words conformably to the Sútras of Páńini: those which follow have adopted other systems.

In the original compilation of the Dictionary, prepared as that was under the superintendence and by the labours of natives of Bengal, the grammatical system used was that of Vopadeva: as this is however of modern origin and limited application, it was considered advisable to discard it for the more generally cultivated method of Páńini, and the entire transposition of all the etymologies has been consequently included in my task. In effecting this object, particularly for all the words contained in the Amara Kosha, the preceding commentators were my chief guides, and Rámáśrama's commentary especially has in these cases been consulted. The etymological analysis of many of the remaining vocables depends upon the authority of the Siddhánta Kaumudí, and that of the rest has been supplied by my Pańdits or myself, in conformity, as exact as our acquaintance with the subject permitted, to the system laid down in the Sútras of Páńini.

The commentary of *Bharata Malla* is the favourite authority of the Bengal school, and of all others in which the grammar of Vopadeva is received: it is an able performance, and is particularly full on the subject of various readings. The author has also compiled a Kosha on this topic, or a vocabulary of words which vary in their orthoepy, styled by the Hindus a Dwirúpa Kosha, a compilation rendered very necessary by the fluctuations in the forms of words, which arise from the arbitrary application of those letters that are considered interchangeable, and from the varieties introduced by different modes of pronunciation in different provinces, and caused, in many cases no doubt, by the blunders of copyists, the multiplication and repetition of which have given to different modes of spelling currency and sanction.* Bharata Malla is considered to have flourished in the middle of the last century, and has written commentaries on many celebrated compositions.†

The *Sára Sundarí* is a commentary which has been occasionally consulted: the author is Mathureśa, who has himself compiled a vocabulary, the Śabdaratnávalí, in speaking of which we shall advert to the few circumstances that are known of him. The commentary is a useful one: it follows the grammar of Padmanábha Datta, the Supadma, a work studied in some parts of Bengal.:

The *Padártha Kaumudí*, by Náráyaṅa Chakravarttí, has been referred to, though not frequently: the Kalápa, a grammar of celebrity in the *Bengal* schools,

---

* [Aufrecht, Catal. Codd. MSS., I, p. 194.]

† [Bharata Malla, or Bharata Mallika, commented e. g. on the Bhaṭṭi Kávya.]

‡ [Aufrecht, Catal. l. l., I, Nos. 439. 40, and pp. 176 and 192.]

has been followed by this commentator in the analytical part of his work.

The *Trikáṅda Viveka*, by Rámanátha Vidyá Váchaspati, a work of considerable merit, and particularly full of orthoepical varieties, will be found frequently cited, and this with two other commentaries, one by Nílakaṅṭha and the other by Ráma Tarka Vágíśa, which are sometimes referred to, complete the number of authorities accessory to the text of Amara, which were employed by Mr. Colebrooke in his publication, and have again been made use of in the following pages.*

Authorities of higher rank, though often of less value, than the commentators on the Amara Kosha, and constituting together with that work and its appendages the bulk of the present compilation, are the vocabularies of different authors. Of these the most valuable are easily and generally procurable, and many others it is asserted exist, though rarely to be found. Those which I have been able to obtain I shall now proceed to enumerate, following as correctly as inference and conjecture will admit the order of their antiquity, and furnishing such slender information respecting their authors as the state of everything like biography in India is capable of affording. The comparative age of various compositions is in many cases ascertainable by the references which the writers make to their predecessors, and the absence of the notice of a celebrated work, where mention of it is likely to be

---

* [Miscell. Essays, II, pp. 54-57.]

found, is a very strong presumption of its not being in existence. The application of this test is very extensive, and conjoined with the information afforded by inscriptions, and that which may be conjectured from the legends of the Puráńas, presents the only chance of our ever being able to extricate the ancient history of India from the labyrinth in which it is at present lost.

The first Kosha after that of Amara, in the copious list of authorities cited by the author of the *Medini*, which has been consulted in the following work, is the *Abhidhánaratnamálá* of Halàyudha Bhatta. It is a vocabulary of limited extent, divided into five books; the first relating to Heaven and the Deities, and the second to Earth; the third to Hell, Water, &c.; the fourth to miscellaneous objects, and the last contains words of various signification. The author cites as his authorities the Amaradatta and the Koshas of Vararuchi, Bhágurí, Vopálita, and others. We may conjecture that his work should be of some antiquity, as he is quoted by Mallinátha, who is certainly prior to Mediníkara. His omission of the Amara Kosha from his list of authorities can scarcely lead us to infer the priority of his own work, but it is possible that the reputation of that vocabulary was not fully established in his time, and that it is therefore included in the appendix *Ádi*, or etcetera, added to his enumeration. Haláyudha Bhatta* has also written on Prosody, and

---

* Asiatic Researches, VII, 233, and X, 891. [Miscell. Essays,

there is a celebrated writer of the same name, on the religious ceremonies of the Hindus: in both instances honourable mention has been made by Mr. Colebrooke of these works. He is said to be a Konkaña Brahman and the pupil of the Mímánsá writer Bhaṭṭa Bháskara. If this last account is correct, he may be placed about the seventh century, as his preceptor is uniformly said to have preceded Śankara Achárya.

Ajaya, or *Ajayapála*, is the next in the list of the Mediní, whose vocabulary has been consulted in the following pages. This is a work of small extent, but of considerable authority: it is confined to the Nánártha, or words of various meanings, and they are arranged according to the initial letters. The author does not specify his authorities, nor does he furnish us with any clue to his age or history. From his introductory stanza he appears to be a sectary, probably a Jaina.*

II, 20; 133. Prof. Aufrecht's preface to his edition of the Abhidhánaratnamálá. London: 1861.]

* In a paper in the Transactions of the Literary Society of Bombay [I, 183] by Lieutenant Macmurdo, which I shall again have occasion to notice, an Ajee Pál occurs, who seems to have taken an active part in the introduction of the Jaina Religion into Guzerat, towards the end of the twelfth century, and who may have been the compiler of the vocabulary, or the patron of its author, who consequently ascribes it to him; a practice frequent in the literary flattery of Hindu writers. [That just the opposite was the case, that Ajaya Pála, the nephew and successor of Kumára Pála, was a fierce persecutor of the Jainas, and can have no possible claim to the authorship of the Nánárthasangraha, is evident from the account of him in the Rásmálá (I, p. 205 ff.).

The work is often cited by the commentators on the Amara Kosha.*

The next in the list of the Medinī is the *Dharaṅi Kosha* or vocabulary of Dharaṅi Dāsa, an author of whom we know nothing further, except that he is considered as a Brahman of Kanouj, and the author of a poetical work, denominated the Kāśi Vīrndāvalī. The vocabulary is of some extent, although it is limited to the words of various meanings, arranged according to their final letters and number of syllables. The author specifies no authorities, and states only generally, that his vocabulary is compiled from older writers. He is himself of some antiquity, as besides the place he holds in the Medinī's list, he is often cited by Mallināṭha.

The *Trikāṅḍa Śesha* is a vocabulary, in three chapters, composed purposely as a supplement to the Vocabulary of Amara, and thence sometimes termed the Amara Śesha; it follows a similar arrangement, and adds a number of words of comparatively rare occurrence. The author was a Jaina, named Purushottama Deva, and he is the author also of several other philological compilations, as an Ekākshara Kosha,† or Vocabulary of monosyllabic words, which I have occasionally referred to, and the Varña-viplava-nāśa, or a collection of various readings. His most celebrated

---

See Lassen, III, 568, and As. Res., XVI, 321 ff. Thomas' edition of Prinsep's Essays, II, 256.]

* [Aufrecht, Catal. Codd. MSS., I, pp. 182. 187. 195 f.]
† [Aufrecht, l. l., I, No. 431. 32.]

work, however, after the Trikáńda, is the following, which indeed takes precedence of it in the list of the Medinf.

The *Háravali* is a collection almost exclusively of uncommon words. It is divided into two parts, the one containing synonymous words, and the other words of various meanings. The first part is again divided into three portions, according to the extent of the synonymes, and their recapitulation through a whole stanza, or a half, or a quarter. The work is of very limited extent, but it is the produce, according to the author's own averment, of twelve years' reading. He states also, that it was compiled at the suggestion and with the aid of his spiritual preceptor, Śrí Dhŕiti Sinha, an Atithi, or religious ascetic known in the spoken dialects by the appellation Aŭt, and he mentions Janamejaya, a Pańdit, as having contributed to the compilation. The authorities he alludes to are mostly of a general and miscellaneous description, but amongst them he enumerates, as the Koshas consulted, and consequently prior to his time, the Śabdárńáva, Utpalini, Sansárávarta, and those of Váchaspati, Vyádi, and Vikramáditya.* The age of Purushottama, according to the order of the Medinì, should be earlier than that of the Viśva,† and he may probably have written in the tenth or eleventh century. He is not however quoted by the commentator Mallinátha, who cites the Viśva Kosha.

---

* [vv. 273-77.] † [Aufrecht, I. l., I, No. 423.]

After the Trikáńda Śesha, we have in the Mediní's list a work entitled the *Ratna Málá*.* I have employed a Kosha of this name, but I am not quite confident of its being the same, the Ratna Málá of Írugapa, entitled Dańdádhinátha, said to imply, as it may signify, a military officer of high rank, and probably the patron rather than the author of the work. It is a compilation of considerable authority, especially in the South of India, and its age may be ascertained with tolerable precision; for it is said to have been undertaken at the desire of Harihara, a prince who conjointly with Bukka Ráya,† his brother, founded the city of Vidyánagara or Bijnagar, about 1340, and reigned there till 1350. The name of its supposed author Írugapa‡ occurs also in an inscription in the Mackenzie collection, as a granter of the Village of Bellagola to a *Jaina* Deity, which grant is dated in the *Saka* year 1284 or A. D. 1362. The vocabulary I have referred to may be possibly the authority alluded to by Medinikara, though it dates rather near to what we may suppose to have been the latter writer's own era, as the title of a vocabulary Ratna

---

* [Aufrecht, l. L, I, Nos. 441-3.]

† Asiatic Researches, IX, 416.

‡ [He is probably identical with Irugadańdeśa, mentioned in an Inscription from Vijayanagara, in As. Res., XX, 21 and 36. See also Lassen, IV, 171. In the printed edition of this work (Madras: 1857) the name of the author is in four places written *Írugapadańdddhinátha*, in one place I. dańdádinátha, and in another I. dańdeśa. The correctness of the first form is attested by the third.]

Mâlâ (a garland of jewels) is very common. I have already noticed the Ratna Mâlâ of Halâyudha, and I shall have occasion to mention a third vocabulary similarly denominated, but confined to medical terms. The work of Daṅdâdhinâtha is a vocabulary of words of various meanings, arranged according to their syllabic length and final letters. The compiler does not specify his authorities.

The next work mentioned, and of the original compilation of which the Medinî is an improvement, appears in the enumeration of this latter; with the epithet *Bahudosham*, or *very* faulty, attached to it. This is the *Viśva Prakâśa Kosha*, a vocabulary of words of various meanings, of considerable extent and merit; and notwithstanding the reproach of Medinîkara, a reproach not wholly undeserved, of great authority in the schools of *Benares* and *Western India*. The words are arranged according to their final letters, their initials, and their number of syllables, but beyond these three points of agreement there is no classification, and the work is therefore consulted with some difficulty. Besides the usual contents of a Kosha, the Viśva Prakâśa includes some useful sections on the occurrence of the interchangeable letters, and on varieties in orthoepy, and the whole is frequently referred to in the following pages.

The Viśva Prakâśa is of great value in the enquiry into the comparative dates of the various lexicons, which I have attempted to institute, being one of the very few compilations which allow us to conjecture the present age of their composition, and furnish us with a fixed point, from which we can take with something like confidence a retrospective view. The vocabularies enumerated above contain no dates, and can only be placed at undefined intervals between the Amara Kosha and the Viśva Prakáśa, upon the authority of the Medini, confirmed as that is in most instances by the enumeration of authorities which occurs in those works, and in which the name of the Viśva never appears: most of them are therefore in all probability prior to the year of Śáka 1033, or A.D. 1111, which the author of the Viśva Prakáśa has given as the date of his compilation.

The author of the Viśva Kosha, Maheśwara, is the most communicative of all the Sanskrit Lexicographers, and we are much indebted to the venial vanity which has induced him to expatiate on his personal history.

He informs us, that he is descended from Śrí Krishña, physician to Súhasánka, sovereign of Gádhipur, a name from which the modern Ghazipur might be supposed to be derived, but which is enumerated by the vocabularies as a synonyme of Kanyákubja or Canouj: Súhasánka also is a synonyme of Vikramáditya, but neither time nor place allow of the persons being identified in this instance,* and some historical notices

---

* As a more etymological speculation I suggest the possibility of Sáhasánka being a title of Śri Chandra Deva, who, according to an inscription published by Mr. Colebrooke (As. Res., vol. IX, 441) [or Misc. Essays, II, 286. See also As. Res. XV, 443. Dr. F. E. Hall's preface to his edition of the Vásavadattá, Calcutta:

of the former might possibly be derived from another composition, which Maheśwara informs us he had written, the history of this prince, or the Sáhasánka Charitra. The period in which the *Viśva Kosha* was compiled was one very likely to have been a season of literary patronage at *Canouj*, as the Muselman princes of the houses of Ghizni and Ghor were for some time, both before and afterwards, fully occupied with those dissensions, which gave the Indian sceptre to the latter, and consequently left the Hindu princes in the undisturbed enjoyment of their patrimonial sway, and tranquil exercise of their commendable privileges. The author of the Viśva cites most of the authorities considered ancient, and which are no longer procurable, but amongst those described in the preceding pages the work of Amara is the only one which he has noticed. The correctness of the date of the Viśva is tolerably well confirmed by its successive citation in the works of Mallinátha, the Medini, and the commentary of Ráya Mukuṭa, the last of which we have seen is little more than three centuries later.*

1859, p. 18], founded the ruling dynasty of Kanouj, about the end of the eleventh century, which *"realm he acquired by his own strength"*. The inscription is unfortunately in *England*, or an examination of the passage in italics in the original might be found connected with the name given to the Prince by Maheśwara or Sáhasánka, compounded as that is of *Sáhasa*, strength or violence, and *Anka*, mark or distinction. [See the references ap. Lassen, III, 810 f.]

* [Aufrecht, l. l., I, No. 428. A. Weber, Verzeichniss der Sanskrit-Handschriften, Nos. 802-4.]

The inference to which I have been led of Amara's having lived in the fifth century, and the position of Maheśwara in the commencement of the twelfth, leave us about six centuries and a half for the appearance of the different vocabularies above specified, and others that have been less fortunate in escaping the ravages of time. The length of this interval appears to be far from disproportionate to the number of similar works published during its continuance, as far as we can judge from analogy; for from the date of the Viśva to that of Ráya Mukuṭa's commentary in 1430, or three hundred and nineteen years, we have but four vocabularies to enumerate, of which one only can be assigned to that interval with any certainty, and the other three may possibly appertain to the division of our subject which comprehends the works anterior to the Viśva Prakáśa, or the beginning of the twelfth century.

In the period that elapsed between the ages of Maheśwara and Ráya Mukuṭa, we fix with certainty the author of the *Medini Kosha*, as he cites the one and is quoted by the other. The work of this writer is an excellent Dictionary of homonymous words arranged according to their final letters and their syllabic lengths, and then further disposed with alphabetical precision: it is a compilation of great accuracy and high authority, and constitutes after the Amara Kosha the basis and bulk of my labours.

The closing section of the Medini recapitulates the authorities employed in its composition, and comprises amongst others the fullest list of Koshas to be met with: on this account and as they appear to be enumerated according to their supposed comparative antiquity, I shall here transcribe the catalogue, accompanying it with such information as to their present existence as I am able to offer from my own knowledge or from oral accounts of the Paṅḍits.

1. The *Utpalini* is one of the supposed authorities of the Amara Kosha; it is certainly of considerable antiquity, and is often quoted by the older writers. It is still procurable,* though not common.

2. The *Śabdārṇava* is often quoted by the commentators on Amara; it is also occasionally procurable, but usually in an imperfect state.

3. The *Sunsárávartta*, a vocabulary often quoted in works of an early date, but supposed to be now lost.

4. The *Náma Málá*, though rare, is yet obtainable: as it is said to be a work of considerable extent, in that case it differs from the short work of Dhananjaya of the same title which I have consulted.†

5. *Bhāguri* is the author of a vocabulary, forming

---

* My remarks on the possibility of meeting with these works apply to Calcutta and Benares particularly, and may be extended perhaps to the tract of India immediately along the Ganges as far as Haridwár: the state of manuscripts in the Dekhan is probably more complete, and it may be expected that the late accessions to the British Indian Empire both to the west and north will be productive of many valuable additions to Sanskrit bibliography.

† One of them was probably the *Nám Málá* of Du Perron, which he terms Dictionnaire Samskretain à l'usage des Sçioures. [? ... See Hindu Sects, new edition, p. 337.]

according to the commentators one of Amara's authorities. The work is not to be met with.

6. *Vararuchi* is also considered as one of Amara's originals, although as one of the nine gems he should be contemporary with him. His vocabulary is not procurable.

7. The *Śáśwata* is often cited, and is said to be procurable in a mutilated state.*

8. *Vopálita* is the author of a Kosha to be met with in scattered portions.

9. *Rantideva* is the compiler of a vocabulary no longer to be found in a complete state.

10. *Hara* is another lexicographer, whose work no longer exists, and who is rarely quoted.

Of the above vocabularies most are cited by the commentators on the *Amara Kosha* and are specified in several of the works about to be enumerated, as the authorities which they consulted. Haláyudha, Purushottama, and Maheśwara make mention of most of them also, corroborating therefore the order of priority in which they are placed by the author of the Medini.

11. *Amara*, the first author of the list, whose work is everywhere obtainable.

12. *Subhanka*, the compiler of a vocabulary rarely to be found.

13. *Haláyudha*, whose work, the Ratna Málá, has been described.

14. *Govarddhana*, author of the Sapta Śatí, or

---

* [Aufrecht, I. I., I, No. 414.]

seven hundred miscellaneous stanzas, from which the idea of the Sat Sai, a similar collection in Hindi, may have been derived in the sixteenth century by Bihárílál, is the author of a vocabulary said to be still procurable in some parts of India.* As he mentions the Vŕihatkathá, of which the antiquity is supposed to be about 700 years, and is thus noticed by Mediníkara, he probably flourished in the twelfth or thirteenth century.

15. *Rabhasa*, or *Rabhasála*, is the author of a vocabulary often cited, but rarely to be found.

16. *Rudra*, an author of whose work the same may be observed.

17. *Amaradatta*, the name of a writer or a vocabulary, often cited, but not known to exist.

18. *Ajaya*, or *Ajaya Pála*, noticed above.

19. *Gangádhara*, an author of whom nothing further is known.

20. The *Dharańi Kosha*, which, as well as the following, has been already the object of our attention.

21. The *Hárávali*.

22. The *Trikáńda Śesha*.

23. The *Ratna Málá*.

24. The *Viśva Prakáśa*, forming with the *Medini* twenty-five vocabularies, all prior to the fifteenth century, and of which my original and myself, aided as we were by Mr. Colebrooke's valuable collection of

---

* [Weber, Handschriften, No. 1381. Colebrooke, Misc. Essays, II, 23. 88.]

manuscripts, have been able to procure no more than nine or ten. They are not however the whole number of works extant in the time of Mediní Kara, and his predecessors, which were either vocabularies themselves, or treated of the forms, inflexions, genders, and meaning of words in a manner that sanctioned their being included in the same class. Thus the author of the Viśva Kosha specifies Sáhasánka, the patron of his family, as the author, the nominal one, it may be imagined, of a vocabulary, and works of a similar character are attributed to the Princes Vikramáditya and Bhoja; the former occurs amongst the remaining authorities of the Mediní, along with works assigned to Bágbhatta, Mádhava, Váchaspati, Dharma, Vyádi, Tárapála, Kátyáyana, Chandra, Soma, and Pániní. There are also other Koshas quoted by Mallinátha and other early commentators, as the Keśava, Yádava, and Vaijayantí, the two latter of which are still found, though not common.

The author of the Mediní gives no account of himself beyond his being the son of Pránakara;[*] his own name Mediníkara appears to be merely an epithet derived from the title of his vocabulary, but the same final syllable Kara is in Bengal the denomination of a family of the Káyastha race[†] and would indicate therefore his being a native of that province; it is also

---

[*] [In a MS. of this work, in the R. Asiatic Society's possession, the author's father is called Pátníakara.]

[†] Asiatic Researches, V, 66.

an appellation common amongst the Mahratta Brahmans, and our author is generally regarded as of that nation. If the Mádhava and Ratna Múlá, he cites, are the same with those mentioned above, he could not have flourished earlier than the end of the fourteenth century.

Besides the authorities anterior to the Medini, I have employed many which are of more recent date; before describing them, however, I shall here pause to advert to some of a doubtful character, and whose comparative age it is difficult to ascertain.

The most important of these guides, and after the Amara and Medini the best work I have had access to, is the *Abhidhána Chintámani* of *Hemachandra*, a Jaina writer of deserved celebrity, and the author also of a series of Jaina hymns[*] and of a Prákrit grammar: as usually met with, and as printed at the Sanskrit press of Calcutta, this vocabulary is divided into two considerable portions, one appropriated to synonymous, the other to homonymous words. The first part is subdivided into six books, according to a peculiar arrangement, and the first book is of great value as a detailed and faithful account of the superior deities or deified hierarchy of the *Jaina* sect. The second part is classed according to the syllabic extent of the vocables it contains, and they are then arranged according to their

---

[*] [The Jaina Mahákávya *Trishashtisaldkápurushacharita*, a copy of which is in the possession of the R. A. S., is also ascribed to him. See Hindu Sects, new edition, p. 283.]

final initial letters. There is some reason to doubt however, whether Hemachandra's original work is not properly limited to the first six books, and whether the Nánártha part has not been added by some later writer.

The introductory lines of this author's vocabulary explain the principles of his arrangement and are confined to the first six sections, taking no notice of that on words of various meanings. Again, this Kosha has been commented on, and the commentary is equally limited to the first six books; and finally, with the exception of the arrangement which is peculiar to it, the second division of the Abhidhána Chintámañi is precisely the same* as the Viśva Kosha, following that in every word and interpretation, and repeating its obscurities and its mistakes. One of these works must therefore be a transcript of the other, and as there is every reason to believe the originality of Maheśwara's work, it follows that the Nánártha part of Hemachandra's vocabulary is borrowed from the Viśva.

If the Nánártha chapters be the work of Hemachandra himself, their being borrowed from the Viśva establishes the priority of the latter work; on the other hand, as Hemachandra is quoted by Mallinátha,

---

* [That this is not the case, is the well-founded opinion of Prof. Goldstücker; see his Sanskrit Dictionary s. v. *abhidhánachintámañi*. On Hemachandra comp. Lassen, Ind. Alt., III, 567. 1195; IV, 803 f. Colebrooke's Misc. Essays, II, 206 ff. According to the Rás Málá (I, 189-204) Hemachandra died in 1174 A.D., eighty-four years old.]

and as the Commentary on his hymns is dated in the year 1292, it is likely that he lived at a period not long subsequent to Maheswara, or in the course of the twelfth century; the accuracy of which inference is confirmed by works current in Guzerat, that ascribe the conversion of the sovereign of that country to the Jaina faith to the influence of our author in the Samvat year 1230 or A. D. 1174:* and it is further corroborated by the time falling within those limits, during which the sect of which Hemachandra was so distinguished a member flourished in many parts of Hindustan.

The concurring traditions of the Brahmanical, Bauddha, and Jaina sects report a two-fold persecution of the second, by each of the others severally, although they are not agreed about the order of their occurrence. If I have conjectured rightly, the priority seems due to that instigated by the members of the orthodox

---

* "About 2500 years from the first promulgation of the Parisnath (Párswanátha) worship, Heema chaarge Juttee (Hemácháyra Yati), a follower of Parsow, much respected by the Shrawuks (Srávakas or Jainas) for his learning, and who had great authority in all matters concerning religion, resided in Puran Puttur, a celebrated city in the district of Neherwalla, which was at that time governed by a Rajepoot Rája, named Goonmar Pall, who lived about the year of Vikrimajut (Vikrámáditya) 1230, or A.D. 1174, Heema Chaargo succeeded in converting the Raja to the Shrawak religion." Account of the *Parisnath Gowricka*, worshipped in the Desert of Parhar, by Lieutenant Macmurdo, Transactions of the Bombay Literary Society. It is only necessary to add that Hemachandra is generally called by the Jainas Hemácháyra, or, as it is pronounced in several of the dialects, Hemácbárj.

faith, and they effected a partial suppression of the
Bauddha heresy about the fifth and sixth centuries;
they were far from extirpating the schism, however,
as the Bauddhas are noticed on the Coromandel Coast
by the Arabian travellers in the eighth and ninth centuries,[*] in Guzerat by Al-Edrisi in the twelfth century:[†] and we have a family of princes who appear
to have followed the doctrines of Buddha, ruling in

---

[*] Asiatic Researches, I, 166. It might be questioned whether this really proves what it has been supposed to establish, the *Bod* of Renaudot being possibly nothing more than the *But* (بت) of the *Persians*, [which is the Sanskrit भूत] or an idol in general: on the other hand, although the Persian term has that meaning, the word is not an Arabic one, and its occurrence in the work of an Arabic writer renders it likely to be the representation of some particular Hindu deity. The turn of the sentence also, if rightly translated, is in favour of its being a proper name. "Il y a dans les Indes des femmes publiques appellées femmes de l'Idole. L'origine de cette coutume est telle: Lorsqu'une femme a fait un vœu pour avoir des enfans, si elle met au monde une belle fille, elle l'apporte au *Bod*, c'est ainsi qu'ils appellent l'idole qu'ils adorent, auprès du quel elle le laisse, &c."

[†] .... نجروارة فطلخيا ملك عظيم يسمى بلهرا وند جيوش وفيلة وعبادته صنم انبذ 'Rex autem Nahroaræ maximus est, et vocatur Balahara, possidetque exercitus et elephantos, colitque idolum Bodda.' [Jauhert's French translation. Paris: 1836, Vol. I, p. 176.] The Nubian geography of Al Sharif al Edrisi, where this passage occurs, was translated by the *Maronites* and published at Paris in 1619; the text of the original was printed at Rome in 1592. According to his translators, Al Edrisi wrote about the middle of the twelfth century or 1152. Consequently the *Bauddha* faith preceded that of Jina in Guzerat, and was subverted there by the latter, soon after Al Edrisi wrote; a course of events very consistent with the view I have taken in the text.

Bengal about the same time.* This seems to be their limit.

I have already observed that Mádhava, a writer of the fourteenth century, places them no nearer than in *Kashmir*, and Abúlfazl,† writing in the sixteenth century, under the reign of a highly tolerant prince, and assisted in his enquiries by Akbar's curiosity as well as power, declares that he had never met with a follower of Buddha in Hindustan and had only encountered some old men of that faith in his third visit to *Kashmir*. Later periods are out of the question; for in the present day I never heard of a person who had met with natives of India proper of this faith, and it does appear that an utter extirpation of the Bauddha religion in India was effected between the twelfth and sixteenth centuries.‡ By whom then was this important revolution brought about? I cannot answer this question with confidence, but think it highly probable that the Jainas performed an important part in the event, especially as there is reason to suppose that the period assigned for the overthrow of the Bauddhas was that in which the Jainas had attained in many parts of India their highest pitch of power and prosperity.

An enquiry into the origin and history of the *Jaina*

---

* Asiatic Researches, V, 131, and IX, 197. [Misc. Essays, II, 282.]

† Gladwin's Ayeen Akbary, vol. III, 151, Calcutta edition.

‡ [Lassen, I. I., IV, 709 f. Rás Málá, I, 12 ff. Mackenzie Collection, I, lxv.]

sect, of whose number and consequence so many
vestiges still remain, would be inconsistent with the
object of the present disquisition, and would in the
actual state of our materials be but imperfectly and
unsatisfactorily prosecuted. Something has been done
towards illustrating the subject by Mr. Colebrooke,
and Colonel Mackenzie; and it is to the latter gentleman we must look for its further prosecution with any
hope of success, as he possesses amongst his invaluable
collection of inscriptions and manuscripts many docu-
ments calculated to throw light upon the investigation.*
My own conclusions are at present in opposition to
those views which assign a remote era to the commencement of the Jaina schism, and I am inclined to
regard it as a scion of the Bauddha heresy, which
sprang into existence during the early centuries of the
Christian era. But whatever may be thought of this
opinion, it may be confidently asserted, that the entire
downfall of the Bauddhas was preceded by several
ages of *Jaina* ascendancy, and it may consequently
be conjectured that the relative position of the two
sects was not without its influence upon the final result.

The *Jainas* appear to have been in possession of
the consciences and patronage of the Ballála Rájás†
from the eighth up to the middle of the eleventh century when Vishńu Vardhana was converted it is said
to the faith of Vishńu by Rámánuja.‡ The petty Rájás

---

* [Mackenzie Coll., I, lxvi ff.; 144 ff. Lassen, l. l., IV, 755 ff.]
† Buchanan's Mysore, vol. III, 110.
‡ Wilks (vol. I, 511) says in 1133; but this would make Rá-

of Tuluva, or part of the sovereignty of Vishńu Vardhana, however still continued attached to the Jaina faith, and many temples, statues, and inscriptions in the twelfth, thirteenth, and fourteenth centuries were met with in that province by Dr. Buchanan. In a list of Colonel Mackenzie's inscriptions, which the liberality of the proprietor has enabled me to consult, I find also the eleventh and succeeding centuries particularly rich in grants, made to *Jaina* establishments in the peninsula; I have already adverted to a grant made by Irugapa, an officer of rank in the Vijayanagara court in the fourteenth century, to the Bellagola establishment, and we are satisfied, that the sect professed considerable influence in that court, by another document which has been published, an edict promulgated by Bukka Ráya, dated Śáka 1290 (A.D. 1367),* the object of which is to effect a reconciliation between the contending parties of the *Vaishńavas* and *Jainas*, and in which it is declared that there is no distinction nor contradiction between the two religions.

The Literature of the *Jainas*† has yet been too little investigated, for us to be able to form any conjectures as to the period at which it especially flourished. But the few data we are in possession of tend to corrobo-

---

mánuja rather ancient, if, as there is reason to believe, that reformer was born about 1008. See Asiatic Researches, IX, 270. [Lassen, IV, 126 ff. Hindu Sects. New edition, p. 35.]

* Asiatic Researches, IX, 271.

† [A. Weber, Ueber das Śatrunjaya Máhátmya. Leipzig, 1858, p. 6 ff. Lassen, IV, 758 ff.]

rate the idea, that from the tenth to the fourteenth century was the season of the Jaina prosperity.

It is said generally of Pújya Páda, a celebrated grammarian of the sect, that he flourished about 1000 years ago, Amita Gati, a Jaina astronomical writer, dates his work in 1050.[*] Hemachandra writes his grammar, vocabulary and hymns in the twelfth century. A commentary on those hymns is dated in the thirteenth, and there is great reason to suspect that the Kalpa Sútra, the great authority of the sect in the north of India, was composed in that century also.[†] We may therefore conclude that the patronage of these periods produced their due fruit, and was accompanied by the appearance and succession of many of the most celebrated writers amongst the Jainas. The modern and present condition of the Jaina sect appear to be additional confirmations both of its late origin and recent prosperity. In the sixteenth century, according to Abúlfazl, they were numerous and powerful, and the open and confident enemies of the Brahmans and their system. In the seventeenth a Jaina monument was erected at Bhagalpur,[‡] the construction

---

[*] Colebrooke's Algebra of the Hindus, Preliminary Dissertation. [Misc. Essays, II, 462 f.]

[†] Besides other reasons for this conjecture, there is one that appears conclusive: amongst the subjects of Mahávíra's juvenile studies the Lilávati is mentioned, a work that was not composed earlier than the middle of the twelfth century. [But compare Lassen, l. l., IV, 769, and Weber, l. l., p. 12.]

[‡] The Páduká of Vásupújya; repeated copies of this inscrip-

of which is attributed to the Rájá of Jayapur; and in the last century the Jainas could boast of such opulent and powerful members as the Seṭs of Múrshídábád.* In the south of India several corporate bodies of their priesthood still exist,† and in many places in the north and west of India they are yet numerous and respectable; their actual condition therefore, although a fallen one, is not so far declined as to indicate a long period of persecution, and, as contrasted with the utter annihilation of the Bauddhas in India proper, argues the more recent possession of influence and power, and renders it probable that those advantages were exerted to the detriment of their fellow dissentient sectaries, and contributed to their final expulsion from the plains of Hindustan.

To return from this digression however to the immediate subject of our enquiries, the information that is obtainable of Hemachandra's history; we find that little or nothing is known of him beyond his writings.

---

tion have established the date of the monument Samvat 1693 or A.D. 1637.

* Of whose immense wealth the author of the Seir Mutaqerin characteristically remarks that, when Mír Habíb with a party of Mahratta horse surprised Múrshidábád, and carried off from Jagat Seṭ's house two crore of Arcot rupees, this prodigious sum did not affect the two brothers more than if it had been two trusses of straw.

† As at Śravaṇa Bellagola in Mysore (Asiatic Researches, IX, 256) and at Biddery in Canara (Buchanan's Mysore, III, 75). I understand from Colonel Mackenzie that there is also an establishment of Jaina priests at Chittamoor [Hindu Sects, p. 333 ff.]

If we may trust a work entitled the Samaya Bhúshaṅa, he was originally an inhabitant of Páṭaliputra or Patna, and according to the passage we have already cited from the Transactions of the Bombay Society, he appears to have finally settled in Gujerat, and to have performed an important part in the religious revolutions of that country.

Another of my authorities which appears to be prior to the Mediní, though not therein enumerated, is the *Śabda Málá* of Rámeśwara Śarmaṅa.* The chief reason for my inferring its priority to the Mediní is its citation by Mallinátha, who is himself apparently anterior to the latter by his no where making mention of it, an omission of which so careful and excellent a commentator as Mallinátha unquestionably is could scarcely have been guilty, had so well qualified a guide as the Mediní been within his reach at the time he wrote. The Śabda Málá is a work of limited extent and value, and is little better than a supplement to the Amara Kosha, the order of which it follows, and to which it adds a few words of uncommon occurrence. The *Náma Málá* is another of my authorities of which the age is uncertain. The title occurs in an early part of the Mediní's list, as I have already observed; but the work I have referred to under the name of its author Dhananjaya appears scarcely worthy of a place in that enumeration, as it is a very limited collection of synonymes strung together without any order or

---

* [Aufrecht, l. L, I, No. 437. 38.]

arrangement. The want of order however is perhaps an argument in favour of its antiquity. The vocabularies that remain to be noticed are all of a date subsequent to that of the Medini, and may be considered as posterior to the fourteenth century. The character I have assigned to the Śabda Málá of a supplement to the Amara Kosha applies still more forcibly to them, as they follow the arrangement of that work, repeat the whole or nearly the whole of its contents, and merely add to them a few new synonymes, varieties of reading, or terms of uncommon occurrence. The *Nánártha* chapters present the chief difference, as they are very scanty in the compilation of Amara, and as the Viśva and Medini afford great facilities to subsequent Koshakáras. As original and independent compositions they are consequently of little comparative value, and of inferior authority to the standard compositions which precede the fourteenth century. The principal of these modern works, and to which reference will be found in the subsequent pages, are the *Bhúri Prayoga*, *Śabda Ratnávalí* and *Jatádhara Kosha*.

The author of the *Bhúri Prayoga* is Padmanábha Datta, the son of Dámodara Datta, apparently the same as the author of the Supadma, a grammar on an original plan, and the basis of a particular school in some parts of Bengal. He professes to render his work a supplement to the Amara Kosha, and accordingly divides it into three similar sections. He has furnished a few additional vocables, but none of much importance. As he enumerates the Medini amongst the vocabularies consulted by him, he is subsequent to the author of that work.*

The *Śabda Ratnávalí* is the compilation of Mathureśa, one of the commentators on the Amara Kosha, and follows that work in arrangement, and contents. It is chiefly useful for its introduction of various readings amongst the synonymes, but has made very little addition of any other kind. This work was composed according to the date in Sáka 1588 or A. D. 1666, and under the patronage of a Musselman chief whose name, as written in the manuscripts, appears to be Múrchhán Khán.. It should be more probably Músá Khán, a name common amongst the Musselman chiefs of the seventeenth century.†

The vocabulary of *Jatádhara* is for the most part a mere transcript of the Amara Kosha, and it is an impudent transcript, for the author acknowledges no authority. He probably thought the remoteness of his position screened him from detection. As he informs us, he was an inhabitant of Chatu-gráma or Chittagong. He has added a few terms occasionally to those extracted from Amara, and for these his work has been referred to. The date of the compilation is not specified, but it is no doubt comparatively modern.‡

---

* [Aufrecht, l. l., I, No. 435.]
† [Aufrecht, l. l., I, No. 439. 40.]
‡ [Aufrecht, l. l., I, p. 191, proves that it was composed before the time of Ráya Mukuta.]

Some compilations have been made of late years, chiefly at the suggestion, and for the use of European patrons. Of these the Śabda Sandarbha Sindhu, containing the words of the Amara Kosha, Hemachandra, Viśva, and Medinî, was compiled by Káśinátha Śarmaṅa for Sir William Jones. A compilation from those and other authorities, but left incomplete, was latterly prepared for Mr. Colebrooke by different hands, one of whom, Vidyákara Miśra, was for some period one of my assistants; and a very voluminous work, the Śabdártha Kalpataru, has been recently compiled for the use of the Madras College.* The first of these is readily obtainable and was purchased by me in Calcutta. Mr. Colebrooke transferred the second to me, and for the third I was indebted to the kind politeness of the late Mr. Ellis, and of Mr. Campbell. The first will be found referred to, though but very rarely, as it offered no additional matter. From the second I have taken some meanings of monosyllabic words, which were quoted from the Ekákshara Koshas, and of which the originals were not in my possession; and from the third I have extracted a number of vocables for which I could find no other authority. This work would have been as valuable as it is copious, had there not been reason to question its accuracy; but the greater part of its references are wholly fanciful, and the Amara Kosha is given as authority for very many terms, which it does not contain. None of these com-

* [ib., No. 455.]

pilations have yet any weight or authority with native scholars.*

The works I have thus enumerated are not the only vocabularies I have consulted, though forming the whole number of those of which the contents and application are of a general nature. Besides these I have employed several medical vocabularies, which comprise also copious lists of plants and drugs, and include a small number of general terms. Those which have been referred to in the following publication, are the *Ratna Málá, Rája Nighańtu, Bháva Prakáśa,* and *Śabda Chandriká.*

The only copy of the *Ratna Málá* I have been able

---

* A compilation of a superior character to any of these modern works, and indeed to any of the more ancient works, is now in progress in Calcutta: it is entitled the *Śabda Kalpa Druma,* and is a Sanskrit Dictionary alphabetically arranged, with references to the authorities, and with copious explanations in the Sanskrit language. It is printed in the Bengali character. It is the work of a young native gentleman of fortune and family, Rádhákánta Deb, with the assistance of the best Pańdits, and is printing at his own expense, and is an occupation which singularly contrasts with the low luxury, in which Hindus of his age and rank ordinarily expend their time and money. The politeness of the author has favoured me with the first sheets of the work; but, I regret, it was not sufficiently advanced for me to benefit by its contents. He has also obliged me with many critical remarks on the earlier part of my own Dictionary, of which, where practicable, I have availed myself. The Śabda Kalpa Druma must take some considerable time before it is completed. [The seventh volume, completing the original work, was published in the year 1851; and six years after a supplementary volume appeared under the title '*Śabdakalpadrumapariśiśhtah*'.]

to procure contains no specification of its date or author, although from the invocation we may conjecture that the latter was a Bauddha or Jaina sectary. It is a useful list of the names of drugs, both vegetable and mineral, with the common Hindu denomination appended, and is regarded as a work of some antiquity and authority.

The *Rája Nighańtu* is the work of Narahari Pańdita, who states himself to be descended from a family of Kashmirian Brahmans. From the frequent occurrence of Dakhiní terms in explanation of his Sanskrit text it is inferred, however, that he was an inhabitant of the south of India. Besides the medical works which he refers to he comprises amongst his authorities Amara, Haláyudha, and the Viśva Prakáśa, and by his stopping at the latter it appears probable that he wrote during the interval between the appearance of that work and the Medini, or some time in the twelfth or thirteenth century. The compilation is almost wholly limited to the Materia Medica of Hindu physicians, or the synonymes and properties of various vegetable and mineral products considered to possess medicinal virtue.

The *Bháva Prakáśa* is a compilation of a more general character, and includes the anatomy, pathology, and therapeutics of the Hindus. It is a very useful work, but not particularly full in the nomenclature of those subjects which come within the scope of the present publication, and is therefore not frequently adverted to. It is the work of Bháva Miśra, the son of Latakana Miśra, and is about two centuries old. The copy I have used, and which belongs to the Library of the Asiatic Society, is dated in the year Samvat 1725, or 150 years ago.

The *Śabda Chandriká* is a vocabulary of vegetable and mineral substances, with a tolerably copious list of animals, and a chapter on compounds, both in medicine and diet. It is accompanied by an interpretation in Bengali and is a useful work. The author is Chakra Páñi Datta, and the compilation is comparatively modern.*

The list of vocabularies which constitute my authorities is not yet completed, and I have to add to their number the *Dwirúpa Kosha* of Bharata Malla, and *Uńádi Kosha* of Ráma Śarmana. The first of these is a collection of various readings, pointing out the different orthoepy of the same word, and is a compilation of a writer whom we have noticed amongst the commentators on Amara. It is not very frequently referred to in the following work, as similar varieties are abundantly furnished by the author's commentary on the Amara Kosha, which afforded a more ready reference, and most of the examples are also met with in the Śabda Ratnávalí, whence they have been likewise extracted.

The *Uńádi Kosha* is an explanation of the irregular derivatives formed with the affixes Uń and others, or Uńádi, the construction and import of which being

---

* [Aufrecht, l. l., No. 453.]

reducible to no positive system, they have been formed into a class by themselves. The vocabulary I now speak of has the advantage of being elucidated by a comment written by the author, and I have therefore found it sometimes usefully consulted; but as the comment is constructed according to Vopadeva's system of grammar, I have preferred in all cases where I had a choice the five Uńádi chapters of the Siddhánta Kaumudí, the entire contents of which, constituting a very full series of these derivatives, will be found embodied in the subsequent sheets.*

Of the above works the whole were employed in the original compilation, with the following exceptions: most of the commentators on Amara, the Náma Málá, the Rájo Nighańtu, Bháva Prakáśa, the Uńádi chapters of the Kaumudí, and the compilations I have particularised as absolutely modern. In the other instances my only task has been collation, and whether the object of this collation was reconciling different readings in manuscript copies of the same work, comparing the differences of separate vocabularies, or correcting the inaccuracies of my original, it was a task of which the labour can scarcely be computed, except by those who have engaged in similar undertakings. It can be a subject of little interest to the reader to accompany me through any detailed exposition of this part of my labours, or to follow the slow and painful steps, by which I have worked my way through a path

* [Ujjvaladatta's commentary on the Uńádi-Sútras, ed. T. Aufrecht. London, 1859, preface p. xxi.]

so intricate and irksome, often terminating in utter perplexity, and I have no doubt, in spite of all my care, frequently ending in mistake. To the Sanskrit student, however, it may not be unserviceable to convey some idea of the condition in which Hindu manuscripts, and indeed all oriental manuscripts, are found: and I may be perhaps indulged for dwelling with some complacency on a part of my labours, of the character and extent of which so little can be known to any one else. I shall therefore proceed to offer one or two examples of the different descriptions of difficulty, by which this province of my labours has been harassed and obstructed.

Of variations in different manuscripts of the same work abundant specimens might be presented; but it will be sufficient to confine them to the Viśva, of which I had four different copies. One of these, under the term वरर, explains it by केदग, another by वादग. Three copies assign to केगट as one sense of it शोवव, and a fourth शेवव, whilst there is reason to think that they are all wrong, and that the correct reading should be शोकव. Under the word घगा, one copy has गाविव, another वाङ्गा, and a third घिविगा, and in many instances the four copies present as many different readings, and every one erroneous. This is the case with the manuscripts of all the Koshas, and it is to be regretted that the printed editions of those which have been published, are very far from correct, with the single exception of the Serampore edition of the Amara Kosha. Printed copies however, as editions multiply, are likely to become more accurate, whilst from the carelessness and ignorance of transcribers in general the multiplication of manuscript copies is only the propagation and augmentation of inaccuracy.

The varieties of reading presented by different works are still more numerous and embarrassing, than those I have noticed. Thus under the word फिफि, one of the interpretations occurs in the Medinī and Viśva मदेश, in the Nánártha Ratna Málá मदेश,* and in Ajaya मदेष. Under the term महार्ष, we have in the Medinī नारष, in the Viśva and Hemachandra नारष; Jaṭádhara writes a passage जलिसमुषते, the Bhúri Prajoga जलि-समुषते. One meaning of हय, as given by my original, is written नारष, Hemachandra has it नारष, the Viśva नारष, the Medinī नारोष, the Dharaṇi जरिष, the Śabda Ratnávalī नारष, and the Trikáṇḍa भारष, Ajaya Pála has नारष, the Śabda Sandarbha Sindhu नारष, and the Nánártha Ratna Málá* has भारिष, offering ten varieties in as many works on a word of three syllables, not one of which is satisfactory. Differences to a like and even greater extent are numerous, and there are some instances in which I have had occasion to notice not fewer than thirteen equally puzzling varieties on one short word. †

---

* [The confusion becomes still greater by the varieties of reading met with in different copies of one and the same work as mentioned above. Thus in the printed edition of the Nánártha-ratnamálá we find *prakáśa* instead of *praveśa* (I, 154), and *ndíaka* instead of *ndńika* (I, 251).]

† As a specimen of my attempts at unravelling some of these

TO THE SANSKRIT DICTIONARY.   241

There is great confusion also in the gender of nouns;
thus वहृ in one passage of the Amara Kosha is termed

---

intricacies, which may be amusing to those readers who take an
interest in philological riddles, I here subjoin the interpretation
of the word वहुर, accompanied by the note which, for my own
satisfaction and for the better understanding of the subject, it has
been my uniform practice in all such cases to prepare and preserve.

वहुर n. (-रं) 1. An arbour, a bower, &c. 2. An uncultivated
field. 3. A sand, a desert. 4. A field. 5. A compound pedicle.
Hem. Ná. 6. A solitude, a wild. 7. A thicket, a wood. Dhar.
vide in loco.

Note: great confusion prevails regarding this and the next
word वहुर, and the original has increased it by adding a third
word वहुर, misquoting the Dharaṇí for it, in which the reading
is correctly वहुर. The authorities differ considerably, and there
is reason to presume that not one of them is uniformly accurate
in the interpretations of these two words. The following are the
passages:

वहुर बाहुलचयें महनीयधवीरपि ॥ Med. [212.]
वहुर कुञ्जमरूयों: चेये ऽनवधि चाहुनि ।
वहुरम् बवचेरें बाहुलीचरचीरपि ॥ Hem. [Nán. 598.]
वहुर तु निर्मनञ्जानें पिन्मुचरें च वहुरम् ।
वहुरं महने कुञ्जे ॥ Dhar.
वहुर: पुंसि महलमरचेचीपरेऽपि च ॥ Śabd. R.
वहुरं बाहुलमचेरें बाहुलीचरचीरपि ॥ Viś.
बाहुचरें चनचचें वहुरं महनें ऽपि च ॥ Tri. [III, 370.]

The first inference to be drawn from these readings is that
besides the meanings peculiar to वहुर it has those of वहुर also;
and the next is that, though वहुर may sometimes occur as a noun
masculine, yet properly it is neuter, all the authorities agreeing
in making it so except the Śabda Ratnávalí. As for the interpretations, the Medini is wrong in बाहुलचयें, which should be
either बाहुलें and चेयें, or बाहुलचयेरं; also in चीवध, which should
be उचरं, from the concurrence of the Hem., Viś., and Śabda
Ratnávalí, and the analogy of the other senses. Hemachandra

musculine, and in another is a noun, of three genders, whilst again Mukuṭa asserts that it is never feminine, and Mathureśa, that it is an error ever to make it neuter.* As to the various readings arising from confounding the different nasals and sibilants, and above all from the perpetual interchange of the letters B and V (ब and व) they are innumerable, and of almost impracticable adjustment. The difficulty of separating them indeed seems to have been long ago insurmountable and to have given rise to the following convenient rule, which renders their distinction a matter of perfect indifference:

एलयोर्डलयोर्बह्वयोर्वर्ववोरपि ।
ब्रह्वयोर्मनयोर्ज्ञाने सविसर्गाविसर्गयोः ।
सबिन्दुकाविन्दुकयोः क्वादभेदे न कस्यचर ॥

"The letters R and L, D and L, J and Y, B and V, Ś and S, M and N, a final Visarga or its omission, and

---

seems the most accurate, except that बाहृन is put for बहृन; the बिन्दुदरे of Dharaṇi is what? and its निर्वेनज्ञान, though admissible, is more probably निर्वेनज्ञान; the मर्वेन of the Śabda Ratnávali is evidently a mistake for बनवेन. The Viśva has बाहृन also where the rest have बहृन, being as usual the same essentially with Hemachandra. The Trikáṇḍa has ब्रवरे for ब्रवरे, and बनवेन for बनवेन. The Śabdártha Kalpataru has under this word बहृन and बीनवे for बहृन and ब्रवरे; and the Śabda Sandarbha Sindhu, misquoting its originals, writes बाहृन for the बाहृन of Viśva and Hemachandra. [A MS. copy of the Medini, in the R. A. S.'s possession, reads ब्रवरे ज्ञाहृनवेन बहृनीद्रयेरपि, and in the Śabdakalpadruma s. v. we find the remark बिव्रवरे-विव्रवदैदाननिन मदरमिनि पाठ :]

* [Bhánudikshita ad Amar. K. II, 1, 10. He does not mention or comment upon the śloka III, 4, 31.]

a final nasal mark or its omission, are always optional, there being no difference between them."* Notwithstanding the latitude which this doctrine permits, the adjustment of these letters, and of व and ब especially, has occasioned me infinite trouble. I may here observe that the classification of words beginning with a B or V, which I have adopted, rests chiefly on the authority of the commentators on Amara, and the chapter of the Viśva on the subject, extended by analogy to those cases to which their specifications do not apply.

To censure the faults of the original compilation with any undue asperity, would ill become one who is conscious of being liable to a similar accusation. Bayle says, it is well in works of this kind, if there are not more than seven errors in a page, and perfection in a Dictionary, according to Dr. Johnson, is the dream of a poet doomed at last to wake a Lexicographer. Both these illustrious men have likewise pointed out the difficulties arising from the mere extent of an undertaking, as well as the impossibility of bestowing the same attention upon many objects, that might be devoted to a few: and the former has justly remarked that, although the first writers of Dictionaries have committed many faults, yet they have done great services, and deserve a glory of which they ought not to be deprived by their successors. That

---

* [See the Sáraswatí Prakriyá. Súrat: 1829, I, Sútra 15, where the śloka reads thus:

एवतीर्षत्वीचैव सुववोर्यचोक्ष्मा ।
वह्नेषां च व्यापर्यंसर्ववारविद्यो ज्ञा: ॥]

errors would therefore occur in the original compilation, might have been expected, and they might also have been visited with a lenient spirit; they exceed however all reasonable limits, and it is in justice to the encouragers and conductors of the work, as well as to myself, that I am induced to notice them. I have corrected at the least several thousand mistakes, and I am confident that, had I engaged to prepare an original compilation, and not to collate and rectify that of the guide I adopted, I should have finished my task in less time, and with less trouble, in a more complete manner, and with more satisfaction to myself. The errors were of every description: words were inserted as original terms, which proved to be merely misspellings of others, and many were assigned to authorities in which they did not occur; the etymologies were mostly fanciful, often erroneous, and not seldom invented to support a word of the compiler's coinage; the interpretations were frequently most grossly inaccurate, and the passages quoted from the different authorities constantly referred to those, to which they did not belong. There were also many faults of omission, and a number of words, even in the Amara Kosha, left out of the compilation: in short the book was put together with an utter indifference to literary reputation, and a dishonest disregard of the duty, which the Paṅdits employed undertook to discharge.

Besides the words extracted from the vocabularies I have specified, and to which an appropriate reference is annexed, a number will be met with without such an appendage: these are additions of my own, consisting chiefly of useful grammatical derivatives, taken from the *Siddhánta Kaumudí*, and a few law terms, from *Manu*, and the *Mitákshará*; in the latter pages of the work, I have also inserted many words which occurred incidentally in the course of such miscellaneous reading as my very restricted leisure has permitted me to indulge in. As improvements and additions of minor importance, I may here mention that I have attached to the nouns the initial letters denoting the gender, as well as the termination of the nominative case singular: and I have referred by appropriate syllables to the several authorities consulted. To those of my originals which have been printed, as the *Hemachandra*, the *Trikáńda*, and *Hárávalí*, I have subjoined the numerals, expressing the chapter, section and verse, in which the word is to be found, agreeably to the mode in which those Koshas are divided. To the printed *Medini*, and the second portion of *Hemachandra*, and to the Serampore edition of *Amara*, such a particular reference was unnecessary, the two first following a partially alphabetical arrangement, as I have already observed, and the last being provided with an alphabetical index, by which its contents can readily be consulted. For the manuscript authorities I have contented myself with the indication of the name, as indeed a more precise reference would neither be serviceable nor practicable.

I have now accounted for all the nouns and particles contained in the following work, and the only classes of words admitted into the original vocabularies of the Sanskrit tongue. To the European student of Sanskrit, however, a Dictionary would be of little value, that should not offer any intepretation of the verbs, and particularly when they are identified, as they are in Sanskrit, with the roots of the whole language. I have therefore embodied the *Dhátupátha*, or catalogues of roots, with the other divisions of the general work.

The Sanskrit root, or *Dhátu*, appears to differ from the primitives of other languages in its fulfilling no other office, and being incapable of entering into any form of speech: to fit it for this purpose, it must undergo many preparatory modifications, and it is then evolved with the aid of additional particles into a noun or verb at pleasure. At the same time, as a matter of convenience, the Hindu grammarians have connected it more directly with verbal than nominal inflection, and in the classification adopted in their lists it wears a more determinate shape, and may then be regarded as the crude verb. The import of the Sanskrit root is as undefined as its character, and it is in fact only the general sign of all the possible varieties of action or being that are referable to a common nature. It is usually explained by a noun, and the noun most frequently is in the seventh or locative case: thus (भू) *Bhú* is explained by (सत्तायाम्) *Sattáyám*, in being; (ज्ञाद्) *Illád* by (व्यक्तशब्दे) *Avyaktaśabde*, in inarticulate sound, &c.* Many roots also have a

---

* [i. e. in the sense of being, in the sense of inarticulate sound.]

great variety of meanings, thus (अव) *Av* has nineteen acceptations, (कल) *Kal*, generally signifying numeration or counting, is susceptible of any meaning a writer may chuse to employ it in, and this indeed so far applies to every other radical, that in derivatives of which the form is clearly traceable to a root of a very different signification the difficulty is immediately solved, by the general law नानार्थेष्वार्वसात्, that roots are capable of various interpretations. These varieties of sense, however, are either rendered perfectly intelligible in books from the context, or they are explained in the commentaries, and most of the verbal inflections are of an application sufficiently precise. As to the individually exact import of the root, it is of very little consequence, as, although it may be a question whether each should be interpreted by an abstract or infinitive noun, this uncertainty is removed at once in practice by the conversion of the root into one or other form: its conversion into the crude verb is the method I have preferred, and it appears in the following pages translated by the English verb in the infinitive mood, with which, however, it must not be confounded, as the Sanskrit root takes an indeclinable infinitive form, which corresponds in power with our infinitive, as designated by the particle *to*.

The Sanskrit roots, as identified with crude verbs, are arranged in ten *Gañas*, or classes, differing in conjugation through a part of their inflection, and consequently discriminated in grammatical works: the arrangement of the *Dhátupáṭha* is however alphabetical. The number of the roots can scarcely be estimated with precision; for, as crude verbs, they may be inflected in several of the conjugations, and they are usually considered as then forming distinct roots. There are also many roots called *Sautra*, from being noticed in *Sútras*, or rules, of etymological analysis, constructed for the occasion by authors of reputation, and there are many peculiar to the Vedas, which, as well as the preceding, are not always included in the enumeration of the *Dhátupáthas*. In general the number of radicals in the ordinary lists is about 1700, as repeated in different classes they exceed 2000. In the following pages the number is something more than nineteen hundred, and they occur as nearly as possible in the following proportions:

  Class the first, 1020
  — — second, 73
  — — third, 23
  — — fourth, 128
  — — fifth, 29
  — — sixth, 154
  — — seventh, 25
  — — eighth, 10
  — — ninth, 59
  — — tenth, 411.

I do not mean to assert that these numbers are faultlessly accurate, but they are sufficiently so to convey a correct notion of the proportion of which the various classes consist: of the whole number, a very considerable proportion also are of rare occurrence.

Although the Sanskrit root is with a few doubtful exceptions* monosyllabic, yet as the crude verb it often appears to consist of several syllables, by the annexation of certain supernumerary letters, which are rejected from every inflection, and serve only to denote the class to which the verb belongs, or the necessity of some peculiar modifications in it or its derivatives. These *Anubandhas* or adjuncts, or indicatory letters, I have in general thought it unnecessary to retain; as, on the one hand, the class is specifically mentioned, and its characteristic formation shewn, by the insertion of the third person singular of the present tense; and, on the other, the appropriate evolutions of the most useful derivative form occur under the respective derivatives. I have however retained some of them, as the letter र for instance, as not only accounting for some singularity in the construction of the present tense, but as sometimes furnishing a useful distinction between two roots of otherwise similar form, and yet of very different meaning and classification.

For the roots contained in the following pages I am indebted chiefly to the labours of Mr. Colebrooke. Those of the first and most numerous class are published in the first volume of his Sanskrit grammar, but the other classes existed only in manuscript, which he had the kindness to complete for my use. The accuracy of his compilation and excellence of his authorities have left me little to do but to transcribe, and al-

* [See Benfey's "Vollständige Grammatik der Sanskritsprache." Leipzig: 1852, p. 71 £.]

though I have consulted the lists in the Grammars of Mr. Wilkins and Dr. Carey, and in Mr. Forster's Essay, as well as occasionally adverted to the works of Mádhava and Vopadeva and the roots given in the Mugdhabodha and Kaumudí, I have found occasion to make but few additions to the copious and satisfactory catalogue Mr. Colebrooke had prepared. I have added to some of the roots, however, a variety of modifications of meaning, depending upon the addition of inseparable prefixes or prepositions, the application and effect of which in Sanskrit compositions are of a very various and puzzling character. It would be almost impossible indeed to collect all the shades of import occasioned by the use of these particles, the application of which seems frequently to depend upon the caprice of the writer. They are often also accumulated to eke out measure without regard to meaning, and leave the radical unaffected, a circumstance that forms one of the great objects of the commentaries by which all Sanskrit works of merit are accompanied, and without which, for some time at least, they will scarcely be perusable with any satisfaction or certainty. The examples I have given are taken chiefly from the Mágha, Bhagavad Gítá, and Megha Dúta; they are comparatively but few however, and I soon found it vain prosecuting the collection, as far as poetical license, or the निरंकुश कवयः, the uncontrolled poets of Sanskrit Grammarians, were likely to lead me.

The whole extent of the Dictionary from these various sources is but indifferently proportioned to a language, which it may be safely said has no limit, and the extent will be thought still less, when it is found that it for a great part consists of the language of Botany and Mythology. For so great a portion being thus appropriated it would be sufficient for me to say, that it is the case with my originals; but there is a still better reason, and incidental reference to a Deity by some of his many titles, and fanciful allusions to a flower or plant, constitute half, or more than half, of the poetry of the Hindus. Their mythology is the main structure, their botany the chief decoration, of their poetical compositions, and I have no fear of being found by the student unnecessarily copious on these two themes. As far as affects my translation of the names of plants and objects of science, I do not mean to be responsible for its accuracy: Mr. Colebrooke's Amara Kosha has been my chief guide, and in other cases I have made use of the Bengali and Uriya vocabularies published at the College, and of Dr. Roxburgh's Catalogue of the Botanical Gardens, as published by Dr. Carey, with the Bengali and Hindi names of a large portion of its contents.

Although the number of vocables contained in the Dictionary is comparatively scanty, yet its application may, with a little attention to the genius and grammar of the language, be almost indefinitely extended. Compound words not found in it may be easily resolved into their component parts, and those parts, if not occurring, may be traced to their radicals, and their import thus be ascertained. The obvious meanings of words as derivable from their etymology, though frequently not assigned to them by any authority, and therefore only not inserted, may of course be always admitted, and they may also be extended as epithets to other senses not expressed, to which their analysis makes them applicable. Names of properties and virtues will often be met with used attributively, when their application will be easily understood; and the conversion of simple nouns into a variety of possessive and attributive shapes by the use of regular affixes will easily be conceived by adverting to some of the analogous formations the work itself contains. As to the effect of negative and privative prefixes, and the addition of the abstractive terminations, there can be no difficulty in these respects, as the modified meaning is too palpable to be misconceived, and by attention to these points, and by a knowledge of the elements of the language, without which all attempts at study must be abortive, I trust the Dictionary now offered to the Public will afford every desirable aid to the student of the Sanskrit Language.

XIV.

NOTICE

OF

EUROPEAN GRAMMARS AND LEXICONS

OF THE

SANSKRIT LANGUAGE.

From the Transactions of the Philological Society, Vol. I (1843), p. 13-36.

It has been thought to contribute to the fulfilment of an object which was suggested at the General Meeting in May last for the Society's earliest consideration, namely, the ascertainment of the actual condition of philological inquiry, to offer a short notice of those publications which within the last half century have been designed to promote, amongst Europeans, an elementary knowledge of the Sanskrit language. It appeared to me that the suggestion to which I had adverted, and for which the Society was indebted to a highly valued colleague, whose opinions must ever be entitled to attention, could be followed out successfully only by a division of labour. A comprehensive whole, consisting of many parts, appears to demand for its investigation the acquirements of different members of the Society, of whom, while there are many who might feel themselves equal to undertake some one subdivision, there are probably few who would not distrust their ability to grapple with so vast an undertaking as a universal survey of the present state of philological research. Under the impression, therefore, that an object, which was indisputably of no small importance in the outset of the Society's career—the determination of a fixed point from whence to start—the knowledge of what has been done as a necessary preliminary to what remains to be done—could be most readily attained by separate exertion, he had been induced to enter upon a department which he thought might reasonably be assigned to him, and as prefatory to other branches of an investigation into the existing state of Sanskrit philology, he purposed to submit a brief account of those means of acquiring an acquaintance with the language, which we owed to the talents and industry of European scholars. He might take a future opportunity of offering some notice of the grammatical works of native authorities, and of the labours of European writers, in the elucidation of the affinities which connect the Sanskrit with other cultivated forms of speech.

For a considerable period a notion prevailed that the learned amongst the natives of India were obstinately averse to the communication of instruction in their sacred language to foreigners, and that this was the reason why so many years elapsed before an attempt to acquire it was made by those Europeans, who from one motive or other had sojourned in India. The notion was not altogether unfounded, although the reluctance which no doubt was encountered was less insuperable than was imagined, and originated in a misconception from which the most enlightened native scholars were free. There is nothing in the laws or institutes of the Hindus which authorizes a monopoly of a knowledge of the Sanskrit language by any one caste or order of the people. The only monopoly insisted upon by the Brahmans was that of tuition. They allowed no other caste to teach—they enjoined the military and agricultural castes to learn, even the holy books, the Vedas. They prohibited the Śúdra or servile caste from hearing the sacred books, but they permitted even the mixed castes to read and hear the great historical and mythological poems, and consequently never thought of excluding them from a knowledge of the language in which those books are composed. Their monopoly of tuition, which they most rigorously guarded against aggression, was so far disinterested that it brought with it no pecuniary profit. Even to the present day it is considered derogatory to the purity of the Brahmanical character to give instruction for hire, and although in the service of Europeans the scruple is surmounted, teaching Sanskrit to native pupils is very generally gratuitous. The Brahmans had no doubt a design in thus reserving to themselves the seemingly unrequited duties of instruction, but it is not necessary on the present occasion to inquire what their objects were. It is sufficient to have shown that there was no law to prevent them from expounding the mysteries of their sacred tongue to ears profane, and that Europeans, although no doubt regarded as amongst the lowest of castes, might have become familiar with them at an earlier period had they entertained the wish and adopted the means of obtaining instruction.

It might appear somewhat unaccountable that the Mohammedans of India should have been blended with the Hindus for centuries, and should have paid no attention to the literature of their fellow-subjects, did we not know the disdainful intolerance with which they regard the languages and literature of all nations that profess a different religious faith. The first sovereigns of Delhi would have incurred the imputation of being infidels had they shown any favour to the Pandits; and in truth they were not in much danger of undergoing such a censure, as they were of a rude race, more addicted to arms than to letters, and commonly dependent upon the former for their thrones and their existence. Their conduct and example were ill calculated to win the confidence of the Hindus, and they were no doubt as backward to impart, as the Mohammedans were careless to seek for, information. The reign of Akbar, in the latter half of the sixteenth century, first wrought a change in this state of public feeling. A friendly intercourse was then first established between both classes of the people, and in imitation of the patronage bestowed by the monarch upon Hindu literary men, the nobles of his court condescended to express curiosity concerning the national literature, and became the scholars of the Brahmans. The rapidity with which the scruples and reluctance of the latter yielded to the sunshine of imperial favour, must have appeared so marvellous to the Mohammedans, that a fable was invented to account for the alteration. It was said that by the command of the king, Sheikh Feizí, the younger* brother of Akbar's able minister Abúlfazl, had been palmed in early life upon the Brahmans as an orphan youth of their own caste, and that he was initiated by them unwittingly into their learning and doctrines. The tale, though still current, is not very probable. Feizí is the reputed and, in part no doubt, real author of various translations from Sanskrit into Persian: other translations were made under his superintendence.† His competency to the task, and the assistance which he commanded, may easily be accounted for without having recourse to fiction. The enlightened encouragement and royal munificence of Akbar were the keys that unlocked the treasures of Hindu lore. The taste which he introduced survived his reign, and in Dárá Shekoh, the unfortunate son of Sháh Jehán, he found a worthy successor. The speculative and supplementary portion of the Vedas, the Upanishads, were translated by his order into Persian.‡ With the accession of Aurangzib the age of Mohammedan bigotry revived, and the

---

* [According to the Tárikh-i-Badaúni, the elder brother.]

† [See Sir H. Elliot's Bibliogr. Index to the Historians of Muhammedan India. Calc., 1849, I, 221. 259 ff.]

‡ From the Persian a translation into Latin was made by Anquetil du Perron, who published it under the title of Oupnekhat, seu Theologia Indica. Paris, 1801. 2 vols. 4to. [Prof. Goldstücker's 'Páṇini', p. 141 f.]

Hindus fell back into their defensive attitude of silence and suspicion.

The first European settlers in India were merchants and soldiers, who troubled themselves little about the intellectual products of the country. The missionaries, however, who followed on their track, speedily perceived the necessity of making themselves familiar with the native languages and writings, and diligently applied themselves to the study. Their purposes were not literary, and they did not deem it incumbent upon them to impart any of their discoveries to the European public, although it is not unlikely that the archives of the Propaganda Society at Rome may contain specimens of the early labours of the missionaries of the Roman church. At any rate, it has been recently evidenced by the voluminous compositions in Sanskrit verse upon Christian subjects by members of the Jesuit mission at Madura, discovered at Pondicheri not many years ago, and of which an account[*] was published in the Researches of the Asiatic Society of Bengal, that some of the members of this mission attained an extraordinary command over the language, and composed in it with an accuracy and an elegance unsurpassed by any later Europeans, and even by modern native scholars. The same proficiency was attained by them in Sanskrit, which they acquired in the vernacular tongues, and which has placed Robert de

---

[*] Account of a Discovery of a modern Imitation of the Vedas, by F. Ellis. Asiatic Researches, XIV, p. 1.

Nobili and Father Beschi amongst the classics of Tamil literature in the estimation of the natives of the south of India. Indications of this successful study however were few and faint in the west, although they were at length manifested in such meagre compilations as the 'Alphabetum Brahmanicum', and 'Alphabetum Grandonico-Malabaricum', published at Rome in 1771 and 1772 by the Propaganda Society.

The first systematic attempt to impart a more extended acquaintance with Sanskrit to European students, was the publication by Paulinus a S. Bartholomeo, a German missionary[*] of the name of Wesdin, of a short and imperfect grammar of the language, to which he gave the title of 'Siddharubam, seu Grammatica Samscrdamica', Rome 1790. This was followed by a number of works on the Indian languages, and the mythology and history of the Hindus, in which the information given, although tinted by colouring of local origin, and blended with fictions peculiar to the Peninsula of India, where Paulinus spent fourteen years, is in the main correct, and might have been useful had it not been overwhelmed by an accompanying mass of crude conjecture and misapplied erudition. A more copious and correct grammar was published by Paulinus in 1804, entitled, 'Vyácarnuam, seu locupletissima Samserdamicæ Linguæ Institutio'. The original of this was a native grammar, a copy of

---

[*] See a biographical notice of Paulinus in the Nouveaux Mélanges Asiatiques, par M. Abel Remusat, vol. II, p. 305.

which had been translated in India by a Danish missionary of the name of Hanxleden, who seems to have been a much better scholar than Paulinus. His papers having come into the possession of the latter, were either published by him as in the present instance, or employed by him for other works, as in the case of the first book of the Lexicon of Amara Sinha, also published by Paulinus with a Latin translation, which he was enabled to execute, it appears, chiefly by the aid of a manuscript Lexicon, Latin and Sanskrit, compiled by Hanxleden, and appended to the Vyácaranam.

This first grammar of the Sanskrit language, being a translation of an original work, is accurate, although not comprehensive. It is printed with Roman letters in all except the first section, in which the Sanskrit words are expressed in the characters of the Tamil alphabet, of very indifferent typographic execution. The Roman representation of the words in accordance with the original Tamil, is disfigured by corruptions derived from the peculiar pronunciation of the natives of that part of the Peninsula of which Tamil is the vernacular idiom, by whom soft labials are substituted for hard, and soft dentals or semivowels for hard dentals, in certain situations. Thus *Somabá* is written for *Somapá*, and *bhavadi* for *bhavati*, and *vrikshál* for *vrikshát*. With respect also to the Roman orthography, a most barbarous-looking equivalent is not unfrequently given for the original, depending partly upon German and partly upon Italian pronunciation, and which it often requires some consideration to identify;

kashtásrita is not at once recognisable in *kaszdaschrida*. The grammar is followed by two vocabularies, one Latin and Sanskrit, arranged according to the analogous senses of the words; the other, Sanskrit and Latin, arranged alphabetically. It is not stated by whom they were compiled, but it is probable that both were the work of Hanxleden. The 'Vyácarana' is not without merit,* and opened the way to the study of Sanskrit by the scholars of the continent; and Paulinus by its publication established a claim to grateful commemoration, although he cannot be considered to have done more than rendered the labours of a brother missionary accessible to the European public.†

Although not yet known in Europe, the labours of our own countrymen in the East, for the dissemination of an accurate knowledge of the Sanskrit language, had preceded the publication of the Vyácarana. The encouragement given to oriental studies by Warren Hastings, the institution of the Asiatic Society by Sir William Jones, and the foundation of the College of Fort William by the Marquis Wellesley, had communicated a powerful impulse and a right direction to the exertions of European scholars in India. Philology could not fail to receive the attention it deserved, and the Asiatic Researches were at an early period enriched

---

* [For less lenient opinions on the 'Vyácarana' compare Sir H. Elliot, l. l., p. 265, Note †.]

† Schlegel questions his fully understanding the writings of Hanxleden: "der Pater Paulinus theilte mit was er nur sehr unvollkommen verstand." Indische Bibliothek, I. l. 9.

by the observations of Sir William Jones and Mr. Colebrooke on various points regarding the structure and nature of the Sanskrit language. The compilation of elementary works expressly for the use of English students was necessarily one of the first objects of the institution of the College, and it was for the benefit of the junior civil servants of the East India Company attached to the College, that the two first published English grammars of the Sanskrit language, those of Dr. Carey and Mr. Colebrooke, were compiled and printed in Serampore and Calcutta.

Dr. William Carey was a member of the Baptist mission in Bengal. After a residence of eight years in the country, during which he had studied with unwearied assiduity the Bengali and Sanskrit languages, he was appointed Professor of both in the College of Fort William early in 1801. He immediately set about compiling a grammar,* and the first part of this work was published in 1803.† It was completed in 1806. It forms an immense volume, extending to a thousand quarto pages. This is in great part ascribable to the size of the Sanskrit types employed, which in the first stages of Sanskrit printing in India were of unnecessarily gigantic dimensions. With a due allowance on this account, enough remains to constitute the grammar a singular monument of in-

---

* Letter to Dr. Ryland, June 15, 1801. Memoir of Dr. Carey, D. D., p. 454.

† A Grammar of the Sungskrit language, by William Carey. Serampore, 1806. Reviewed, Quarterly Review, vol. I.

dustrious application. The work is divided into five books. The first explains the forms and powers of the letters of the alphabet, and then treats of what is termed in original grammars *Sandhi*, or combination; a series of rules providing for the coalescence or modification of letters when they come into junction or juxtaposition, so as to avoid harshness or hiatus in their articulation; a subject more minutely investigated and more systematically regulated in Sanskrit than in the grammar of any other language. The second book is appropriated to what native grammarians designate *Śabda*, literally a sound, or as here understood, an articulate sound, a word; under which head are comprised declinable words, whether substantives, adjectives, or pronouns; and indeclinable words, adverbs, prepositions, and conjunctions. The third book treats of the *Dhátus* or roots, as capable of verbal inflexion; first, as simple verbs in the ten classes or conjugations under which they are arranged in original works; and secondly, as derivative verbs, causals, desideratives, and frequentatives. The fourth book of 'Carey's Grammar' describes the formation of derivative words and of compound nouns, and treats of the genders of nouns. The fifth book comprehends the syntax and a few pages of exercises. To the whole is added, by way of an appendix, an alphabetical list of roots.

The Sanskrit Grammar of Dr. Carey is modelled upon the plan of the native grammars, and for the most part follows a similar order. The native authorities also are those chiefly current in Bengal, and he was assisted in the compilation by Bengali Pandits; he therefore speaks their language and adopts their technical phraseology to an extent that is not a little embarrassing to a mere European scholar. It is also inconveniently troublesome in use to a beginner, especially from the separation which it admits between the rules and the examples, so that many pages invariably intervene before the application of the precept, by which alone its purport is rendered intelligible, occurs. Numerical references from the examples to the rules are inserted, it is true, at the foot of the page in which the former are met with, but the verification imposes extra trouble upon the student, and is likely to be carelessly made: the want of a definite impression in the first aspect of a rule is seldom subsequently supplied. The section which treats of the formation of derivative words is broken up into unnecessarily multiplied subdivisions, which, with an appearance of classification, only render the subject more complicated and reference more uncertain. The exemplifications of the syntax are meagre and uninteresting. On the other hand, the chapters on conjugation are very copious and instructive, affording examples of a number of the most useful verbs in more or less detail. There are some inaccuracies, but they are not of a nature or extent to detract materially from the usefulness of an ample exhibition of conjugational varieties, as the conjugation of the verbs is the only real difficulty in Sanskrit grammar. The list of roots is a very serviceable and important addition. The whole is provided with a comprehensive index. The 'Grammar' is in truth a compilation of very great merit, although, from its adhering so closely to native technicalities, it cannot ever be of much advantage to European students. To scholars more advanced it is calculated to be of frequent service, and to any one who should propose to make himself acquainted with an original grammar of the Bengal School it would prove an invaluable auxiliary.

Shortly prior to the publication of Dr. Carey's complete Grammar appeared the first part of a grammar, compiled by the late Henry Thomas Colebrooke, a member of the Civil Service of Bengal, who throughout a long and active public life in India, in the course of which he ascended to the highest distinctions of the service, cultivated the language and literature of the Hindus with singular ability, untiring diligence, and unrivalled success. Succeeding to the position occupied by Sir William Jones, he proved himself worthy to be his successor, as, if he brought with him to the study an inferior order of scholastic attainments, and a less poetical imagination, he surpassed that distinguished orientalist in the profundity and exactitude with which he accomplished all he attempted, and for which he was indebted to a severer turn of thought and a predilection for scientific and mathematical investigation. At the time at which the College of Fort William was established, Mr. Colebrooke held the important office of one of the Judges of the High Court of Appeal of Bengal, but the interest which he felt in the institution induced him to allow himself to be named as Professor of Hindu Law and the Sanskrit Language, and he acted for some time as Examiner in the Persian, Hindustani, Bengali, and Sanskrit Languages. From his connexion with the College originated the grammar now noticed, which was published in 1805.

Mr. Colebrooke's 'Sanskrit Grammar' forms a small folio volume, extended beyond its due proportion by the same circumstance which magnified the bulk of Dr. Carey's work—the unnecessary size of the Devanagari types. The general arrangement is much the same as that of Dr. Carey, being regulated by the nature of the subjects explained. There are many essential varieties however in the details. The letters, their several powers, and the changes which they undergo in connexion with each other, are first described. Then follows the declension of nouns. Three chapters succeed, of which one treats of the genders of nouns, one of the formation of the feminine gender, and one of indeclinables. The rest of the work is occupied with the general rules of conjugation, exemplified by a rich collection of the Paradigms, in more or less detail, of all the verbs of the first conjugation, as derived from the best standard authorities, whose variations are carefully pointed out in accompanying annotations. No further portion of the grammar was ever published, Mr. Colebrooke considering that, after other entire grammars had been provided, it was not necessary to finish his own work, and his time and interest being engaged in other occupations and inquiries. The only materials which he seems to have collected were the remaining conjugations of the simple verbs, of which he gave the author a manuscript copy. The Paradigms were less fully developed than they would have been if they had been designed for publication. The subjects of derivation, composition and syntax were untouched, much to the regret of all those who are familiar with Mr. Colebrooke's labours in various departments of Hindu literature and science.

The grammar of Mr. Colebrooke, like that of Dr. Carey, is based upon the writings of Hindu grammarians. He has followed however the authorities of a different school, that of which Benares is considered to be the high seat, and which in its origin is more ancient than the school of Bengal. He has consequently adopted their terminology in the technicalities which he employs and the precepts which he enunciates, but he has arranged the rules according to a classification of his own. The technical language of his rules, as of those of Carey's grammar, is startling and perplexing to a European student, and almost incomprehensible without the aid of an interpreter. The difficulty here also is enhanced by the want of contiguous examples, by which the rules may be at once illustrated and rendered intelligible. The examples are in a different and sometimes in a distant part of the volume, and although references are sometimes specified numerically, yet they are not always inserted, and are never of ready applicability from the nature of the divisions into books, chapters and sections. Thus, as an example both of the phraseology and of the separation of rule and illustration, let us take the following—it is one out of some hundreds. Section 7. chapter IV. of Book I. treats of the permutations of finals. Rule I. runs thus: —" A blank (*lopa*) is substituted for *n* final of a crude noun that is denominated *pada*, except the vocative singular, unless in the neuter gender." Now here we have first the theoretical peculiarity that a letter is said not to be elided or expunged, but a blank is said to be substituted for it; and secondly, the use of the term *pada*, by which is meant the crude noun before all inflexional terminations beginning with a consonant, exclusive of those of the nominative case in the three numbers, and of the accusative singular and dual, and also before affixes forming derivatives, and before other nouns forming compounds. The first application of this rule occurs after an interval of forty pages, under the declension of nouns ending in *n*, as *rájan*, a king, which loses its final *n*, agreeably to the precept, before the inflexional terminations beginning with consonants, as *rájabhis*, by kings; *rájasu*, in or amongst kings; but keeps it in the vocative, as *rájan*, oh king. The other applications do not occur in the volume at all, as the work does not comprehend the construction of derivatives and compounds, in which the final of *rájan* is equally lost, as *rájya rájatva*, royalty; *rája-dharma*, the duty of a king. Had these exemplifications been attached to the rule, the obscurity would have been dissipated, and a definite and permanent impression of a very extensively useful precept would have been effected. Where, however, familiarity with the arrangement and with the phraseology is acquired, Mr. Colebrooke's grammar becomes of inestimable value from its extreme precision and remarkable comprehensiveness. The rules provide most accurately, and in the shortest possible space, for every contingency of inflexion, whether of nouns or verbs.

Although not exactly in the order of publication, yet it will be convenient, whilst yet in the regions of the East, to notice two other productions of the Calcutta press upon the subject of Sanskrit grammar. The first of these was as early in point of compilation as either of its predecessors, having been prepared in 1804. The author, Mr. Forster, declares however, that subsequently to the appearance of the grammars of Carey and Colebrooke, he was so sensible of the inferiority of his own that he had allowed it to slumber longer in the press than was necessary, with a view to its eventual suppression. Mr. Forster was also a member of the Civil Service of Bengal, and was a distinguished Bengali scholar. He was a man of a vigorous and active mind, but without Mr. Colebrooke's scholarship and perspicacity, and of a more mechanical than even methodical turn. His work is entitled, 'An Essay on the Principles of Sanskrit Grammar',* and is

---

* 1 vol. 4to, Calcutta, 1810. Reviewed by Bopp in the 'Heidelberger Jahrbücher, 1818', No. XXX.

illustrative of the author's peculiarities, displaying great labour and considerable ingenuity. It is, to a great extent, an attempt to give a tabular form to Sanskrit grammar, the exemplifications of the rules for the permutation of letters, the inflexions of declension and conjugation, and the development of derivative verbs and nouns, being collected in tables to which the rules refer. The construction of these tables, the relations that some of them bear to others, and the connexion between them and the rules they exemplify, are not always happily contrived, and the complex and troublesome system of the references from the rules to the tables, and from one table to another, renders the work wholly unavailable for elementary study. It contains however a vast number of useful specifications, and may be occasionally consulted with benefit by riper students. The work, as far as printed, comprises the usual divisions of the grammar; but it was the intention of the author to have given a second volume, in which he was to have inserted a translation of the 'Mugdhabodha', the native grammar, which is the standard authority in Bengal, and which is ascribed to Vopadeva, a grammarian of the twelfth century.*

The other Sanskrit grammar published in Calcutta is of comparatively recent date. It is the work of Mr.

---

* There is, in the library of Trinity College, Cambridge, a neatly written copy of Mr. Forster's essay, including, it is believed, the materials of the second portion of his work.

Yates, a member of the Baptist mission, a body which for its number has furnished a greater proportion of first-rate Sanskrit and Bengali scholars than any other class of persons in Bengal. Mr. Yates's grammar is constructed upon the plan of popular European grammars, with a view to the simplification of the system and abridgement of time and labour in the acquirement. He has not altogether failed in his object, although it may be doubted if the principles of popular vernacular grammar be applicable to so copious and complicated a language as Sanskrit.* Mr. Yates's grammar forms a moderately sized octavo volume, and may be consulted with facility. It does not seem to have made much way in Europe, its necessity having been superseded by similar productions in this part of the world. At no time however, not even at the present, do any of the publications of the Anglo-Indian press penetrate through what may be termed, to use an Indian illustration, the bound-hedge of English literature.

When the Asiatic Society of Calcutta was first instituted, and for a few years following, the inquiries of our countrymen into the languages and literature of India seem to have excited some attention and interest. Much of this was owing to the European reputation of Sir William Jones, acquired in an English university, and maintained by his correspondence on

---

* Indische Bib., vol. II, p. 11.

oriental subjects with the most eminent of the continental orientalists. The novelty of the objects investigated, and the attractive though erroneous tendency of some of the Society's fancied verifications of ancient mythology and scriptural history, contributed also to awaken and to keep interest alive. The public mind was also then at leisure to receive new impressions, as little of novelty or importance in literature was offered for its amusement or instruction about the period when the first volume of the 'Asiatic Researches' appeared, or in 1788. In a very brief time, however, came the all-absorbing interest of the momentous events springing from the revolution in France, and when literature revived it assumed a more inviting form than archæological conjecture or philological speculation, busying themselves with a distant people and remote antiquity. It is not surprising therefore that no note was taken of the grammatical labours of Englishmen residing in the East, and that they found their way slowly and with difficulty even to the few who stood in need of their aid and longed for their appearance. A striking instance of this occurs in the case of the late Professor Chézy, who until 1810 had not heard of the existence of Carey's 'Sanskrit Grammar'. In the preface to his excellent edition and translation of 'Sakuntala' he has described, in an animated and interesting tone, the wretched means and the unremitting application by which he acquired his first knowledge of Sanskrit, and the delight with which he welcomed the bulky volume of Carey, and the more elegant and available grammar of Wilkins, which had been published in London at the end of 1808.*

The publication of the grammar of the late Sir Charles Wilkins constitutes an important era in the annals of Sanskrit philology. Its European origin and complexion, its distinct and elegant typography, and the higher merits of method and perspicuity, recommended its contents to the notice of continental scholars, and tempted as well as enabled them to embark in a study from which they had previously been repelled by the uncouth form and inadequate structure of the vessels provided for their conveyance. From the appearance of the grammar of Wilkins may be dated the impulse given to the cultivation of Sanskrit, and, as an obvious consequence, of comparative philology both in France and Germany, and the somewhat tardy, though it is to be hoped not unpromising, emulation which the labours of the philologists of the continent have at length aroused amongst ourselves.

Sir Charles Wilkins, like Colebrooke and Forster, reflects lustre upon the civil service of Bengal. Stimulated and encouraged by the example of Mr. Halhed, also a Bengal civilian, the first Englishman who directed his attention to Sanskrit, although better known by his

---

* "La bibliothèque du roi possédait bien à la vérité un essai informe de grammaire, un manuscrit composé, à ce que je crois, par quelque Missionnaire Portugais, mais ne renfermant que le paradigme du verbe substantif, le tableau de déclinaisons, une partie du vocabulaire d'Amera et une liste des dhatous; le tout fourmillant d'erreurs les plus grossières."

grammar of the Bengali language, Mr. Wilkins engaged about the year 1778 with ardour in the study, and, in despite of the absence of all elementary assistance, soon became profoundly acquainted with the structure of the language, and with its standard literature. An undeniable proof of the success which had rewarded his diligence was manifested in 1784 by the publication of his translation of the philosophical episode from the 'Mahábhárata', the 'Bhagavad Gítá', which was printed in London under the patronage of the Court of Directors, at the recommendation of the most illustrious governor-general that British India ever obeyed, Warren Hastings. The difficulty of acquiring the knowledge of a difficult language, such as Sanskrit, without any other appliances and means than grammars and lexicons in the language itself, and preceptors ignorant of English, and unfamiliar with our notions of elementary tuition, can be conceived by none but those who have been placed in similar circumstances. Fortunately the author's experience of the difficulty was brief, for had not the grammar of Sir C. Wilkins come to his rescue, whilst guessing at the obscurities of the 'Mugdhabodha' through the equally puzzling interpretation of a Pańdit, he would probably have relinquished the task in despair. Such as it was, the experiment qualified him to do justice to the perseverance and industry by which his precursors in the path have enabled others to follow their route. Upon the return of Mr. Wilkins to England, he brought with him translations of three popular native grammars, and from these, and other original authorities, he compiled a grammar, of which the first pages were printed in 1795. The types of the 'Devanágarí' letters employed were cut and cast under his personal direction; and for the more accurate execution of the work he set up a printing press in his own house. When his preparations were complete, and, as stated, the first pages of the grammar were printed, the house was set on fire; the manuscript books, matrices and punches were saved, but the types and press were destroyed, and the prosecution of the work was stopped. So many causes of delay retarded its resumption, that Mr. Wilkins at last had determined to abandon his design, when the establishment of the East India College at Haileybury supplied him with a sufficient inducement to renew and complete his labours. The grammar was accordingly finished, and was published towards the close of 1808.

The general plan of Wilkins's grammar is, like that of his predecessors, suggested by the arrangement of native grammarians. To the alphabet and laws of Sandhi succeed the declension of nouns in the order of their final letters, and then the declension of pronouns. The conjugation of verbs, simple and derivative, follows, and then the formation of participles and analogous nouns. The remaining chapters treat of the formation of miscellaneous derivative nouns, of indeclinable words, of the construction of compounds, and of the genders of nouns, and the work ends with the syntax.

The main objects, which Mr. Wilkins professes to have had in view in the classification of his grammar and the enunciation of its precepts, are perspicuity and correctness, and it must be admitted that, with some few exceptions of comparatively trivial importance, he has accomplished both. The principal defects of the grammar are an insufficient provision of general principles, and in some respects an inconvenient classification. The examples are numerous, and for the most part well selected, but the rules which they exemplify do not adequately define existing analogies of construction, a knowledge of which is essential to reduce, connect and simplify what in its present state appears as a somewhat unwieldy and unretainable mass of incoherent details. An unnecessary multiplication of declensions is one consequence of this want of a connecting principle. In the conjugation of the verbs the separation of the four tenses, to which the analogy of conjugational modification is restricted, from the other six tenses, which according to the author are common to all conjugations, scatters the component members of an individual body over a number of pages, so as to render it a matter of extreme difficulty, and to a beginner almost an impossibility, to trace and reunite them so as to form an entire verb. It is to be remarked, as a consequence of this plan, that the whole grammar does not furnish a solitary example of an entire verb inflected throughout in its various moods, tenses, and persons, an omission that is particularly embarassing to a beginner. In regard to the indefinite preterite tense, one of the most perplexing parts of conjugation, an attempt has been made to reduce its multiform construction to a fixed number of modes, but not with much success, as no general principle has been laid down, whilst it is very evident that all the essential modifications are resolvable into no more than two, or that this tense comprehends the præter-pluperfect and the aorist past— the inflexions of each of which are diversified upon principles not difficult to be detected. The chapters on the derivation of words are totally devoid of method, and it might be objected to them that the examples are needlessly copious, but that, as no printed dictionary of the language existed when the grammar was published, this copiousness of words was of infinite value, as in some degree supplying the deficiency. Finally, is may be objected to the chapter on syntax, that it is not so simple as could be wished, nor are the illustrations in general interesting or striking; notwithstanding these exceptions, however, the justice of which may possibly be with reason called in question, the grammar of Sir C. Wilkins is undeniably a work of great merit and utility, and must ever be regarded as of standard authority.*

---

* Schlegel thus speaks of it: "Finally, Wilkins has with uncommon clearness and ingenuity reduced, if I may use the expression, the Algebra of Sanskrit grammar to familiar arithmetic. It is true that we miss many things in his book, the absence of which, considering the large scale on which the work is planned, cannot well be excused. His terminology also is not always hap-

The facilities now afforded by the grammatical works on Sanskrit published in the English language were immediately and zealously applied by men of the highest literary character upon the continent to the acquirement of a knowledge of the language and literature of the Hindus. The success that attended their diligence was speedily displayed in the publication of various interesting disquisitions, either upon subjects of a general nature, or the structure and affinities of the language, especially by those accomplished scholars, Frederick and Augustus Schlegel, by Professors Chézy of Paris, Bopp of Berlin, and Frank of Munich. Some time, however, elapsed before a complete Sanskrit grammar was attempted.

The first Sanskrit grammar published on the continent, after the publication of Wilkins's grammar in England, and the arrival in Europe of the grammars published in Calcutta, was the work of the late Professor Othmar Frank,* then attached to the University

---

pily chosen; but nevertheless, as a beginning, the grammar is exceedingly convenient and serviceable."—*Ind. Bib.* [I, p. 10]. Burnouf observes: "Parmi ces ouvrages (the different Anglo-Sanskrit grammars) c'est encore celui de Wilkins qu'on peut consulter avec le plus de fruit, et quelques reproches que l'on soit en droite de lui adresser il reste encore comme un beau monument du savoir de la patience de l'auteur."—*Journ. As.* Mai 1825. He quotes also Chézy's opinions, as expressed in the 'Moniteur', 1810, No. 30, and says, "qu'il n'a pas trop dit quand il parle de l'étonnante perfection qui règne dans ce travail, et quand il ajoute que malgré quelques fautes il n'est pas moins digne de l'admiration et de la reconnaissance des savants."

* "Grammatica Sanskrita: edidit Othmarus Frank."

of Wurtzburgh, a scholar of the most extensive erudition, and a critic of the most candid and amiable temperament, but whose judgment was sometimes carried away by that turn for metaphysical speculation which is not uncommon amongst his countrymen. From the cultivation of Persian literature and philosophy he passed with avidity to Sanskrit philology and metaphysics, and in the former department took the lead in the compilation of a grammar for German students. It was written in Latin, and published at Wurtzburgh in 1823. The want of a fount of moveable types compelled the author to have recourse to lithography to represent the Devanágarí letters; and as they were not written in the best style, nor always accurately, they are very injurious to the appearance of the volume and inconvenient in use. Professor Frank acknowledged his obligations to the works of Colebrooke and Wilkins, but he had also consulted the original grammars printed in Calcutta, which by this time had reached Europe—the 'Sútras' of Páńini, and the 'Siddhánta Kaumudí'. He has however chiefly followed the arrangement of Wilkins, modifying, it may be doubted if judiciously, the order of the declensions, and abridging, but not always improving, the chapters on conjugation and derivation. He is equally deficient in the enunciation of general principles, and his rules are assertions of the bare fact that words assume certain forms, without any attempt to explain how or why. His principal additions consist of tables exhibiting the inflexional changes of nouns and verbs in a convenient and readily consulted manner. The table of conjugations however limits the paradigms of nine out of the ten classes of verbs to the persons of the present tense of the indicative mood, and is of proportionably restricted usefulness. This part of the grammar is open to the objection made to that of Wilkins, that the tenses are distributed in various places, accordingly as they are formed with what Prof. Frank denominates primary or secondary inflexions,* and that no example is given in the whole grammar of an entire verb. Prof. Frank has taken some pains to explain the meaning of the principal grammatical terms used by native grammarians, derived chiefly from Carey. He has also attempted to build upon the doctrines of the original authorities a theory of the language generally, and of the analogous construction and offices of the different parts of speech, but he has not developed his views in sufficient detail, or with sufficient distinctness, to admit of their being fully comprehended; and it may be doubted, as he has not specified his authorities, whether the original grammarians have anywhere suggested, what he imagines he discovers in them, a typical genius of the language, or its relation to the distinctions of matter and spirit. Speculations of this nature were favourite themes with Prof. Frank, and have sometimes perhaps impaired the beneficial results of his unquestionable abilities, industry, and learning.

---

* "Flexus primi," "F. secundarii."

The grammar by which German scholars have been chiefly introduced to the acquirement of Sanskrit in their several universities, is that of Prof. Bopp of Berlin. This, which was originally written in German,* was published in parts at the several dates of 1824, 1825, and 1827. The Professor's own Latin version† of the more considerable portion was published in 1829, and the remainder, with some emendations and improvements, in 1832. The grammar was again published in an abridged and amended form in 1834. This last edition is, like the first, in German.

The first German edition, and the first part of the Latin version, were founded, the author states, upon the grammars of Wilkins and Forster; and he expresses his opinion that the structure of the language may be more fully developed from the materials which they furnish than from any advantage or assistance derivable from the study of the native Sanskrit grammarians. This avowed depreciation of the authorities on which the works that served Prof. Bopp as guides were declaredly based,‡ contrasted with the title he

---

* "Ausführliches Lehrgebäude der Sanskrit Sprache".
† "Grammatica Critica Linguæ Sanskritæ".
‡ "Cum grammaticam hanc conscribere instituerem, magnaque viderem Wilkinsii et Forsteri de lingua Sanscrita merita, facile intellexi, has litteras non tam accuratiori et copiosiori Grammaticorum indigenarum studio augeri et adjuvari posse, quam libera adhibita critica arte, quæ rationem et leges, quibus lingua in formationibus suis sit usa, examinare et explicare studeat." [See Lassen's criticism in the "Indische Bibliothek", III, p. 22 ff.]

had given to his own work of 'A Critical Grammar', has exposed him to some rather severe animadversion on the part of his countrymen; one good effect of which, however, was to induce Prof. Bopp to direct his attention to the original grammar of Páṅini at least, and to enrich the second portion of his Latin version, and the second German edition of his work, with many important observations derived from that source. It may be doubted, however, if the prejudice which he seems to have early contracted against native grammarians has not been injurious to the comprehensiveness of his views and the perspicuity of his arrangement.

Although entitled an abridgement, the last German edition of Prof. Bopp's 'Grammar' can scarcely be regarded as an abbreviation, except typographically. It is printed in a smaller type and more compact shape, but it contains much additional matter, and the differences which it exhibits are rather alterations than omissions or curtailments. The grammar has, in fact, been remodelled in many important respects, and so materially improved, that it may be considered to have superseded the earlier editions; as it also presents the author's latest conclusions upon the subject, it will be sufficient to confine our attention to a brief notice of this particular publication.*

The general arrangement of Bopp's 'Grammar' conforms to that of Wilkins's, but differs in some of the

---

* [The second edition appeared in 1845, and the third in 1863.]

details. To the account of the alphabet succeed the rules of literal combination, or *Sandhi,* or as they are termed of Euphony. Under this head, however, Bopp has included changes not simply euphonic, nor properly comprised within the limits of combination as proposed by the original grammarians. The terms *Sandhi* or *Sanhitá,* which are applied to this portion of grammar, both denote a holding together, a coalescence or combination, which can, of course, alone take place between two or more letters when they are in contact or contiguity. The object proposed by such laws of combination is, to avoid any harshness or hiatus occasioned by the actual or proximate concurrence of incongruous sounds. Prof. Bopp has extended his rules to changes which occur in single letters in the middle of words, having no regard whatever to the sounds by which they are preceded or followed, but dependent upon inflexional provisions, upon laws affecting declension and conjugation. How far these are to be treated as merely euphonic changes may admit of question, but most assuredly they are not changes resulting from the contact or contiguity of incongruous letters, and are so far inconsistently included under the denomination *Sandhi.* It may be convenient to bring these literal changes together under one head, and anticipate in some degree the laws of inflexion; but on the other hand, it confounds things essentially different, and is a departure from the precision and simplicity of the original system.

Some remarks on the character of Sanskrit roots,

and the prepositions with which they combine to form compound verbs, precede the chapters on declension. In the earlier editions, Prof. Bopp, after specifying the general principles upon which nouns were inflected, classed them under six declensions, but in the last edition he has reduced these to one, to which he has subjoined a long series of what he designates as irregular nouns, classing them in the order of the declensions of Wilkins according to their final letters. The reduction of all nouns to one declension is perfectly consistent with the doctrines of the native grammarians and with their scheme of terminations, which is more or less applicable to every case of nominal inflexion. It may be doubted, however, if the irregular nouns of Bopp can be always regarded as deviations from rule, and their being given separately prevents their analogy of construction, mutually or universally, from being so evident as it might be. There are two principal sources of varieties in inflexion, changes of those letters or syllables which are subjoined to the inflective word or base to express cases or persons, and changes of the inflective word or base itself. The former constitute the essence of declension, and there is little irregularity in them. The changes of the base are peculiar either to individuals or to classes of nouns, but in the latter are founded on common principles, and these can scarcely be denominated irregularities. Prof. Bopp has not thought it necessary to advert to this distinction, attaching little or no importance to the scheme of terminations given in original grammars;

he has looked to the inflected noun, not in its elements, but as a whole, and has considered any special modifications which it may undergo as deviations from general rules. This method is, no doubt, more conformable to European notions, but it appears to be less simple and less easy of recollection than that of the original authorities.

The declensions of adjectives, numerals and pronouns follow those of substantive nouns, and useful tables are inserted in all the editions exhibiting the forms of various nouns in their several cases, in a convenient and serviceable manner.

The subject of conjugation is next treated of. More importance is here attached to the technical inflexional terminations of the original system than was assigned to those of declension. It may be questioned however if even in this instance the terminations are sufficiently prominent. There is also a departure from the technical scheme even as represented by Wilkins, in omitting without remark the indicatory letters of the terminations, that is, certain letters added to the actual termination which are not used to construct the inflexions, but which denote certain invariable modifications of the base to which the inflexional terminations are attached. Thus the terminations of the three persons singular of the present tense are called by Bopp *mi, si, ti*; in original works they are *mip, sip, tip*. The *p* is indicatory, signifying that, for the radical vowel of the base, a Guña letter or diphthong is to be substituted, which substitution does not take place before the terminations of the dual *vas*, *thas*, *tas*, or of the plural *mas*, *tha*, *anti*. Is is true that this is an instance of what Schlegel calls the Algebra of Sanskrit grammar, and the use of such indicatory letters is purely technical and arbitrary. But what else than technical and arbitrary are significant words when they are employed in a specific and conventional acceptation? Instead of the Sanskrit sign *p*, the presence of which requires a definite change, and the absence of which prohibits that change, Prof. Bopp is obliged to propose different words for the two contingencies, and to give to those words significations which they do not naturally bear, in order to apply them to the object in view, and which senses are in this application of the words merely conventional. Those personal terminations before which the vowel of the base may be changed he calls light—*leichte*—*leves*; those before which it is unchanged he terms heavy—*schwere*—*graves*. It is obvious that these terms can convey, *à priori*, a no more precise notion of the influence exercised by the terminations upon the base than any given letter or syllable. Until explained their purport is unintelligible, and they have this disadvantage, that when explained their fitness is liable to be disputed. What is the meaning of a light or heavy syllable? Why is *mi* lighter than *mas*, *ti* than *tha*? The single indicatory letter, the algebraic sign, has its conventional significancy and no other, and its intention being once defined, it cannot be mistaken or misapplied. However unphilosophical therefore it may be thought, the short-hand of the Sanskrit grammarians has in these respects a decided advantage over the proposed designations. It has its own office and no other.

In the classification he first adopted, Prof. Bopp distributed the verbs amongst four conjugations. In his last work he reduces the number to two, which is an improvement. He follows however, in regard to the tenses, the same course as Wilkins, dividing the four conjugationals, which he calls special, from the other six, which he terms general. The rules which he prescribes for the structure of the former under their several classes or conjugations, are illustrated by comparatively few examples, but he has added useful tables of the personal terminations of both orders of tenses, so that the construction of a complete verb may be effected with comparative facility. It is however in this part of Sanskrit grammar that the only serious difficulty lies. The peculiarities in the modifications of verbal bases, not of the terminations, are so numerous and anomalous, that when they are scattered over a wide space, and are to be picked up piece-meal, they are very apt to elude the search, and slip from the recollection of the student. It seems preferable therefore to adopt the arrangement observed by Mr. Colebrooke with regard to the first class of verbs, and give examples of all those most frequently recurring, in paradigms, more or less copious, according to the circumstances of each verb. The peculiarities of every verb are thus brought together under their common original, and that may be readily remembered as a whole which can scarcely be acquired by the separate contemplation of its *disjecta membra*. Prof. Bopp seems to have felt this difficulty, and in order to enable the student of his Grammar to advert more promptly to an anomalous construction in various instances, he has added to the conjugations an alphabetical list of what he terms irregular verbs, with numerical references to the paragraph in which the irregularity is described. The cases may be thus more easily referred to, no doubt, but such reference implies previous knowledge of the irregularity. The reader must know, for instance, that the verb *Anja* does offer an anomaly, before he attempts to find what that anomaly may be. In fact, he must have already learnt, although he may have forgotten it, and the index is therefore only a supplement to the recollection. Upon the whole, although it cannot be denied that Prof. Bopp's treatment of this branch of his subject is much more satisfactory than that of his predecessors, Mr. Colebrooke excepted, it leaves much to be desired.

As a specimen of Prof. Bopp's mode of dealing with the conjugation of Sanskrit verbs, the following view which he takes of the personal inflexions may be cited.

1. "The characteristic signs of the persons are the following:—The first person has in the singular and plural *m*, and in the dual *v*, the connexion of which, with the essential elements of the first personal pronoun, or *m* in different cases of the singular, and *v* in the nominatives of the dual and plural numbers, as

explained in a preceding passage, is very obvious. In the imperative singular of the active voice the first person substitutes *n* for *m*, and the deponent voice drops the consonant in all the persons of the singular number, so that *me* becomes *e*; *ma* becomes *a*; *mi* becomes *i*, and *ai* is substituted for *mai* or *nai*. The syllable *as* in the plural ending *mas* is, I doubt not, identical with the termination of the plural nominative of *as*, since the personal endings of the verb correspond as to their purport to the nominatives of nouns. The termination *mas* is therefore to be resolved into *m* and *as*, and the latter appears also in the terminations of the first person dual *vas*, as *ad-vas*, we two eat.*

"The dual termination of the nominatives of nouns, or *au*, is derived from *as*, of which it is merely an emphatic amplification. (Comp. Gr. § 206.) The abbreviated terminations *ma*, *va*, in the subordinate tenses, are dependent upon the unabridged terminations *mas*, *vas*, as neuters on masculines and feminines. (Ibid. § 231.) As neuter, and in fact dualistic, the dual endings of the middle voice *âthe*, *âte*, are in my opinion to be considered as agreeing with the nominative dual of regular neuter nouns, the primitive of which ends in *a*. So *te* from *âte* is identical with

---

* [It is needless to state that some of the views quoted above have been considerably modified in the two later editions of the Sanskrit grammar, and in the second German edition of the Comparative Grammar.]

the isolated pronoun *te*, they or those two, formed from *ta* with the affix *i*. Also *te* and *the* agree with the masculine nominatives plural of the pronouns through the analogies comprehended in rule 243-4.

2. "The second person has, through all varieties of number and tense, these characteristic elements, *t, th, dhv, dh, h, sv, s*, of which the last is the widest deviation from the pronominal primitives *tva, tve*, subordinate from *te* (in like manner as *sv* is formed out of *tv*, and *s* third person out of *t*); the closest analogy to the pronoun being *dhve, dhvam*, of the Átmanepada, the *v* of which, again, in the second person of the imperative singular is connected with *s*, as *sva*. *S* in truth predominates in the singular, as *tudasi*, thou tormentest; *atudas*, thou hast tormented, &c. *Th* and *dh* are common substitutions for *t*, as *prathama* for *pra-tama*, the first; *adh-ara* for *a-tara*, lower; and *adhama* for *a-tama*, lowest: as further exemplifications of these in the second person take the following. From *tud*, active voice, second preterite, second person singular, *tuloditha*; present, second person dual, *tudathas*; plural, *tudatha*; middle voice, present, second person plural, *tudadhve*; imperfect, second person singular, *tudasva*. *Ad* in the second person singular imperative makes *ad-dhi*. The transition of *as* into the dual ending *thas*, and *as* in the third person into *tas*, depends upon the same principle as the formation of *mas* and *vas* in the first person of the plural and dual numbers, that is, it is the annexation of the plural termination of the nominative case of nouns to the

especial sign of the third personal pronoun, as they were of the same termination to the signs of the first and second personal pronouns *m* and *v*.

3. "The third person has, in the three numbers in both voices where the terminations undergo no contraction, the letter *t* for its characteristic element, the conformity of which with the pronominal *t* is as open as day. The development of *ám* in the dual of the potential, &c., we elucidate through the principle of *ávám*, we two; *yu-vám*, ye two; as also in the second and third persons of the Atmanepada, the endings *áthám* and *átám*."

The chapters on conjugation in Prof. Bopp's grammar contain some interesting analogies between the Sanskrit and Greek inflexions of the verb, but these belong to the subject of comparative philology. There is also some bold and ingenious theory upon the construction of some of the general tenses, such as the two futures and the conditional, which he regards as compounded, not simple tenses; also of the complete development of the substantive verb *as*, *esse*, to be; which is always considered elsewhere as defective. Some of Prof. Bopp's views are rather startling at first, but they are not therefore to be hastily rejected, and may upon further investigation prove to be well-founded.

Consideration is also due to Bopp's theory of the formation of the infinitive mood, which Sanskrit grammarians always treat as a verbal derivative indeclinable noun; also to his views of the formation of the indeclinable past participle ending in *twá* and *ya*, and the adverbial participle ending in *am*. All these are regarded by Bopp as the objective or instrumental cases of nouns, of which the other cases are defective or obsolete, although traceable possibly in the ancient Sanskrit of the Vedas, of which he has given some proofs; others may be perhaps discovered when our acquaintance with the texts of the Vedas is more extensive.

After disposing of those derivatives, which are commonly held by us to be parts of a verb, the Grammar proceeds to describe other verbal derivatives, to which, as well as to the preceding, Bopp gives the name of Primitives. To them succeed derivative words formed from nouns, as patronymics, possessives, and the like. In both classes he has adopted an arrangement equally simple and convenient—an alphabetical list of the suffixes employed by native grammarians to construct derivative upon primitive words, illustrated by examples of the words formed upon this principle. In doing this, however, Prof. Bopp has omitted what might by some be considered as the most useful part of the classification. These suffixes, as well as those used in forming the inflexions of declension and conjugation, are composed of two elements, the letter or letters which are really added to or substituted for the original ending of the base, and a letter or letters which are merely indicatory of certain changes in the body of the base: the latter Prof. Bopp omits. Thus, in the first part of his Taddhita, or nominal derivatives, he gives the letter *a* as forming patronymics, abstracts, collectives and adjectives from primitive nouns, as *vásishtha*, son of Vasishtha; *sauhrida*, friendship, from *suhrid*, a friend; *kápota*, a flock of pigeons, from *kapota*, a pigeon; *rájata*, silver or silvery, from *rajata*, the metal, silver. In these examples it will be noticed the original short vowel of the base is transmuted to a long vowel or diphthong; it is exchanged, in technical language, for its vṛiddhi, or augmented substitute. The rule that says such change takes place has to provide for each separate case separately, but in the notation of the original scheme it is a general rule that an indicatory nasal of the cerebral class in any suffix whatever denotes the increase or vṛiddhi of the vowel of the base. Accordingly, the affix is here said to be not *a*, but *aṅ*, the *ṅ* being the indicatory, the *a* the essential element; consequently, *aṅ* being applied to the words particularized, *a* is either added to or substituted for the proper termination of the primitive, the radical vowel of which also undergoes a definite modification. There is another important consideration to recommend the preservation of the indicatory letter. The essential letter of a suffix may be the same, but the effect upon the base may be different; in one instance its addition may require, in another prohibit, any change of the radical vowel; two opposite results proceeding from the same adjunct, as it stands in Bopp's scheme. The cause of the difference is at once seen when the indicatory letter is inserted and its influence is known. Derivatives formed with *a* alone may or may not change the vowel of the base, but those formed with *aṅ* do require the change; those formed with *añ*, or *a*, and the nasal of the guttural class of consonants, never admit it. *Śiva* with *aṅ* must make *śaiva*; *chiti* with *aṅ* makes *chintá*. It would therefore have been of benefit to the student, as furnishing him with a key to similarity and dissimilarity of derivation, if the indicatory had been added to the essential elements in the alphabetical lists of the suffixes.

The chapters on derivation are followed by those on compound nouns and indeclinables; no chapter on syntax is included in either of the editions. The author in the first edition announced his purpose of delaying it until after the publication of the glossary to his edition of Nalus. It has not yet however appeared, and no notice is taken of the omission in the last edition. The subject could not fail to derive interesting and important elucidation from Prof. Bopp, although, as he justly observes, Sanskrit syntax may be disposed of in a very moderate compass, as the principles of construction are for the most part conformable to those of general grammar or the grammars of kindred languages, and rarely deviate from the limits prescribed by the nature of its own copious and perfect system of grammatical forms.*

---

* "Syntaxin nondum absolvere potui, ne tamen extensum hac de re opus expectent lectores; Sanskrita enim lingua apud antiquiores inprimis auctores locupletissimæ et perfectissimæ suæ

From this brief and necessarily imperfect sketch of the Sanskrit grammar of Prof. Bopp, it will no doubt be evident that he has treated the subject with profound attention, and has given to Sanskrit students a most valuable and instructive work. The last edition is in particular to be recommended as a compendious and comprehensive guide to the study of Sanskrit grammar, and it fully merits the character which was given to the first edition of it by another distinguished German scholar and critic, Prof Lassen, when adverting to the authorities which Prof. Bopp professed to have followed; he described it as more systematic than the grammar of Wilkins, more perspicuous than that of Forster, and more concise than either.

But one other grammar remained to be mentioned, concerning which the author could say little, as it was his own. It was published in 1841.[*] Its especial object is to render the acquirement of Sanskrit easy to beginners. How far this is effected remains to be determined. From the remarks which had been hazarded upon some portions of Prof. Bopp's Grammar, it would be readily inferred that the author had made more use than Prof. Bopp had done of the methods of native

---

grammaticæ raro transgreditur fines a natura constitutos, ita, ut qui ea repetere noluerit quæ ad generalis grammaticæ pertinent principia, et eodem jure in cujusvis alias ex eadem familia linguæ compendio locum habeant, 'paucis capitibus absolvat syntaxin Sanskritam."

[*] [Second edition 1847.]

grammarians, and he had only to hope that he might not thereby have merited the sentence which was pronounced upon Mr. Colebrooke's Grammar, that "whilst it is of value as an introduction to the study of native grammars, it is insufficient and excessively obscure as a grammar of the language."

Several works connected with the objects of the grammars which have been adverted to, and which are in an especial degree subservient to the acquirement of the Sanskrit language, have been compiled and published by European authors regarding the Sanskrit radicals. Lists of these are attached to Carey's 'Sanskrit Grammar', and to his 'Bengali Dictionary', and as identical with verbs they are particularized by Wilkins and Forster. The former also published a separate work, in which the roots are arranged in alphabetical order, with the meaning as expressed in original lists, the translation of the original term, a short sentence illustrative of its use, and the indicatory letters denoting peculiarities of conjugation. The chief defects of this publication are occasional inaccuracies and general poverty of exemplification.

A work of a similar purport, but superior execution, was subsequently published by the late Dr. Rosen, and was characterized by that ability, judgement, and learning which he displayed still more conspicuously in his edition and version of the first part of the 'Rigveda', and which have ensured to his too brief career the admiration and regret of all Sanskrit scholars. In this compilation the roots are arranged alphabetically by their final and then their initial letters. Their Sanskrit equivalents, as given by two standard native writers, Kásinátha and Vopadeva, are inserted and translated by the Latin infinitive. The classes in which they are conjugated are specified, and short paradigms of the principal tenses are supplied. The most novel and useful feature of the work is the exemplification of the senses of the radicals as they occur in their inflected forms in short but well-chosen passages extracted from the different books which had been printed at the period when the work of Dr. Rosen was compiled. The same plan of illustration is then adapted to another and important novelty, the most useful of the compound verbs, or those in which the inseparable prepositions are prefixed to the radicals, constituting the great body of the verbs that occur in Sanskrit compositions. The examples are referred to the originals whence they are extracted, and are translated into Latin with fidelity and elegance.

A still more elaborate description of Sanskrit radicals has been subsequently published. It was printed at Bonn in 1841, and is the work of Mr. Westergaard, a young but distinguished scholar, whose ardour in the cause of Sanskrit has induced him to repair to India in order to prosecute his studies to still higher proficiency. He has deservedly received for this purpose the patronage of the Danish government. The materials of his list of roots were derived from this country. Mr. Westergaard laboured for some time with most extraordinary diligence in the Library of the East India

Company, and drew his information and examples chiefly from the manuscript volumes of the Company's collection. The roots are arranged alphabetically according to their final and initial letters. The class and voice in which each is conjugated are specified, and a paradigm more or less complete, according as authorities warrant the forms, is available. The meanings are then stated and exemplified by citations from published and unpublished texts, and the structure and use of the derivative verbs are also shown and exemplified. To them succeeds the series of compound verbs according to the order of their prefixes, with passages illustrating their application. Reference to the authorities whence the forms and examples are derived is constant and careful. As the examples are very numerous, and as no facilities exist in Sanskrit manuscripts, such as verbal indices, or any similar auxiliars, the labour and research by which they were collected must have been very great and persevering. They are for the most part judiciously selected, but they are not translated, and this is a serious drawback from the value of the compilation; for passages detached from the context of a work not familiarly known and not easily accessible do not always admit of ready and confident interpretation. It would no doubt have materially augmented Mr. Westergaard's trouble to have given translations of all the passages he has quoted, but it would have proportionably enhanced the usefulness and interest of the compilation if he had followed Dr. Rosen's example in this respect. A translation by himself is also necessary to support his rendering of the purport of a simple or compound verb, and secure its being acquiesced in by others. It is of infinite importance in the early stages of Sanskrit study, that in all books of an elementary character radical words should be rendered by unquestionable and unexceptionable European equivalents. When the native grammarians give the sense of a radical by a word of obvious import, then the European interpreter is tolerably safe, although even here he may be unlucky in his translation, and fail to make use of the most appropriate expression. When, however, he has to deduce the sense of a radical from his own understanding of some of its inflexions as they occur in composition, and where usage, licence, or metaphor may have given their own colouring to the primitive signification, it is very possible that the translator may mistake or may be misled as to the sense, and confound a lax or general with a literal and particular meaning. It is true that Mr. Westergaard defines the sense which he ascribes to the verb that he inserts as he understands its use in the example quoted, but then comes the question whether he has understood the passage rightly; the answer to which, although no doubt in most instances affirmative, may sometimes be given with doubt and hesitation.

Of subordinate contributions to the elucidation of Sanskrit grammar, independently of the attempts made to illustrate such original works as have been printed in Europe, or to develope the affinities of the language, the author could offer but a brief and passing intimation. They are scattered through a variety of continental publications on Oriental or general literature, many of which are little known in this country, and of various merits and character, from the Transactions of the Imperial Academy of St. Petersburgh to the 'Mercure de France' of Paris. Amongst the richest in articles on Sanskrit philology, not comparative, may be especially noticed a periodical conducted by the illustrious William Augustus von Schlegel, the 'Indische Bibliothek', a work which has been discontinued for some years. Its place in Germany has been latterly taken by a periodical of a more comprehensive character, the 'Zeitschrift für die Kunde des Morgenlandes', embracing the literature of the East, not of India alone, and conducted by an association of the most eminent German oriental scholars. In the former of these collections may be especially particularized, 1. the observations of Prof. Schlegel himself upon the actual state of Sanskrit philology in 1820;* and 2. a general view of the state of Sanskrit literature in 1824;† 3. a remarkable and most elaborate dissertation on the verbal derivatives formed with the suffixes *Ya* and *Twá*, intended to establish their analogy to the gerunds of the Latin verb by Baron William von Humboldt;‡ and 4. a review of Prof. Bopp's Grammar by Prof. Lassen.§ In the 'Zeitschrift' we have a theory of the

---

* Vol. I, p. 1, and Vol. II, part 1. † Vol. II, p. 1. ‡ Vol. I, part 4, § [Vol. III, p. 1.]

formation of compound nouns with the interrogative pronoun by Dr. Nesselmann, and a paper on the substitution of the cerebral for the dental nasal under certain circumstances, by Dr. Boehtlingk. There are no doubt communications of like tendency and value in other collections with which I am unacquainted. The 'Journal Asiatique' of the Asiatic Society of Paris is less rich in contributions to Sanskrit philology than to other branches of Asiatic literature.

Less has been attempted in the collateral branch of lexicography than in grammar. The character of native lexicons will be more particularly adverted to on some other occasion. It would be sufficient at present to state that they correspond in their arrangement to vocabularies as we employ the term, rather than to dictionaries, the words being classed in them according to analogy of meaning without regard to alphabetical order. They omit also many words of popular currency, as being too familiar to need explanation, and withhold consequently much that is most wanted by a European student. The best work of the class was selected at an early period for publication and translation by Mr. Colebrooke. The 'Amara Kosha', or lexicon of Amara Sinha, was printed at Serampore in 1808, accompanied by a marginal translation into English, by illustrations and additions derived from the numerous commentaries on the original text, and by a most useful alphabetical index. A reprint of the text with a French translation at the foot of the page has recently been published at Paris, the work of a young and highly promising Sanskrit scholar, also prematurely lost to the cultivation of Hindu literature, M. Loiseleur des Longchamps.

At the same time that the vocabulary of Amara Sinha was published, a dictionary on a more extended scale, and alphabetically arranged, was compiled, under the instructions of Mr. Colebrooke and the immediate supervision of one of the most celebrated native scholars in Bengal, by a number of Paṅḍits. The main object of this compilation was to bring together the contents of as many of the original Koshas, or vocabularies as were procurable, to arrange them in alphabetical order, and add their etymology, according to grammatical authorities. Soon after its completion the author obtained a copy of this work, and having carefully collated all the words with the authorities whence they were taken, incorporated with them the whole of the radicals as well as other words omitted in the compilation, and transferred the etymologies from the Bengali to the Benares terminology. He made a translation of the work, and with the encouragement of the Bengal government published it in 1819. The plan of the original compilation necessarily left many deficiencies. Shortly before he left India, however, he had an opportunity of making more extensive additions, which remedied in some degree the imperfections of the first edition, although no doubt still leaving many accessions to be made. This second edition was published in 1832. Such as it is, this dictionary is the only one yet published; and although no person could be more sensible than the author how far it falls short of such a lexicon as the study of Sanskrit demands, yet he had the satisfaction of knowing that it had materially contributed to the extension of a knowledge of Sanskrit in Europe. Although no other dictionary has been published, its place has in a great measure been supplied by useful glossaries attached to some of the books edited by European scholars, particularly by Prof. Bopp in the glossary to his edition of 'Nalus', and Prof. Johnson of the East India College in his editions recently published of the first book of the 'Hitopadeśa', 'Selections from the Mahábhárata', and 'Megha Dúta'. Prof. Bopp is also engaged upon a glossary on a large scale, of which the first part only is published. When glossaries of this kind, and when verbal indices to standard works shall have been sufficiently multiplied, it will then be comparatively easy to compile a Sanskrit dictionary that shall place its compiler on a level with Facciolati or Stephens.

The author had thus endeavoured to bring before the Society a general view of the advance that had been made in the rudimental cultivation of Sanskrit philology; and it would probably be admitted, even from this brief and imperfect notice, that, considering the period within which the study of Sanskrit had been prosecuted by Europeans, the progress had been creditable, and that no lack of intelligence or activity had been displayed in clearing away the impediments by which the first steps of the acquirement were beset. The facilities provided were no doubt far from sufficient; the approach might still be embarrassed by perplexing labyrinths, dark passages and cumbrous obstructions; the first labours of the pioneer must be necessarily rough and incomplete; but the path had been laid open, and it remained for succeeding exertions to smooth, to level, and to embellish it.

XV.
REVIEW
OF
PROFESSOR MAX MÜLLER'S "HISTORY
OF
ANCIENT SANSKRIT LITERATURE".

Second Edition, London: 1860.

From the Edinburgh Review, Oct. 1860, p. 361-85.

Towards the close of the last century great interest was excited, among the scholars of Europe, by the information that the Hindus are in possession of a sacred literature which is the most ancient and authentic in the world, and which exhibits a view of the creation and government of the universe wholly subversive of the records on which Christianity was founded. This literature is embodied in a work, or series of works, collectively termed the 'Veda', written in an old dialect of Sanskrit known to only a few of the most learned of the Brahmans—a class who at that time regarded Europeans with mixed feelings of terror and contempt, and whom no inducement whatever could prevail upon to communicate to strangers and outcasts any knowledge of their venerated scriptures.

The curiosity thus excited was naturally further stimulated by the difficulty of its gratification, and repeated efforts were made to break through the barrier, but without success; in the genuine native spirit evasion was grafted upon direct refusal, and fraud was had recourse to to appease the eagerness of the European inquirer, who was ill qualified to detect imposition. Thus Mr. Holwell,* in his 'Interesting Historical Events', published in 1766, gives a long account of what he terms the contents of the 'Chartah Bhade' and 'Aughtorrah Bhade', intending thereby the 'Chatwára Veda', or four Vedas, and 'Atháráh Veda', eighteen Vedas; the latter being no Vedas at all, but the eighteen Puránas, from which the particulars he details are evidently derived through a very inaccurate medium in Persian or Hindustani. He also affirms that a translation of the Vedas existed by Baldæus, a chaplain in the service of the Dutch East-India Company, in Ceylon, in 1760: this is equally inaccurate—no such translation was ever published: in the description of Malabar and Ceylon, published by the learned chaplain, in 1762, he has a chapter on the 'Afgoderey der Oost Indische Heydener'; but this, like Holwell's own account, represents the mythology of the Hindus agreeably to the Puránas, modified by popular superstitions and practices. Again, Colonel Dow, in the preface to his History of Hindustan, published in 1768, prints as specimens of the Vedas a few verses which are in reality taken from a work on rhetoric. Mr. Walker, in the preface to his translation of 'The Code of Gentoo Laws', shows himself more accurately informed than his predecessors, but his information is still imperfect. 'The

---

* [Compare K. J. H. Windischmann, "Die Philosophie im Fortgange der Weltgeschichte". Bonn: 1832, p. 585-634.]

'Pańdits,' he says, 'who compiled the code were to a 'man resolute in rejecting all solicitations for instruc-'tion in Sanskrit; and even the persuasions and in-'fluence of the Governor-General, Warren Hastings, 'were exerted in vain.'

The Brahmans, who supplied Dow with surreptitious passages from the Vedas, were not the sole manufacturers of such pious frauds, and very extensive compositions in Sanskrit were put forth in the south of India, under that designation, by the missionaries of the Propaganda, showing a wonderful amount of industry and extraordinary command of the language, but written in the style of the Puráńas—not of the Vedas. They were discovered by Mr. Ellis, of the Madras Civil Service, at Pondicheri, and are described by him in the 14th volume of the 'Asiatic Researches': amongst them was the original of a work of which a translation had been printed in Europe, in 1778, at Yverdon 'L'Ezour Vedam traduit du Sanscretan par 'un Brame.' The original had been brought from Pondicheri, and presented to Voltaire, who, transferring it to the Royal Library, expressed his belief that it was four centuries older than Alexander, and that it was the most precious gift for which the West had been ever indebted to the East;—how little he knew of the matter is evident from the work, which is an attempted refutation of Hinduism by a Christian author.

The unsatisfactory nature of these attempts augmented the desire of European scholars to procure authentic copies of the originals, and the failure to do so suggested a doubt whether they were any longer in existence: this suspicion was dissipated by Colonel Polier, who at last procured a copy from Jaypur, through Don Pedro de Silva, the Portuguese physician of the Raja. Colonel Polier brought it to England in 1789, and presented it to Sir Joseph Bankes, by whom it was transferred to the British Museum, where it is preserved. It is a handsome M.S., but is limited to the text, which without the scholia is of comparatively little use. Subsequent research, in which Sir Robert Chambers, one of the Judges of the Supreme Court of Calcutta, was pre-eminently successful, multiplied copies of portions, at least, of the Vedas, which, with other MSS. collected by him, were sold many years after his decease to the King of Prussia, and are now at Berlin. A catalogue by Professor Weber was published in 1853. As Sir Robert was not a Sanskrit scholar, he contributed no further to our knowledge of the originals: even Sir William Jones was but little acquainted with the original text.

In the meantime Mr. Colebrooke, a member of the Bengal Civil Service, who had been diligently raising himself to that pre-eminence as a Sanskrit scholar which was eventually undisputed, engaged, amongst other pursuits, in the study of the Vedas, for which his position as a civilian at Benares and the relaxing scruples of the Brahmans offered him favourable opportunities. In 1805 appeared the first authentic analysis of the Vedas from his pen, in his essay on the Vedas, published in the eighth volume of the Asiatic

Researches, conveying as copious a description of their contents as the scope and extent of his dissertation permitted, and characterised by that care and precision by which all Mr. Colebrooke's contributions to Hindu literature are distinguished. The notice was avowedly of a general nature, and the materials were in some instances admitted to be imperfect, but the result was a distinct appreciation of the character of the four works known as the Vedas,—the Rich, Yajush, Sáman, and Atharvan, with specimen translations of a portion of their contents of a curious and interesting purport; the first precise information of some of their chief supplements or Bráhmaṅas, and of their principal commentaries; arguments in proof of their authenticity, and a speculation as to the probability of their dating as early at least as the 14th century B.C. Here our knowledge was suspended, and Mr. Colebrooke's essay continued for thirty years our only authority on the subject of the Hindu Vedas. Notwithstanding the fulness and accuracy of Mr. Colebrooke's essay, it was always felt that an actual translation of the Vedas, or of their principal portions, was still wanting as the only guide upon which reliance could be placed for a comprehensive and correct appreciation of their contents; and at last, upon the institution of the Oriental Translation Fund, the late Dr. Rosen was encouraged and assisted to translate the Rig-Veda, the most important of the four. Of the eight books in which this work is arranged Dr. Rosen translated the first only into Latin; it was published in 1838 with the text in both Nágarí and Roman characters. Unfortunately his premature death put a stop to the erudite and conscientious execution of his task.

The next step towards the illustration of the Vedas was made by the Oriental Text Committee, in co-operation with that of the Translation Fund, by the publication, in 1842, of the text and translation of the Sáma-Veda, by the late Rev. Mr. Stevenson, of Bombay, who had previously published at that Presidency an English version of the two first sections of the first Ashtaka or eighth of the Rig-Veda. The Sáma-Veda is short, and is a repetition or recast, for the greater part, of the Rig-Veda. It has been since reprinted, with a German translation, a copious glossary, and most laborious illustrations by Professor Benfey, of Göttingen.

For the study of the Hindu Scriptures had now been taken up in France and Germany with that intense zeal and indefatigable assiduity which characterise continental literary erudition. In 1842 M. Nève, of Louvain, a pupil of Burnouf, published his 'Études sur le Rig-Véda'. Professor Roth, of Tubingen, another pupil of Burnouf, who, in various communications addressed to the Oriental Society of Germany, had afforded novel and interesting information respecting Vedic literature, published in 1846 his three dissertations 'Zur Literatur und Geschichte des Weda'; a publication of no great extent, but entirely new, and of the highest interest and value, and which has evidently given an electric impulse to the study of the Vedas upon the Continent, extending, although with much less intensity, to this country.

The next publication was also by Professor Roth, the text and partial explanation of the Nirukta by Yáska, an ancient commentator on passages of the Veda, and an author of a short glossary of Vedic terms. M. Nève, of Louvain, next published his 'Essai sur le Mythe des Ribhavas', 1847, and detached hymns were published, with translations by Professor Lassen, of Bonn, and the late Eugène Burnouf, of Paris. More important works are the original texts. That of the Sáma-Veda has been alluded to. Professor Weber, of Berlin, has just completed, in three large quarto volumes, the texts of the Yajur-Veda, (that portion called the White Yajush,) of the Satapatha Bráhmaña, and of the Sútras, or Precepts of Kátyáyana, both of which are illustrative of the Yajur-Veda. The text of the Atharva-Veda has been printed by Professors Roth and Whitney: the latter an American Sanskritist; and the most voluminous and important, the Rig-Veda, with an elaborate commentary by Sáyaña Achárya, who flourished in the 14th century of our era, is in course of publication by Professor Max Müller, of Oxford, under the authority and at the cost of the Home Government of India. Three volumes have been published;* it will be completed in two, or at most in three more, and is an extraordinary specimen of diligence, acumen, and scholarship which does infinite credit both to the editor and his patrons, who have thus preserved

---

* [Vol. IV, 1863.]

from the risk of decay a most venerable memorial of human belief. A French translation of the whole work from manuscript has been published by the late M. Langlois, and an English version, by Professor Wilson, proceeds *pari passu* with Professor Müller's text. Three volumes containing half the Rig-Veda, or four out of its eight Ashtakas, have been published.

Speaking of the Vedas, it is usually assumed that a collective or homogeneous work is intended; but, as above intimated, the works to which the designation is applied, are four in number,—the Rig-Veda, the Yajur-Veda, the Súma-Veda, the Atharva-Veda, each of which is a Sanhitá or collection complete in itself, of detached hymns and prayers, mixed up in the Yajush with ritual directions. But these four works, constituting the mere utterance of the Vedic religion, form but a small portion of the religious literature even of the Vedic period. In addition to the Sanhitás, we have Bráhmañas, Súktas, Upanishads, Prátisákhyas, Vedúngas, and scholia of the most minute and profound description, all professing to spring from, and illustrate and carry into effect, the worship taught by the Vedas, a more or less extensive acquaintance with which is essential to a thorough understanding of the Veda, although it is rarely, if ever, now mastered by the Brahmans, and is manifestly beyond the reach of the European Sanskritist. Such acquirement is fortunately not indispensable to the determination of the great outline of the primitive system of religious belief inferable from the texts which are now before us, but it is no doubt of great importance to an accurate estimate of their purpose and their history. A sense of their value in these respects has induced Professor Müller to bring his immense reading and unequalled research to bear upon the subject, and has given to the public the subject of our present notice, 'A History of Ancient Sanskrit Literature, as far as it illustrates the primitive religion of the Bráhmañas'.

Referring to the light which the cultivation of Sanskrit in its philological bearings has reflected upon the history of mankind, identifying, through the incontestable testimony of language, races long separated by half the globe, and diametrically opposed in complexion, constitution, laws, and religion, and pointing out the necessity of beginning with the beginning, Professor Müller observes:—

'It is with the Veda, therefore, that Indian philology ought to begin if it is to follow a natural and historical course. So great an influence has the Vedic age (the historical period to which we are justified in referring the formation of the sacred texts) exercised upon all succeeding periods of Indian history, so closely is every branch of literature connected with Vedic traditions, so deeply have the religious and moral ideas of that primitive era taken root in the mind of the Indian nation, so minutely has almost every private and public act of Indian life been regulated by old traditionary precepts, that it is impossible to find the right point of view for judging of Indian religion, morals, and literature without a knowledge of the literary remains of the Vedic age. No one could fairly say that those men who first began to study Sanskrit, now seventy years ago, ought to have begun with reading the Veda. The difficulties connected with the study of the Veda would have made such a course utterly impossible and useless. But since the combined labours of Sanskrit scholars have now rendered the study of that language of more easy access, since the terminology of Indian grammarians and commentators, which not long ago was considered unintelligible, has become more familiar to us, and manuscripts can be more readily procured at the principal public libraries of Europe, Sanskrit philology has no longer an excuse for ignoring the Vedic age.' (P. 9, 10.)

Consistently with this view of the subject, the *Vedas*, as we have observed, must mean something more than a single work, and in Professor Müller's opinion 'it 'would be much nearer the truth to take Veda as a 'collective name for the sacred literature of the Vedic 'age, which forms, so to speak, the back ground of the 'whole Indian World.' With regard to this literature, although no doubt some has perished, yet a large proportion still remains, and until it shall have been more completely investigated, a work of very many years, it would scarcely be safe to take a comprehensive view of the whole age. Professor Müller modestly observes that what he has to offer are but Prolegomena or treatises on some preliminary questions which may be determinately answered from the materials now available to Sanskrit scholars: his principal object, he adds, is 'to put the antiquity of the Veda in its proper light;' meaning thereby not only the chronological distance of the Vedic age from our own, measured by the revolutions and progress of the heavenly bodies, but also and still more the distance between the intellectual, moral, and religious state of men as represented to us during the Vedic age, compared with that of other periods of history,—a distance which can be measured by the revolutions and the progress of the human mind.

After some interesting observations upon the unity of the Aryan races, and their divergence west and east at a period prior to history, Professor Müller proceeds to trace the development of the religious speculations which have given to the Hindu mind its predominant character, and have rendered them regardless or contemptuous of the ephemeral transactions which constitute political history. Adopting as a starting point the separation of Buddhism from Hinduism in the 6th century B.C., he proceeds from thence through three periods up to that which he regards as the earliest period, describing the different classes of literature bearing upon that point. The copiousness of detail with which he elucidates the various stages is far beyond the limits of a notice like the present; and we must be content to advert briefly to the principal stages through which the Professor traces the upward ascent of the system, distinguishing them into what he terms the Chhandas, Mantra, Brāhmaṅa, and Sūtra periods.

The first or *Sūtra* period; a Sūtra, literally a thread, is applied to a short and often obscure didactic rule, the peculiarities of which, as Professor Müller observes, it is not easy to explain to one who has not worked his way through the Sūtras themselves: they are the groundwork of all the systems of philosophy as well as of grammar, as in the case of the Sūtras of Pāṅini, and are only intelligible by the assistance of commentators who amplify their language and expound its purport. In this place the Sūtras intended are those only which are connected with the Vedas, but which do not purposely belong to the Vedic age, being included within the order of Smṛiti works, or those handed down by memory or tradition, and not of the Śruti or the literature of revelation,—the Mantras and Bráhmañas. One great distinction is that the authors of the latter when named are said to be *seers* of the prayers and hymns—not the authors—whilst the Sútras are attributed to human authors, all of whom, according to Professor Müller, are anterior to Buddha.

Under the head of Sútras or Precepts Professor Müller classes the works called *Vedángas* or members, angas, of the Veda, usually enumerated as six, although perhaps on insufficient authority. We are not, however, to look for the Vedángas to those small and barren tracts which are known by this name, and which represent only the last unsuccessful attempts to bring the complicated and unintelligible doctrines of former ages into a popular form. They are Śikshá, pronunciation; Chhandas, metre; Vyákarańa, grammar; Nirukta, explanation of words; Jyotisha, astronomy; and Kalpa, ceremonial. The first two are considered necessary for reading the Veda, the two next for understanding it, and the last two for employing it at sacrifices. Under the first division *Śikshá*, Phonetics, or Pronunciation, comprising rules regarding letters, accents, quantity, organs of enunciation, delivery, and euphonic combinations, Professor Müller has entered into a detailed account of a class of Vedic literature first made known to us by Professor Roth, in his essay on the Literature of the Veda. This consists of works termed *Prátiśákhyas*, being respectively (prati) intended for the use of the branches or Śákhás of the Vedas. Every such Śákhá, it is to be presumed, had its own Prátiśákhya, but at present only four are known to exist, one for each Veda.

That for the Rig-Veda is considered as belonging to the Śakala Śákhá; but, as Professor Müller observes, there is not a single instance of a MS. of the Rig-Veda at present known to which the rules of this Prátiśákhya apply. Probably the same may be said of the other three, for the rules of the Prátiśákhyas were not intended for written literature, they were only to serve as a guide in the instruction of pupils who had to learn the text of the Veda by heart and repeat it as part of their daily devotions. The text of this Prátiśákhya, with a commentary, has been printed by Professor Müller, as far as the sixth book, with a German translation; and the whole has been printed and translated into French in the Journal Asiatique by M. Regnier. The Prátiśákhya of the White Yajush has been edited by Professor Weber, in his Indische Studien.[*] Such laborious minutiæ and elaborate subtleties relating to the enunciation of human speech are not to be met with in the literature of any other nation.

The standard authority for the *Chhandas* or metre of the Vedas is an author named Pingala, who can

[*] [Vol. IV, p. 65-160; 177-331. The Atharva-Veda-Prátiśákhya was published, with a translation and notes, by Prof. Whitney in the 7th vol. of the Journal Am. Or. Soc. Compare Prof. Goldstücker's "Páńini", p. 183-214, and A. Weber, Ind. Studien, V, p. 89-135.]

scarcely however be regarded as belonging to the Sútra period, nor does he confine himself to the metre of the Vedas or even of Sanskrit, giving rules also for Prákrit prosody. A very full account of his system is given by Mr. Colebrooke in the tenth volume of the Asiatic Researches.* As Pingala is the authority for the prosody, so is Páṅini for the grammar of the Veda; but, as remarked by Professor Müller, there is an obvious inconsistency in this, for the main body of Páṅini's grammar relates to the post-Vedic development of the language, and the Vedic peculiarities are only occasionally specified. There were, however, many grammarians prior to Páṅini, as Mr. Colebrooke, in the first and only published volume of his Sanskrit grammar, remarks, and to some of them we might look for a more accurate representation of Vedic grammar if they had not perished.

The next of the Angas is termed *Nirukta*, and, as generally met with, is a short vocabulary of synonymous words found in the Vedas, most of which are now unused or obsolete. The author to whom it is ascribed, Yáska, has added to it two sections, in which he explains various texts of the Veda, and enters largely into the etymology of the language. The text has been published by Professor Roth, with an explanation of particular portions. The Nirukta, together with the Prátiśákhyas, and Páṅini's grammar, supply the most interesting and important information on the growth

---

* [= Miscell. Essays, II, 62 ff.]

of grammatical science in India—a science cultivated by only two nations in antiquity, the Hindus and the Greeks, as here pointed out by Professor Müller, who has also indicated some interesting points of agreement and difference in their treatment of the subject. The following are selected from his remarks as of general interest:—

'There are only two nations in the whole history of the world which have conceived independently, and without any suggestions from others, the two sciences of Logic and Grammar, the Hindus and the Greeks. Although the Arabs and Jews, among the Semitic nations, have elaborated their own system of grammar, in accordance with the peculiar character of their language, they owe to the Greeks the broad outlines of grammatical science, and they received from Aristotle the primary impulse to a study of the categories of thought and speech. Our own grammatical terms came to us from the Greeks; and their history is curious enough, if we trace them back through the clumsy and frequently erroneous translations of the literary statesmen of Rome, to the scholars and critics of Alexandria, and finally to the early philosophers of Greece, the Stoics, Aristotle, Protagoras and Pythagoras. But it is still more instructive to compare this development of the grammatical categories in Greece with the parallel, yet quite independent, history of grammatical science in India. It is only by means of such a comparison that we can learn to understand what is organic, and what is merely accidental, in the growth of this science, and appreciate the real difficulties which had to be overcome in the classification of words and the arrangement of grammatical forms. The Greeks and Hindus started from opposite points. The Greeks began with philosophy, and endeavoured to transfer their philosophical terminology to the facts of language. The Hindus began with collecting the facts of language, and their generalisations never went beyond the external forms of speech. Thus the Hindus excel in accuracy, the Greeks in grasp. The grammar of the former has ended in a colossal pedantry; that of the latter still invigorates the mind of every rising generation throughout the civilised world.'

Again :—

'It is in the Sútra literature that we meet with discussions on language of a purely scientific character; and what we do find in the Prátiśákhya, in the Nirukta and Pánini, is quite sufficient to show that at their time the science of language was not of recent origin. I can only touch upon one point. It is well known how long it took before the Greeks arrived at a complete nomenclature for the parts of speech. Plato knew only of Noun (ὄνομα) and Verb (ῥῆμα), as the two component parts of speech, and for philosophical purposes Aristotle too did not go beyond that number. It is only in discussing the rules of rhetoric that he is led to the admission of two more parts of speech, the σύνδεσμοι (conjunctions) and ἄρθρα (articles). The pronoun (ἀντωνυμία) does not come in before Zenodotos, and the preposition (πρόθεσις) occurs first in Aristarchos. In the Prátiśákhya, on the contrary, we meet at once with the following exhaustive classification of the parts of speech (XII, 5).

'The noun (náma), the verb (ákhyáta), the preposition (upasarga), and the particle (nipáta) are called by grammarians the four classes of words. The noun is that by which we mark a being, a verb that by which we mark being; the latter is called a root (dhátu). There are twenty prepositions, and these have a meaning, if joined with nouns or verbs. The rest of the words are called particles. The verb expresses an action; the preposition defines it; the noun marks a being; particles are but expletives.' (Pp. 159-62.)

The *Kalpa Sútras* constitute the next division of the dependent branches of the Veda, and, as extended in their application to all precepts regulating the ceremonial observances of the Hindu which are of Vedic origin, form an extensive series of works which for practical purposes are the most important of the whole. They are distinguished into three classes, as *Śrauta*,

Gŕihya, and *Sámayáchárika Sútras*: the first prescribe the especial Vedic ceremonials or sacrifices, such as those to be celebrated on the days of new and full moon; the second enjoin the household or domestic rites, practised at various stages of the life of the Hindu from conception to death. The third regulate the daily observances of the twice-born; they are comparatively of little note, but the Sútras of the two first orders are of much greater moment. The Śrauta ceremonials are now rarely if ever performed, but the Gŕihya or domestic rites are more or less regularly observed, and the prayers derived from the Vedas are still repeated at their celebration; the Vedic texts are taken from the several Vedas on which the Sútras are considered to be dependent, each Veda having its own Sútras. Professor Müller enumerates as still extant and entire three of the Black Yajush, one of the White, three of the Sáma, two of the Ŕich, and one of the Atharva. Many more are quoted in different compositions, which are no longer procurable. The chief Sútrakáras of the Black Yajush are Ápastamba, Baudháyana, Satyáshádha Hiranyakeśi, and Manu, whose Sútras exist in fragments only. Kátyáyana is the author of the Sútras of the White Yajush. Maśaka, Láṭyáyana and Dráhyáyana are the authors of those of the Sáma, Áśvaláyana and Śánkháyana of those of the Ŕich, and the Atharva has the Kuśika Sútras. Professor Müller attributes to these Sútras an important part in the development of the Hindu religion.

The Kalpa Sútras, Professor Müller observes, mark

a new period of literature and a new purpose in the literary and religious life of India. They were adopted by different schools, and came in time to supersede the authorities on which they were founded. Professor Müller enumerates nineteen (p. 211) works of this class as either actually existing, or quoted by different scholiasts.

The last of the Angas is the *Jyotisha* of the Vedas; but here also the tract or tracts that pass under this designation are brief and meagre and of little authority. They are not, however, without interest, especially in connexion with indications of a knowledge of astronomical phenomena found both in the Mantras and Bráhmañas. As Professor Müller notices, notwithstanding the modern form of the Jyotisha tracts, the doctrines represent the earliest stage of Hindu astronomy, and show that the lunar mansions and the solar-lunar year were part of their system.*

The next subject to which the work relates is a description of the systematic indices or *Anukramañis* of the Veda. The most perfect of those still extant is that of the Ṛig-veda, attributed to Kátyáyana, which specifies the first words of each hymn, the number of verses, the name and family of the author, the name of the deity to whom it is addressed, and the metre of every verse. Before this there had been separate indices for each of these subjects, and it was from com-

---

* [A. Weber, Ueber den Vedakalender, Namens Jyotisham. Berlin: 1862.]

prising all of them that the index of Kátyáyana was termed the Sarvánukrama or Universal Index. The separate indices were ascribed to Saunaka, and some of them exist at least as quotations, or, in one instance, entire. One of his peculiarities and a proof of the minuteness with which the texts were studied, is a specification of the Mańdalas, the Anuvákas, and the number of Súktas or hymns in each, giving 1017 of the latter. Another enumeration is that of the Vargas and verses, as 10,417 of the latter; there are other enumerations, showing some, though not a very wide difference, as 10,409, 10,616, 10,622. There is even an enumeration of all the words, reckoning them at 153,826. One advantage of these calculations is their precluding the possibility of any wide deviation from the original text. The other Vedas have also their indices, but the only authors handed down are Saunaka and his pupil Kátyáyana, who is the author of one of the indices of the Yajush, as well as of the Rich.

As with these works we take leave of the Sútra period, in which the authors of the different compositions, although reputed saints, are mortals, and are named, we may pause to inquire how far it may be possible to ascertain the date of their existence, and so far the era of the more modern contributions to the literature of the Vedas. Saunaka is an important personage in Hindu legend, not only in connexion with the Rig-veda, but with the Mahábhárata, being one of the Rishis to whom it was related. In connexion with the Veda his immediate pupil was Áśvaláyana, whose

Sútras we have, and from whom Kátyáyana derived his knowledge. We have no means of tracing the date of Śaunaka and Áśvaláyana, except as preceding Kátyáyana, of whose period we have some indications, although not perhaps entitled to much reliance. But Kátyáyana is the reputed author of the Várttikas, additions and emendations of the grammatical Sútras of Páńini, and if the same person be intended, which is more than questionable, he is the same as Vararuchi, whom Hindu tradition makes cotemporary with Nanda, the predecessor of Chandragupta, Rájá of Pátaliputra, —the Sandrocoptus to whom Megasthenes was sent ambassador by Seleucus. If we can trust to the tradition, then we have a final point for the date of Kátyáyana, the second half of the fourth century before the Christian era.*

The identity of the Sandrocottus or Sandrocoptus of the Greeks, with the Chandragupta of the Hindus, first pointed out by Sir Wm. Jones, was subsequently more fully developed by Professor Wilson in his introduction to the drama of the Mudrá Rákshasa, of which he is one of the principal characters. For it is not now called in question and is regarded by Professor Müller as the sheet-anchor of Indian chronology. He has entered into very copious details on the subject, not only from the classical and Hindu authorities, but those of the Jains and Buddhists, to the latter of whom Chandragupta is a person of historical interest,

---

* [Goldstücker, l. l., p. 89 ff. Weber, Ind. Stud., V, 43 ff.]

as the grandfather of Aśoka, their great patron. There is some discrepancy as to dates between their chronology and that of the Brahmans, but not of very irreconcilable character. The dates of Buddha's Nirvāṇa vary considerably, but are reducible to two classes. The Chinese, Tibetans, and Mongols place it ten centuries more or less B.C.; the Singhalese, Burmans, Siamese, six centuries; and this latter is most consistent with their records of the progress of the religion. Buddha's death is placed by them 543 B.C., but Professor Müller suggests that the date should rather be 477 B.C., which will explain the difference of something more than sixty years between the Buddhist and Hindu and Greek chronology; but as he observes, whatever change may have to be introduced into the earlier chronology of India, nothing will shake the date of Chandragupta; and consequently, if Kátyáyana flourished about his time, we may consider the fourth century B.C. as the period of his Sútras and Anukramaṇis. Reckoning upwards from this time through his predecessors Áśvaláyana and Śaunaka, we may reasonably prove them to have lived in the first half or the beginning of the fourth century B.C.; and as there were authors of Sútras prior to Śaunaka, Professor Müller proposes to extend the Sútra period to the sixth or seventh century:—prior to which we have the literature that is considered by the Hindus as constituting the periods of their inspired or scriptural Vedas.

Having assigned to the latter literature of India the

upward limit of six centuries B.C., Professor Müller proceeds to examine another and confessedly more ancient class of Vedic writings, differing in style both from the Sútras which are posterior, and from the Mantras which are anterior to them. These are the *Bráhmaṅas*, whose currency constitutes a distinct stage in the progress of the religious history of the Hindus.

According to the generally recognised classification of the Vedic literature it comprises two great divisions, the Karma Káńda and Jnána Káńda, the practice and speculation, the ceremonial and the philosophical sections, the liturgy and theosophy, or in the language of the commentators, the Mantra and the Bráhmaṅa; meaning by the first the prayers, hymns, charms, and other formulæ to be cited or chanted at the sacrifice; by the second inquiries into the nature of man and God, and the relations of matter and spirit. The definition of the Bráhmaṅa is, however, very far from definite, and the scholiasts are driven to the conclusion that it is no otherwise to be characterised than that whatever in the Veda is not Mantra is necessarily Bráhmaṅa,* a very vague and unmeaning distinction, and much too comprehensive to constitute a special characteristic. It would be difficult indeed to assign any specific attribute to the Bráhmaṅas as we have them, the Aitareya Bráhmaṅa of the Rich, the Satapatha Bráhmaṅa of the White Yajush, which has been

---

* [Goldstücker, l. l., p. 69 ff. Haug, Ait. Br., I, p. 1-7.]

published by Professor Weber, and of which an analysis is given by Professor Müller, and the Gopatha Brāhmaṇa of the Atharva, also described by our author: in none of these does philosophical speculation take any prominent share; their object is usually to illustrate the ceremonial or the Mantras, by explaining their origin and import, and repeating legends illustrative of both, citing summarily the texts which are used on a particular occasion. These old stories form the most valuable portion of the sacrifice of Śunaḥśepha, for instance, in which his own father offers him as an immolation. As told in the Aitareya Brāhmaṇa, it is a very remarkable legend; it is translated by Professor Müller, but had been previously published by Professor Wilson in the Journal of the Royal Asiatic Society.[*] Again, in the Śatapatha, we have the Hindu version of the escape of Manu from the deluge. The original of the story is repeated in the Mahābhārata and the Matsya and other Purāṇas,[†] and was originally translated by Sir William Jones. Many other interesting particulars occur in these Brāhmaṇas which are of great value to both the political and religious history of the Hindus, but little or nothing to justify

---

[*] [Ait. Br. VII, 3. Journal R. A. S., Vol. VIII, p. 96 ff. H. H. Wilson's Essays and Lectures, Vol. II, p. 247-69. See also the references in Muir's Sanskrit Texts, I, 104 ff.]

[†] [Mahābh., III, 12746 ff.; Matsya Pur. 2; Burnouf, Bhāg. Pur., III, p. XXIII ff.; Weber, Ind. Stud., I, 161 ff.; Kellgren, de ovo mundano (1849), p. 45-62; Muir's Original Sanskrit Texts, II, 329 ff.]

their character of Brahma Káńḍa or theosophy of the Veda.

Where then is this to be found? In works termed *Áraṅyakas* and *Upanishads*, which may be considered as belonging to the class of Bráhmaṅas, and which are often found as integral portions of them, or even of the Sanhitá, or collections of the Mantras, although at the same time held to be distinct. The Áraṅyakas* are so called, according to Sáyaṅa, because they were to be read in the forest, as if they were the text-books of the anchorites, whose devotions were spiritual. Several of these have been published in the Bibliotheca Indica, especially the Bṛihad-áraṅyaka and Taittiríya-áraṅyaka, the former of which is also translated by Dr. Roer. The mystical philosophy of this class of literature may be seen from the translation; it is also evident that the Áraṅyakas, however sometimes confounded with the Bráhmaṅas, intimate their prior existence.

A still more numerous class of works, although in some instances of rather equivocal date and authenticity, is the chief repository of Hindu speculation. These are the *Upanishads*, the Mysteries of Theosophy. Of these some fifty were translated into Persian by order of Dárá Shakoh, and from the Persian by Anquetil du Perron, into Latin, under the title of 'Oupnékhat', or 'Theosophia Indica'. The double translation makes wild work of the original, but their number is

---

* [Goldstücker's "Páṅini", p. 129. Weber, Ind. Stud., V, 49.]

by no means complete; and besides other lists there is one by Mr. Elliot, in the Journal of the As. Soc. of Bengal,* which specifies 108 works, which are known as Upanishads to the Brahmans of the south of India. Many, probably most, of them are no doubt of modern date, originating with the tenets of particular sects or individuals; those that are apparently the most ancient and authentic are the Bṛihad-áraṅyaka, Aitareya, Chhándogya, Taittiríya, Íśa, Kena, Praśna, Kaṭha, Muṅḍaka, and Máṅḍúkya; all which have been printed in the 'Bibliotheca Indica', edited by Dr. Roer, who has also translated the greater number. Translations of several have been made by other hands, especially by the late Rammohun Roy, who hoped that through the Monotheism of the Upanishads he might wean his countrymen from idolatry. Although their general tendency is Monotheistic, or rather perhaps Pantheistic, yet, as Professor Müller observes, there is so much freedom and breadth of thought in them, that it is not difficult to find in them some authority for almost any shade of philosophical opinion. Notwithstanding this vagueness, however, the Upanishads that wear an authentic aspect may be regarded as well as the Áraṅyakas as the Jnána kánda, or philosophical portion of the Veda, although it may be doubted if they immediately succeeded the Mantra or Karma period. They may even be regarded as subsequent in some respects to the Bráhmaṇas, not only because they oc-

---

* [for 1851, p. 607. Weber, Ind. Stud., III, 324 ff.]

casionally repeat or refer to their legends, but because the Bráhmañas are more practical and have a more near relation to ceremonial rites, the practice of which is in all religions prior to speculation. The further history of the Bráhmañas as belonging to various *Charañas*, schools or fraternities, adopting in preference some divisions of the original texts, is given by Professor Müller, and is followed by a list of the *Gotras* or Brahman families and their branches, constituting what the author calls the Brahmanic Peerage of India. Seven chief families are enumerated in one list, of whom there are forty-nine subdivisions; but there are other lists still more numerous, and Brahmans in various parts of India still profess to draw their descent from some of these ramifications. To prove that these lists were not merely arbitrary compositions, Professor Müller shows their practical bearing on two important acts of the ancient Brahmanic Society,—the common consecration of the sacrificial fires and inter-marriage.

After offering some specimens of the contents of the *Bráhmañas*, Professor Müller proceeds to consider their probable era, and manifest and long-continued posteriority to the Mantra of proper Vedic period, every page containing the clearest proof that the spirit of the ancient Vedic poetry, and the purport of the original Vedic sacrifices, were both beyond the comprehension of the authors of the Bráhmañas. There is also clear evidence that the Bráhmañas are not the work of a few individuals—they represent a complete period through which the whole stream of thought poured in one channel, and was directed to the construction and development of what may be regarded as the system of Brahmanical Hinduism, but faintly if at all indicated by the original Vedic verses.

Professor Müller thinks it impossible to assign a shorter interval than two centuries for the origin and accumulation of the mass of Brahmanical literature that must have existed. We confess that we are disposed to look upon this limit as much too brief for the establishment of an elaborate ritual, for the appropriation of all spiritual authority by the Brāhmans, for the distinctions of races or the institutions of caste, and for the mysticism and speculation of the Áraṅyakas or Upanishads: a period of five centuries would not seem to be too protracted for such a complete remodelling of the primitive system and its wide dissemination through all those parts of India where the Brahmans have spread. There seems no reason to question the general accuracy of the lists of teachers preserved by Brahmanical tradition, and which as Professor Müller remarks would extend the limits of this age to a very considerable degree. These traditions are preserved in different supplementary works or Vanśas, also regarded as Bráhmañas—several of which are extant. There are several of these in the Śatapatha Bráhmaña, which Professor Müller quotes, and he concludes that from their extent it is possible that the limit he suggests will have to be extended. We quite concur in this anticipation, and think there can be little doubt that, instead of two centuries, we may venture to conjecture four or five, and so carry the commencement of the Bráhmaña period to the 10th or 11th century B.C.

We now only come to what is properly the Veda—the *Mantra* period of Professor Müller—the collections of prayers, hymns, formulæ, ritual injunctions, charms—which have been brought together in the Sanhitás or collections of the four Vedas. 'The Hindus themselves are content to look upon the fourth as of an equivocal character, and usually speak of the Vedas as three.

Setting this aside then, we should have for the scriptural Vedas the remaining three; but here also a very important distinction is to be made, and the Yajush and the Sáman are to be regarded as long subsequent to the Řich, originating in a different object and possessing different characteristics connected evidently with the development of the ritual, and approaching, through intervals of greater or less extent, to the period of the Bráhmañas.

The Yajur-veda is two-fold—the Taittiríya or Black Yajush, and the Vájasaneyi or White, originating, no doubt, with a schism of which Yájnavalkya was the probable author. Both these forms indicate their subservience to an established ceremonial; they are liturgies and rubrics interspersing short injunctions of a ritual purport, which are given in prose, with verses to be repeated at the ceremony, many of which are the same that occur in the Řig-veda, from which they are in all probability derived.

In the course of time it had become the practice to

poured in one channel, and was directed to the construction and development of what may be regarded as the system of Brahmanical Hinduism, but faintly if at all indicated by the original Vedic verses.

Professor Müller thinks it impossible to assign a shorter interval than two centuries for the origin and accumulation of the mass of Brahmanical literature that must have existed. We confess that we are disposed to look upon this limit as much too brief for the establishment of an elaborate ritual, for the appropriation of all spiritual authority by the Brahmans, for the distinctions of races or the institutions of caste, and for the mysticism and speculation of the Áraṅyakas or Upanishads: a period of five centuries would not seem to be too protracted for such a complete remodelling of the primitive system and its wide dissemination through all those parts of India where the Brahmans have spread. There seems no reason to question the general accuracy of the lists of teachers preserved by Brahmanical tradition, and which as Professor Müller remarks would extend the limits of this age to a very considerable degree. These traditions are preserved in different supplementary works or Vanśas, also regarded as Bráhmañas—several of which are extant. There are several of these in the Śatapatha Bráhmaña, which Professor Müller quotes, and he concludes that from their extent it is possible that the limit he suggests will have to be extended. We quite concur in this anticipation, and think there can be little doubt that, instead of two centuries, we may venture to conjecture four or five, and so carry the commencement of the Bráhmaṅa period to the 10th or 11th century B.C.

We now only come to what is properly the Veda— the *Mantra* period of Professor Müller—the collections of prayers, hymns, formulæ, ritual injunctions, charms —which have been brought together in the Sanhitás or collections of the four Vedas. 'The Hindus themselves are content to look upon the fourth as of an equivocal character, and usually speak of the Vedas as three.

Setting this aside then, we should have for the scriptural Vedas the remaining three; but here also a very important distinction is to be made, and the Yajush and the Sáman are to be regarded as long subsequent to the Ṙich, originating in a different object and possessing different characteristics connected evidently with the development of the ritual, and approaching, through intervals of greater or less extent, to the period of the Bráhmaṅas.

The Yajur-veda is two-fold—the Taittirīya or Black Yajush, and the Vájasaneyi or White, originating, no doubt, with a schism of which Yájnavalkya was the probable author. Both these forms indicate their subservience to an established ceremonial; they are liturgies and rubrics interspersing short injunctions of a ritual purport, which are given in prose, with verses to be repeated at the ceremony, many of which are the same that occur in the Ṙig-veda, from which they are in all probability derived.

In the course of time it had become the practice to

accompany part of the sacrifice by songs, and hence arose the third or Sáma-veda, of which the verses are to be chanted: a very large portion of its contents are the same as the hymns of the Rich, and perhaps the whole might be identified if we had the whole of the early Śákhás.

It is then to the *Rig-veda Sanhitá* that we must look for the most authentic and primitive representation of the Hindu religious belief. We must not, however, lose sight for a moment of the meaning of the term Sanhitá or collections. The Rig-veda Sanhitá is not a work of one author or of one purport; it is a mere bringing together of a number of metrical compositions, varying in authorship, intention, and date, generally of a religious character but not always, and although offering occasional intimations of ceremonial and priestly worship, yet possessing nothing of a decidedly liturgical character, or direct applicability to either Śrauta or Gṛihya rites. The verses may be employed and are employed at such rites, and they were also recited at sacrifices in praise of the deities to whom any particular act of sacrifice was addressed, usually by priests, termed the Hotṛi, in a loud and distinct tone, and with due regard to the rules of euphony, any deviation from which vitiated the ceremony. Here, therefore, we have evidence that there was a ceremonial in existence when some at least of the hymns of the Rich were composed; and even rites of a somewhat sacred character, as the Darśapúrṅamásau, or sacrifices at the new and full moon, and the whole array of priests, sixteen in number, are alluded to. But these allusions are incidental and transitory; they show that some of the hymns must have been preceded by rudiments of a liturgical ceremony, yet many others have not the slightest reference to anything beyond the simple adoration, by the presentation of butter or some juice to the deities, who are the objects of the praise or prayer. The different issues of the Súktas, so often mentioned by themselves as being old or new, will allow for the gradual evolution of liturgical rites emerging evidently into the rubrics of the Yajush and the chaunts of the Sáma. On this subject Professor Müller observes:—

'We may, therefore, safely ascribe the collection of the Rig-veda, or, as Professor Roth calls it, the historical Veda, to a less practical age than that of the Bráhmaṇa period; to an age, not entirely free from the trammels of a ceremonial, yet not completely enslaved by a system of mere formalities; to an age no longer creative and impulsive, yet not without some power of upholding the traditions of a past that spoke to a later generation of men through the very poems which they were collecting with so much zeal and accuracy.'

Professor Müller conceives nevertheless that there is some priestly influence distinguishable in the Sanhitá of the Rig-veda, as exemplified by its classification into Maṅdalas or Circles, of which seven are attributable to as many different Rishis and their descendants. There may have been such collections in use by different Gotras; but, to say the least, some of those persons to whom they are ascribed are of a rather equivocal character, and the compiler of the whole Sanhitá may have adopted the distinction as handed down by tradition without caring to be very exact as to detail. The question is not of much moment; the priority and posteriority of the Súktas relatively being unquestioned, they are undoubtedly of very various, possibly of very distant, eras, and we know too little of the chronology of the Rishis, their reputed Seers, to base the date of the composition upon that of the author. The Súktas of the Rig-veda had run through a long course of years, possibly centuries, before they were brought together in one general collection. The business of collection must have occupied some considerable time,—according to Professor Müller, two centuries; but we know too little of the process of reducing the scattered Mantras into a collective form, to be able to assign any fixed period to it. It is uniformly ascribed to Krishña Dvaipáyana, surnamed Vyása the arranger, assisted by a number of reputed sages, intending possibly a school or series of schools in which the Sanhitás of the Vedas were brought into their present shape during an interval of the duration supposed, or about two centuries, bringing the compilation, agreeably to an amended compendium, to the 12th or 13th century before the Christian era.

In what state did the several hymns circulate when they were first brought together? Had they been current orally alone, or in writing, and, if the former, were they reduced to writing when they were collected? That the Mantras were for a long time, perhaps for ages, current orally, there can be little reason to doubt. The pains taken to secure their accurate enunciation, and the elliptical style of their composition, are evidences of oral transmission. The question, as stated by Professor Müller, is, was the collection of the ten books of Vedic hymns the work of persons cognisant of the art of writing; were the thousand and seventeen hymns of the Ṛig-veda, after they were gathered into one body, preserved by memory or on paper? Professor Müller answers these questions by an interesting excursus on the probable period when the art of writing was first known to the Hindus, and draws the inference that before the time of Páńini, and before the first spreading of Buddhism in India, writing for literary purposes was not in use. The chief ground for this inference is the absence of any word not only in the hymns, but even in the grammatical lectures of Páńini, which presupposes the existence of writing, whilst in the ancient works of a people like the Jews, to whom writing must have been known from of old, such words as writing, scripture, book, volume, are of constant recurrence. Nothing of this kind occurs in any Sanskrit works older than Manu and the Mahábhárata. At the same time Professor Müller admits that the Hindus were acquainted with the art of writing before the time of Alexander, and the expressions *likhita* and *likhápita*, written, and caused to be written, occur on the inscriptions of Priyadarsi, which are no doubt of the third century B.C., and therefore, as far as is yet known, of Páńini's date, cotemporary with him, or even older; consequently, no argument can be drawn from his omissions or phraseology against a knowledge of the art of writing in his time. The question is not without its difficulties. That the Súktas could be handed down from generation to generation by memory alone we need not hesitate to admit, but if they had not been committed to writing when they were collected and classified into *adhyáyas* and *maṅdalas*, the task of compiling and perpetuating would have been but imperfectly accomplished, if some more durable condition had not been impressed upon the collection than that of being entrusted to the memory alone.*

To the Mantra period Professor Müller adds one still earlier, to which he gives the appellation of *Chhandas*,—the metrical or poetical period; understanding thereby the time at which those hymns or mantras were composed, which may be regarded as of most archaic character, emanating from the first religious sentiments of a simple people, and preceding the institution of a ceremonial, or the organisation of a priesthood. It seems scarcely necessary to make this a distinct era;† it is the same as the Mantra period, in which we have seen a wider space is evidently required for the new, intermediate, and ancient hymns which are recognised by the authors of the hymns themselves, especially as Professor Müller thinks it essential to caution against too hasty conclusions as

---

* [See on this question Prof. Goldstücker's "Páṇini", p. 15-67, and Weber, Ind. Stud., IV, 89 ff.; V, 18 ff.]

† [Haug, Ait. Br., I, p. 23. Goldstücker, l. l., p. 71.]

to the comparative recent date of many hymns, in which sentiments worthy of the most advanced ceremonial, or the presence of philosophical ideas, are to be found; there being, as he observes, very little to guide us in forming a judgment of what is genuine and primitive in the ancient poetry of so peculiar a race as that of the Aryans in India. In this want therefore of a safe criterion we may be content to look upon the Mantra period as one complete in itself, though extending over a long space of time, and in some instances to a very remote antiquity. At the same time even that is not the most distant term to which we may trace the literature of the Vedas; for, as Professor Müller remarks, ages must have passed before the grammatical texture of the Vedic Sanskrit could have assumed the consistency and regularity which it exhibits. Throughout, every tense, every mood, every number and person, of the verb is fixed, and all the terminations of the cases are formally established.

'From this point of view the Vedic language and poetry may be ascribed to a modern or secondary period in the history of the world, if only it be understood that what preceded that period in India, or in any other part of the Aryan world, is lost to us beyond the hope of recovery, and that, therefore, to us the Veda represents the most ancient chapter in the history of the human Intellect. We find no traces in the Veda, or in any Aryan work, of a growing language, growing in the sense 'in which some of the Turanian languages may be said to be still growing at the present day. The whole grammatical mechanism is finished, the most complicated forms are sanctioned, and the only changes of which the Aryan speech, arrived at the point where we find it in the Veda, admits, are those of gradual decay and recomposition.'

Having come to this conclusion that we have in the hymns of the Rig-veda some of the oldest records in the history of man, we may now inquire what was the condition of society which it discloses, and more especially what was the religion of the people? How far it afforded the sanction which the Hindus affirm of it to the religion that has prevailed for at least twenty centuries in Hindustan?

'The Veda', says Professor Müller, 'has a two-fold interest: it belongs to the history of the world and to the history of India. In the history of the world the Veda fills a gap which no literary work in any other language could fill. It carries us back to times of which we have no records anywhere, and gives us the very words of a generation of men, of whom otherwise we could form but the vaguest estimate by means of conjectures and inferences. As long as man continues to take an interest in the history of his race, and as long as we collect in libraries and museums the relics of former ages, the first place in that long row of books which contains the records of the Aryan branch of mankind, will belong for ever to the *Rig-veda*.'

It has pleased some of the most enthusiastic cultivators of the literature of the Vedas, amongst whom our author must be distinguished, to imagine a state of Indian society of a pure, simple, and patriarchal description, in which the feeding of flocks and herds was the main occupation of life, and whose chief recreation was the adoration of the deified elements or the composition of those songs in their honour which constitute a large portion of the actual collection.

'There was a time when the poet was the leader, the king, and priest of his family or tribe, when his songs and sayings were listened to in anxious silence and with implicit faith, when his prayers were repeated by crowds who looked up to their kings and priests, their leaders and judges, as men better, nobler, wiser than the rest, as beings nearer to the gods in proportion as they were raised above the common level of mankind. These men themselves living a life of perfect freedom, speaking a language not yet broken by literary usage, and thinking thoughts unfettered as yet by traditional chains, were at once teachers, lawgivers, poets, and priests. There is no very deep wisdom in their teaching, their laws are simple, their poetry shows no very high flights of fancy, and their religion might be told in a few words. But what there is of their language, poetry, and religion has a charm which no other period of Indian literature possesses: it is spontaneous, original, and truthful.'

For all this there seems to us to be but little warrant in any of the hymns, and the general tenor of them leaves no doubt that at the date of their composition society had assumed a more artificial character, and that the people were not encamped on the borders of rivers, or spacious Havanas, but were collected in hamlets and towns, and that their leaders were neither poets nor patriarchs, but princes whose favour and munificence were sought for and bestowed upon priests and poets. No doubt the principalities were of small political power, but they were independent and constantly at variance with one another, although their contests partook more of a predatory than a national hostility. It is also clear that a considerable portion of India was occupied by races not only of a different character and creed, but actively inimical to the practices of the Hindus, with whom the latter were in a normal state of antagonism. The subjugation or the servitude of these races must have been the work of time. Professor Müller has not entered upon this subject, but confines his attention to the religious condition which the Vedas exhibit as existing at the various periods throughout which the hymns may be traced.

The first and most obvious conclusion to be drawn from the hymns of the Veda, whatever may be their relative antiquity, whether twenty or twelve centuries B. C., is that the religion which they inculcate is not that of the Hindus of the present day. The Brahman who, from the time of the code of Manu as we have it, had arrogated to himself the attributes of a god upon earth, is in the Veda only one of seven, or even of sixteen priests, acting as a sort of master of the ceremonies, but not invested with any superior rank or authority. Of the distinction of caste at all the indications are faint and uncertain, with one exception —that of a remarkable hymn in the 10th Maṅḍala, the tenor and style of which place it indisputably in a comparatively recent stage, and bring it at least to the Brahmanic period, by which time we know that the Brahmanical system had been organised.* There is no mention of temples nor of public worship; the ceremonial is entirely domestic, and so far the formulæ, the language of the Súktas, still constitute the liturgy of the domestic rites of the Hindus. It is very doubtful if images were known, although mention of personal peculiarities, as of the handsome jaws of Indra, might

---

* [Muir, L L, I, 6 ff.; 42; II, 210.]

be suggested by a sculptured representation of him. Something else may, however, be meant; but the great feature of difference is the total absence of the divinities, both nomina and numina, who have for ages engaged, and, to a great degree, engrossed, the adoration of the Hindus. We have no indications of a Triad, the creative, preserving, and destroying power; Brahmá does not appear as a deity, and Vishńu, although named, has nothing in common with the Vishńu of the Puráńas; no allusion occurs to his Avatáras. His manifestation as Krishńa, the favourite divinity of the lower classes, for some centuries at least, does not appear. As a divinity Śiva is not named, nor is his type the Linga ever adverted to. Durgá and her triumphs, and Káli, whom the 'blood of man delights a thousand years', have no place whatever in the hymns of the Vedas. These differences are palpable, and so far from the Vedas being the basis of the existing system, they completely overturn it. It would be an interesting subject of inquiry to discover when, and by what means, the vast mass of the modern mythology of the Hindus sprang into existence and attained its circulation throughout India.

What then was the religion of the Vedic Hindus, as exhibited in the Súktas? Recollecting that these are most probably of widely different dates, and that they were collected and put together without much, if any, regard to system, we cannot expect to find a coherent and systematic form of worship or belief: each Súkta must be taken by itself, expressing its own notions.

By far the greater portion of them are addressed to the personified elements, especially to Agni or Fire, as represented in three phases, in heaven as the sun, in mid-air as lightning and meteoric phenomena, and on earth in the ordinary elementary type. Indra, the atmosphere, is the next in importance, especially as the sender of rain and consequent fertility, and to these two perhaps half the Súktas are addressed. Connected with them are the sun, the two divinities termed Aśvins and the Dawn, and Indra and Varuṅa; and the Viśvadevas, or universal deities, may, without much violence, be brought within the same category. These deities are eulogised and magnified, and they are implored for food, cattle, progeny, safety, long life, and all worldly enjoyments. Varuṅa especially appears to be the punisher of crime, and his protection against wickedness is frequently implored. Indra is, in an especial degree, the god of battles and giver of victory, but his attributes and the legend relating to him are not unfrequently ascribed to other divinities, as to the Aśvins and to Agni. A prominent and rather unintelligible object of praise and prayer is the Soma plant,* a sort of asclepias, the bruised leaves and stems of which yield a juice, which by standing ferments into an intoxicating liquor, which is supposed to gratify the gods and animate them to extraordinary exploits.

---

* [Haug's Essays on the Sacred Language of the Parsees. Bombay: 1862, p. 139 f. Aitareya Bráhmaṅa, ed. Haug, Vol. I, p. 59 ff. F. Windischmann, "Ueber den Somacultus der Arier". München: 1847. F. Spiegel, "Éràn". Berlin: 1863, p. 235.]

That this beverage was partaken of by the assistants can alone explain their elevation of it to the rank of a deity, and can have originated only in a stage of semi-barbarism, such as we can imagine might have won the adoration of the American Indians when first acquainted with ardent spirits. In hymns, too, which are apparently of an early date, we have the details of the Scythian sacrifice of the horse; and there are indications of the occasional offering of human victims, although of rare and special occurrence.* As a general rule, however, the offerings are of an innocent description — the Soma juice, clarified butter, and cakes of barley or other grain fried with butter and poured upon the fire. The same is presented to all the gods alike, and in this, as in other respects, there is so much in common that all the Vedic divinities may be resolved into one, as a general type of one universal being.

What indications do we find of a future existence or a system of rewards and punishments? The Vedic Hindus recognised unreservedly the difference between a material and spiritual state of being, and looked to the survival of the soul, and its occupation of an incorruptible body amongst the Pitris or Manes. There is no detail as to their condition, nor have we any positive intimation of punishment of sin after death, beyond deprecating its consequences during life, and

---

* [A. Weber in "Zeitschrift der deutschen morgenl. Gesellschaft", Vol. XVIII, 262-87.]

the designation of Yama as judge of the dead. It was also part of the Vedic creed that holy men, as in the case of the *Ribhus*, might attain the condition of gods. These intimations, however, are incidental and vague, and all that we can positively conclude from them is that the Vedas recognised, after the dissolution of the body, the life of the soul which animated it, and its continued existence in some heavenly sphere. There is no very distinct reference to the metempsychosis; none whatever to the fact of transmigration; an omission the more worthy of notice that it is the foundation of all the philosophical systems of the Hindus, and consequently proves their being posterior to the Vedas.

Had the Vedas any knowledge of one almighty and all-wise Creator and Ruler of the universe? They had a belief in such a Being, although evidently not unmingled with uncertainty and doubt. Professor Müller has given us a very remarkable Sûkta, in which a state of things before creation is clearly apprehended, the course of creation summarily sketched, and the question stated, Who knows what is the truth? There are several passages of this kind in the Sûktas, but to some of which at least very reasonable suspicions of a later age attach, being of the nature of the mysterious, which is manifested in the Upanishads. We are much disposed to look upon several of those cited by Professor Müller as open to this objection, and to think that in his enthusiasm he has been led to give a value to expressions which is more exalted than they deserve. Thus, for instance, in the hymn above alluded to, and which has been gracefully put into metre by a friend, we have the following passage:—

> 'Darkness there was; and all at first was veiled
> In gloom profound—an ocean without light;
> The germ that still lay covered in the husk
> Burst forth, one nature from the fervent heat;
> Then first came Love upon it.'

Now the term 'love' here appears to us to convey a notion too transcendental to have had a place in the conception of the original author. The word is *káma*, which scarcely indicates love in the sense in which it may here be understood, although not absolutely indefensible; but *káma* means desire, wish; and it expresses here the wish, synonymous with the will, of the sole existing Being to create. It is a familiar Vedic phrase in speaking of the time before creation, to say 'THAT, the one Being, was alone. He said,—May I be 'many!—then sprang the world into existence.' It is the wish, or rather the will, therefore, of God that the world should come into existence that the passage is speaking of, and not any such emotion as is ordinarily understood by 'love'. At any rate, this hymn and various others, particularly two in the tenth Maṅdala, hymns 81, 82, addressed to Viśvakarmá, the Omnificent, establish beyond controversy that the Vedic cosmogony was that of none of the subsequent schools; neither asserting with the Sánkhyas the coeternity of matter and spirit, nor with the Vedántas the existence of spirit alone. However dim the knowledge, however vacillating the opinion, it is evident that the authors of the old hymns of the Veda were disposed to believe in the primary existence of one God when nought else existed, and that the world was created by his fiat, and organised by his wisdom and might.

These are the conclusions to which a careful consideration of the contents of the textual portion of the Vedas, the Sanhitás, reasonably leads; and it is unnecessary to point out how important they are, not only to the history of the Hindu religion, but to that of the religion of the ancient world, at an era prior to any of which we possess a written word, with the exception of the Pentateuch. Students of ancient history and religion will feel greatly indebted to the erudition and laborious research of Professor Müller. It is not possible, in a brief survey like the present, to render justice to a work, every page of which teems with information that no other scholar ever has, or could have, placed before the public; and although many of the details are likely to interest those only who delight to explore the dark paths of antiquity, and to trace the progress of human opinion and belief, yet the work must ever hold a foremost place, not only in the history of India, but in that of the human race.

INDEX.

Abaldraina II, 186.
Abbás II, 93.
'*Abdallah ibn moqaffa*' II, 10. 98 f.
'*Abdu-lmulk nasr ullah* II, 93.
Abhedya II, 307.
Abhidhánachintámani III, 222 ff.
Abbidhánaratnamálá III, 209 f.
Abhimanyu I, 127. 192. 296. 300 f.
Abhindrad I, 127.
Abhinanda III, 204.
Abúlfazl I, 158. II, 78. 91. 111. III, 226. 229. 257.
Abú ya'qúb II, 107.
Áchára III, 87.
Áchárddaráa II, 320.
Áchárarati II, 231.
Áchárya I, 58. II, 36.
Achyuta upádhyáya III, 206.
Adhibhúta III, 140 f.
Adhidaiva III, 140 f.
Adhishíhána III, 152.
Adhiyajna III, 140 f.
Adhyátma III, 140 f.
Adháyáya I, 121. III, 357.
Adhwaryu I, 122.
Ádi purána I, 8.
Ádi parva I, 280.
Aditi I, 12. 33 f. 108.

Áditya I, 12. 46. 105. 127.
Áditya (king) III, 186.
Adwaita III, 146.
Ádya I, 127.
Agada II, 274 f.
Agastya I, 19. 28. 48. II, 224. 332. III, 196.
Aghápuh III, 132.
Ágneya astra I, 307.
Ágneya purána see *Agni purána*.
Agni I, 41 f. 82 ff. 149. 151. II, 352. III, 343.
Agni (fire) I, 382.
Agni purána I, 7 f. 82 – 91. 121. 182. II, 290 f. 293. 298. 301 ff. 306. 308.
Agniákha II, 135 ff.
Agnishthoma I, 127.
Agnishwátta I, 151. 154.
Agnivarchchá I, 130.
Agniveía I, 307.
Agnyastra II, 301.
Agrahára II, 162.
Aguru II, 217.
Ahankára I, 10. 23. 145 f.
Áhárya I, 382.
Ahichchhatra I, 42.
Ahichchhatrá I, 48. 291.

Ahikshetra I, 48.
Ákúti I, 124.
Aindreyaka I, 148.
Airávata II, 231. 328. 361. 372.
Aitareya bráhmaña III, 326 f.
Aitareya upanishad III, 329.
Aja I, 47.
Ajámídha I, 308. 312.
Ajayapála III, 106. 210. 220. 240.
Ajyapá I, 154.
Akarma III, 134 f.
Akarshiká I, 168.
Ákúta I, 145 f.
Akbar III, 226. 256 f.
Akhyáta III, 320.
Akrúra I, 133.
Akshara III, 132.
Akshauhiní II, 212 f.
Ákúti I, 25. 124.
Aidbú I, 383.
Alagardá I, 300.
Alaká II, 224. 328. 372. 375 f. 400.
Alakshmi I, 59.
Alankára I, 346.
Al edrísí III, 225.
Al monsir II, 93.
Alolatwa III, 150.
Aloluptwa III, 150.
Al wd'ez II, 93 f.
Amaradatta III, 209. 220.
Amaradeva III, 166.
Amarakhandaka II, 330 f.
Amarakosha II, 298. 300. 306. 316. 324. 328. 332 ff. 372. 379 f. 111. 118. 126 f. 138. 159 f. 165 ff. — 184. 201 ff. 205. 208 f. 215 ff. 231 ff. 251. 301.

Amarasakti II, 7. 10.
Amarasinha III, 211.
Amarasinha III, 166 ff. 173. 175. 177. 179 ff. 197. 199 ff. 208 f. 216 ff. 232. 236 f. 260. 301 f.
Amarávatí I, 14.
Amarddaka I, 62.
Ambálíká I, 358. 363 ff. II, 186. 189. 205. 209 f.
Ambariska I, 52. 112.
Ambashíká I, 292.
Ambíká I, 261.
Amitagati III, 222.
Ámrakúta II, 329 f. 332.
Amrita I, 125. II, 384.
Amukta II, 289.
Ánaka II, 262.
Ánaka III, 116.
Anámaya III, 148.
Ananta I, 112. II, 302.
Ananta (king) I, 158. II, 111 f.
Anantabhatta II, 79.
Anantakirtti II, 257 f.
Anantasakti II, 7.
Anantasayana I, 69.
Anantasira II, 219 f.
Anantavarmá I, 376 f. II, 280 f.
Anantavijaya III, 112.
Anasúyá I, 150.
Andhaka I, 299. 312.
Andhra I, 374 f. II, 261 f. 269.
Ándhra I, 134.
Andhrabhritya I, 134.
Anga I, 125. 240. 285. 293. 323. 357. 362. 366. 369. 371. 373. 375. II, 136. 188 f. 145. 210. 233. 240. 269. 296.

INDEX. 331

Angdraka I, 199 f.
Angáravati I, 199 f.
Angarakshaka II, 36.
Angiras I, 41. 127. 150. II, 41. 275.
Ángirasa I, 150.
Anikini II, 292.
Anila II, 192.
Aniruddha I, 14. 111. 116 f. 139.
Anjana II, 328.
Anka II, 18.
Ankuśa II, 295.
Annapúrná I, 70.
Ania I, 101. 121.
Anákinda I, 101.
Aniarúpa I, 101.
Anidrátdra I, 137.
Aniunda II, 300.
Antar II, 111.
Antarbhedi II, 306.
Antarrantika II, 35.
Anubandha II, 249.
Anugangam I, 136.
Anugraha I, 118.
Anukrama I, 54. 71.
Anukramoní III, 322. 325.
Anuśásana parva I, 296. III, 16.
Anuśastra I, 387.
Amrodka III, 323.
Amicinda II, 294.
Anvedri sohelli II, 13 f. 27. 91. 94. 144.
Anwikshiki II, 272.
Ap I, 145.
Apahdra III, 16.
Apahdravarmd I, 353. 359 ff. II, 167. 188 ff. 210.
Apahri III, 16.
Aparikshita kdritwa II, 2. 48.
Aparydpta III, 116.
Apastamba III, 321.
Apaviddha III, 48.
Aprajasta III, 49. 51.
Apsaras I, 41. 55. 858. II, 188. 213. 219. 316.
Apsaraloka I, 41.
Apyaya dikshita I, 348.
Ará I, 386.
Arabian nights II, 103 ff. 119. 146. 150.
Áraňgaka I, 50. III, 323 ff.
Arbuda I, 38.
Ardeshir dirdzdast II, 107.
Ardhachandra II, 302.
Arddhadhárá I, 386.
Arddhanáríśwara I, 212.
Argha II, 319 f.
Arghya II, 319 f.
Árhata III, 194.
Arjuna I, 26 f. 53. 133. 192. 278 f. 285. 291. 293 f. 296. 298. 300 f. 304 f. 312. 317 f. 320 ff. II, 60. 296. 302. 356 f. III, 101. 107. 112 ff.
Arjunavrishdda III, 115.
Áriara I, 151.
Artha II, 8. 121 f. III, 131.
Arthopála I, 353. 367 ff. II, 169. 180. 221. 237.
Arthapati I, 361 ff.
Arrdkarotas I, 143.
Áryabhúmi II, 332.
Aryaka I, 151.
Áryaketu II, 287 ff.

INDEX.

Áryáputra II, 287.
Áryávartta II, 332.
Asamhata II, 306.
Asurarsa III, 51.
Ashádha II, 317 f. 397.
Ashtaka III, 310. 312.
Ashtami I, 70.
Asi I, 85.
Asipatra III, 96.
Asura I, 19. 26. 28. 50. 63. 67. 108. II, 174. 347. 352. 366.
Asmaka I, 279. II, 277. 280 f. 286 ff.
Asoka III, 325.
Asoka (tree) II, 195. 216. 378 f.
Asokasundari I, 33.
Asrama parva I, 286.
Asraya III, 151.
Asrita I, 147.
Asrurindumati I, 32.
Asuddhyaksha II, 35.
Aswaldyana III, 321. 323 ff.
Aswamedha I, 38. 42. 48. 52. 78. 286. II, 253. 360.
Aswamedhaja II, 60.
Aswamedhika parva I, 286.
Aswattha I, 69 f.
Aswatthámá I, 308. 317. 319.
Aswini I, 272 f. 278. III, 343.
Atala I, 45.
Átavikáddya II, 35.
Atharva veda I, 129 f. 272. II, 210. III, 112. 310. 311 f. 321. 327.
Atimukta II, 242.
Atiratha II, 294.
Atirátra I, 137.

Atithi III, 212.
Átmá I, 145. III, 142.
Átmabodha II, 396.
Átreya I, 150. 273.
Atri I, 35. 122. 127. 150.
Aurangzib III, 257.
Aurasa III, 47.
Aurva I, 111.
Avanti I, 13. II, 57. 250. 341.
Avantidesa II, 280.
Avantiká II, 312.
Avantisundari I, 356 ff. II, 182. 183 f. 187.
Avasthá III, 151.
Avatára I, 58. 60. 63. 91. 99. 108. II, 366 f. III, 342.
Arimukta I, 84.
Avimukteswara I, 84. 366. II, 221.
Avyakta I, 146. III, 145 f.
Avyaya III, 149.
Aydr dánish II, 27. 78.
Ayini akbari I, 158. II, 112. 328.
Ayodhya I, 47 f. 50 f. 174. 177. II, 19. 25. 151. 342.
Áyur veda I, 97. 271. 274.
Áyus I, 38.

Badariká I, 179.
Badarikásrama I, 60. 67. 179. 185.
Badaríndtha I, 185.
Bagheta III, 205.
Bahár dánish I, 169. 224. II, 15. 17. 142.
Bahlika I, 313.
Báhlika I, 318. III, 194.
Bakrou sháh II, 93.
Báhudantiputra II, 275.

INDEX.

Bahwikdsya I, 154.
Baitdl pachisi I, 157. 372. II, 336.
Bakula II, 216.
Balabhadra II, 20 f. 25. 254 ff.
Bālachandrikā II, 179 ff. 185.
Baladeva I, 116.
Balddhyaksha II, 35.
Bālagopāla I, 84.
Balajd I, 19 f.
Bālakhilya I, 150. 210.
Bālambhatta I, 8. III, 14.
Balarāma I, 14. 133. 332. 341.
II, 357 f. 370.
Bali I, 45 f. 65. 111. II, 267.
Ballāla miśra III, 178.
Ballāla rāja III, 227.
Bāṇa bhaṭṭa I, 157.
Bāṇāndiā I, 20 f.
Bāṇeśvara I, 111. 138.
Bandhaila III, 205.
Bāndhara III, 47.
Bandhumati II, 225.
Bandhupāla II, 179 ff.
Barṣiya II, 90 f.
Bauddha I, 59. 185. 219. II, 20.
31. 76. 195. 202. 257. III, 150 f.
187 f. 191. 193 ff. 197 ff. 224 ff.
324.
Baudhāyana III, 47 ff. 321.
Bhādra I, 70. 117.
Bhadrakālī I, 117.
Bhadravardmārāma III, 205.
Bhadraśākti II, 7.
Bhādrāśramī I, 70.
Bhagadatta II, 291.
Bhāgadheya I, 127.
Bhāgavata purāṇa I, 3. 31. 46.
III.

52 f. 60. 74. 79. 82. 110. 113.
116. 122. 124 f. 177. 134. 296.
II, 60.
Bhagavadgītā I, 62. II, 345. 357.
III, 94–157. 250. 274.
Bhagavadgītā māhātmya I, 62.
Bhagavatī I, 38.
Bhagīratha I, 28. 42. 324. II,
359 f.
Bhāgīrathī I, 124 f.
Bhāguri III, 209. 218.
Bhaimī ekādaśī I, 28.
Bhairava I, 113.
Bhairavānanda II, 57.
Bhairavī tantra II, 34.
Bhakti I, 57. 61. 72. 92. 96.
Bhānudikshita III, 126. 205. 242.
Bharadvāja I, 127. 273. 291. 297.
306. 313.
Bharata I, 40. 75. 126. II, 353.
Bharatamallika II, 325. 336. III,
205 f. 237.
Bhārata varsha I, 12. 192.
Bhārgava I, 150.
Bhartṛihari I, 348. II, 155. 335.
Bhātrunda II, 29.
Bhāhid II, 66. 73.
Bhāskarācārmā I, 877. II, 282.
Bhaṭṭa bhāskara III, 210.
Bhaṭṭāchārya III, 195.
Bhaṭṭa nagara II, 23.
Bhaṭṭikāvya I, 343.
Bhaṭṭojidikshita III, 181. 205.
Bhaṭṭotpala I, 152.
Bhavabhūti I, 345. II, 341. 348.
III, 177.
Bhāva miśra III, 236.

Bhárátí I, 161. II, 247. 353.
Bhadra prabdša III, 235 f. 238.
Bharya I, 127.
Bhedana I, 382.
Bhikshá I, 340.
Bhikshuka III, 119.
Bhilla II, 26. 142 f.
Bhíma I, 279 ff. 317. 324. 333. 356 ff.
Bhímadhanved I, 371 f. II, 243. 245. 247.
Bhímapardírama II, 151.
Bhímasena I, 291.
Bhindipála II, 323.
Bhishak II, 35.
Bhishma I, 23. 30. 66. 285 f. 291 ff. 313. II, 294. 296.
Bhishma panchaka I, 66.
Bhishma parva II, 294.
Bhoga II, 306. III, 120.
Bhoja I, 157. 299. 376. II, 257. III, 168. 173 ff. 221.
Bhojachampú III, 177.
Bhujadeva I, 314 ff.
Bhojaprabandha III, 168. 171. 173. 177 f. 180. 182. 189.
Bhojardja III, 204.
Bhojavansa I, 345 f.
Bhojika I, 166.
Bhram III, 117.
Bhrigu I, 37. 54. 61 f. 106. 150. 308 f. II, 366.
Bhrigukshetra I, 38.
Bhrigupati II, 366.
Bhúmi II, 344.
Bhúmikhanda I, 22. 30 45. 76 ff.
Bhúpálaka I, 200.

Bhúriprayoga III, 232 f. 240.
Bhúta I, 41. 148. III, 295.
Bhúta vidyá I, 274 f.
Bhúti III, 151.
Bhuvanakosha I, 84.
Bhuvanesvara I, 17.
Bidpay I, 156. II, 31 ff.
Bihdri lál III, 220.
Bimba II, 383.
Bindusdra tírtha I, 117.
Brahma I, 23 f. 100. III, 120. 132. 140 f. 152.
Brahmá I, 8 ff. 19. 22 ff. 42. 46. 56. 58. 61. 64 f. 68 f. 71. 93. 95 ff. 119. 146 ff. 161. 272. 310. II, 5. 274. 321. 356. 382. III, 96. 342.
Brahmadatta I, 26. 29. 240.
Brahmagítá I, 22.
Brahmahrada I, 20.
Brahmakánda III, 328.
Brahmaketu I, 44.
Brahmakhanda I, 93-98.
Brahmana III, 303. 312. 315 f. 322. 326 ff.
Brahmándá I, 113.
Brahmándapurána I, 85. II, 321.
Brahmani I, 141.
Brahmapurána I, 7-21. 59. 121.
Brahmardkshasa II, 260.
Brahmasanhitá III, 90.
Brahmasútra III, 105 ff.
Brahmavartta II, 356.
Brahmavairortta purána I, 2. 91-120. III, 96 f.
Brahmottarakhánda I, 21.
Brihad dranyaka III, 328.

INDEX.   355

Brihad draniyaka upanishad III, 329.
Buddha III, 166. 180 f. 183. 187. 198. 225. 316. 325.
Buddhagayā III, 180.
Buddhi III, 123.
Budha I, 41.
Bukka rāya I, 81. III, 192. 213. 228.
Bundela III, 205.

Chākí II, 300.
Chakra I, 112. II, 60.
Chakradhara II, 60 ff.
Chakrānka I, 49.
Chakrapāṇidatta III, 237.
Chakrapāṇidīkshita I, 348.
Chakravedhi II, 381.
Chākshusha I, 126 f.
Chakvad II, 208. 216. 383.
Champa II, 215.
Champā I, 357 ff. 364. 373. II, 186. 189. 195. 241.
Champaka II, 216.
Chamū II, 292.
Chāṇakya I, 87. 177 ff. 354. II, 6. 273.
Chandaghosha I, 367 f. II, 226. 228. 231.
Chāndiddā II, 157.
Chāndiddī II, 157.
Chanilamahāsena I, 198.
Chandasena I, 190 ff. 214. 226. 228.
Chandasinhu I, 367 f. II, 228. 225. 232.
Chandavarmā II, 71. 282.

Chandarikrama I, 266.
Chandi I, 103. 198. 265 f. 353. II, 143.
Chandika II, 165.
Chandra III, 221.
Chandrabhāga I, 137.
Chandragupta I, 133 f. 165. 175. 178. II, 6. 118. III, 324 f.
Chandrakānta II, 376.
Chandrapālita II, 277.
Chandraprabhā I, 260 ff.
Chandrasena I, 371. II, 242. 245 f. 261.
Chandrasekhara I, 324.
Chandravarmā I, 357 ff. 364. II, 180. 185. 188. 209 f. 221.
Charaka I, 89. 273.
Charaṇa III, 330.
Charaṇādri II, 332.
Charchitā III, 187.
Charchitanagara III, 187. 197.
Charmamrati I, 88. 295. II, 354.
Chdaka II, 326.
Chātaka II, 174. 325 f. 334 f. 399.
Chatugrāma III, 233.
Chaturbhuj III, 88.
Chaunrí II, 346.
Chedi I, 230. 297.
Chekitāna I, 297.
Cheruman perumal III, 190 f.
Chetand III, 146.
Chhagala I, 149.
Chhandas III, 215 ff. 337.
Chhāndogya upanishad III, 322.
Chhatradhāra II, 36.
Chhedana I, 382.
Chichukā I, 38.

23*

Chikitsā I, 270. 275.
Chikitsāsthāna I, 274.
Chitragrīva II, 24.
Chitragupta II, 164. 172. See Mitragupta.
Chitrakūṭa II, 315. 331. 336.
Chitrāngada I, 291.
Chitraratha II, 82.
Chitrasena I, 55 f.
Chola I, 68. 241.
Chūrṇa II, 325.
Chyavana I, 37 f. 42.

Dadhīchi I, 28.
Daitya I, 32 f. 45. 59. 65. 200. 267. 319.
Dākinī I, 373. II, 133.
Dakṣa I, 9 ff. 25. 30. 41. 44. 112. 125 ff. 151. 161. 272.
Dakṣa (Jur.) III, 67.
Dakṣiṇā I, 101. 103. 124.
Dāmaliptā I, 371. 373. II, 242. See Tāmraliptā.
Damana I, 42.
Damanaka II, 12. 139.
Damayantī I, 324. II, 135.
Dāmottaradatta III, 232.
Dānadharma I, 286. III, 16.
Dānava I, 33. 45.
Daṇḍa I, 20. II, 206.
Daṇḍādhīndtha III, 213.
Daṇḍakāraṇya I, 29. II, 173.
Daṇḍanīti II, 270. 272.
Daṇḍī I, 157. 344 ff. 379. II, 6. 152.
Dantaśankhu I, 386.
Dantila I, 12.

Danu I, 33.
Dārānagara I, 312.
Dārā shekoh III, 257. 328.
Daridrā I, 70.
Darpasāra I, 356 ff. 368. II, 180. 185 ff. 232.
Darśapūrṇamāsau III, 333.
Dāruvarmā I, 356 ff. II, 180 f.
Ḍāreika I, 187.
Daśakumārachartira I, 87. 157. 169. 187. 342-379. II, 6. 46. 152. 160.
Daśapura II, 355.
Daśaratha I, 17.
Daśārṇa II, 326 f.
Dattaka III, 47 ff.
Dattakachandrikā III, 45. 47. 49.
Dattakamīmāṃsā III, 44. 46.
Dattātreya I, 55.
Dauedrika II, 85.
Dāyabhāga III, 16. 19. 23. 30. 50 ff. 67. 69. 71. 78. 189.
Dāyadā III, 46.
Dāyakramasaṃgraha III, 14. 13. 16. 68 f.
Dāyatattva III, 20.
Dehabhṛit III, 148.
Deśya I, 184. II, 119.
Deva I, 127.
Devadatta I, 185 ff. III, 112.
Devadyuti I, 56.
Devagiri II, 351.
Devahūti I, 124.
Devakī I, 108 ff. 137. 341.
Devakīrtya I, 154.
Devala I, 110. III, 47 f. 50. 51 f.
Devapura I, 50.

Devarakshita I, 136.
Devasarmd II, 13. 22 ff. 51. 141.
Devasena I, 30. 234.
Devasmitá I, 216 ff. II, 122 f. 125 f.
Devatá I, 127.
Devi I, 90. 161. 166. II, 35. 43. 79. III, 182.
Devikd I, 39.
Devi purdña II, 320.
Dhana III. 18.
Dhanaka II, 248.
Dhanamitra I, 361 ff. II, 188 f. 198 ff.
Dhananjaya I, 283. III, 218. 231.
Dhaneśwara I, 69.
Dhanurveda II, 230 f. 294 f.
Dhanushka II, 291.
Dhanvantari I, 89. 112. 273. 276. III, 168.
Dhanvin II, 291.
Dhanyaka II, 248 ff.
Dhdnyaka II, 248.
Dhard I, 109.
Dhdrá I, 341. III, 168. 174.
Dharanidhra III, 211.
Dharanikosha III, 211. 220. 240 ff.
Dhariñi I, 151.
Dharma I, 92. 97. 105. 125. 279. 326. II, 8. 192 f. III, 117 f. 120. 133. 140. 198. 221.
Dharmasútra I, 139.
Dharmabuddhi II, 25.
Dharmadatta I, 216.
Dharmagupta I, 216.
Dharmapdla I, 352. II, 160. 169. 223. 236.
Dharmaputra I, 236.

Dharmaraja I, 236.
Dharmacarddhana I, 370. II, 236.
Dhdtri I, 66. 68. 73.
Dhdtu III, 246. 263. 330.
Dhdtupdtha III, 246 ff.
Dhdturdga II, 394.
Dhrishla I, 127.
Dhrishtadyumna I, 295 ff. 325 f. 331. II, 308.
Dhrishtaketu I, 296 f.
Dhritarāshtra I, 123. 279 ff. 320. 331. 353. II, 308. 357. III, 115.
Dhriti I, 124. III, 146.
Dhruva I, 41. 125. 152.
Dhrurd III, 154.
Dhúmankha II, 136.
Dhúmini II, 248 ff.
Dhundhu I, 42.
Dhundumdra I, 42.
Dhydna yoga I, 71.
Didda II, 112.
Dilpdla I, 41.
Dikshd I, 56.
Dikshita III, 205.
Dilipa I, 46. 54. 56 f. 60. 62. 64. II, 360.
Dindra II, 38. 179. 197.
Dipaddna mdhdtmya I, 64.
Dipakarni I, 181.
Diti I, 33. II, 80.
Divoddsa I, 42.
Dodā I, 162. 215. 281. 307. II, 203.
Dṛdhyáyaña III, 321.
Draupadi I, 281. 284. 287. 289. 300. 311. 324 ff.
Drāvida I, 44. 55. 80. II, 250.

Drāvida (lex.) III, 204.
Dravyābhidhāna I, 270.
Drishadwati II, 356.
Dhūyapura I, 19 f.
Droṅa I, 285. 291. 293. 298. 304 ff. 325.
Droṅa parra I, 285.
Drupada I, 281. 291. 297. 307. 310 ff. 325. 329. 336. 340.
Duhídsana I, 292.
Durgā I, 20. 48. 77. 84. 101. 103. 105. 109. 112 ff. 163. 378. II, 143. 286. 348. III, 176. 163. 342.
Durgapdla II, 35.
Durgasinha I, 183.
Duredsas I, 52. 59. 105. 111 f. 116. 125. 293.
Duryodhana I, 279 ff. 317. 329. 338. II, 214. 296.
Dushmanta II, 317.
Dushṭabuddhi II, 25.
Dushyanta I, 40.
Dwaipāyana vydsa I, 121.
Dwāpara yuga I, 121. 123. 149 f. 152.
Dwārakā I, 14. 31. 53. 60. 66. 115 f. 118. 138. 284. 287.
Dwāravati I, 32.
Dwipa I, 11. 39. 126.
Dwirūpa kosha III, 207. 237.

Ekabuddhi II, 61.
Ekadanta I, 107.
Ekadaushtra I, 107.
Ekādasi I, 15. 69. 72.
Ekākshara kosha III, 211. 234.

Ekdwara I, 12. 17.
Ekavira II, 281.
Eshani I, 386.
Eshya I, 392.

Feizi III, 257.
Firdausi II, 90. 92.

Gddhipura III, 215.
Gajddhyaksha II, 35.
Gajdkhya I, 311.
Gambhira II, 349.
Gaṅa I, 127. II, 292. III, 247.
Gaṅapati I, 114.
Gaṅdaki I, 49. 60.
Gandhāra I, 291. 311.
Gāndhāra I, 291.
Gāndhāra grāma II, 72.
Gandharba I, 41. 97. 118. II, 158.
Gāndharba viedha I, 167. 350.
Gāndhāri I, 287. 292. 815.
Gandhavati II, 345. 349.
Gāndiva I, 294. II, 356 f.
Gaṅeśa I, 93. 104-7. 117 ff. II, 216. 352.
Gaṅeśa khaṅda I, 93. 108-7.
Gangā I, 42. 101. 305 f. II, 333. 352. 358 ff. 372. III, 83.95 f. 142.
Gangādhara III, 220.
Gangādhcdra I, 166. 306. 358.
Gangādhedra māhātmya II, 358.
Gangādgara I, 60. 72.
Gāngeya I, 306.
Garga I, 108.
Gārgya I, 149.
Garuda I, 192 ff. 207 ff. 260. II, 15. 18. 127. 129. 139. 360.

Gauri I, 28. 68. II, 169. 360. 370.
Gautama I, 52. 59. 127. III, 49.
Gautami I, 340.
Gayā I, 26. II, 352.
Gayā māhātmya I, 85.
Gāyatri I, 28.
Ghanṭākarna II, 19.
Ghaṭa II, 147 ff.
Ghaṭakarpara II, 335. III, 167 f.
Ghaṭotkacha I, 226 f. 333.
Ghī I, 140.
Ghora I, 151.
Ghṛitāchī I, 97.
Guḍ II, 66. 78.
Gītagovinda II, 370.
Gochandand I, 390.
Goddrari I, 60. 62. 162. 180. 241. II, 28. 153. 332.
Goji I, 387.
Gokula I, 53. 110. 112. 115. 120.
Goloka I, 98. 103 f. 115.
Gomedhā II, 358.
Gomini II, 248. 250.
Gomūtrika II, 307.
Gopa I, 97 f. 108. 118.
Gopakanyā II, 225.
Gopāla I, 65. 84.
Gopālaka I, 226 ff. 239. II, 156. 158.
Gopatha brāhmaṇa III, 327.
Gophaṇ II, 300.
Gopī I, 53. 95. 97 f. 106. 118. II, 15.
Gopīnātha I, 131. 319. 379.
Gorambha II, 13.
Gosdin I, 120.

Goshtika karma II, 77.
Gotra III, 330. 334.
Govardhana III, 44. 178. 204. 219.
Govinda I, 84. 95.
Govindadatta I, 184 f. 189.
Grahamanjari I, 158.
Grāma II, 66. 77.
Grihagupta II, 254. 256.
Grihya III, 333.
Grihyasūtra III, 321.
Grishma II, 373.
Gūdhotpanna III, 48.
Guha I, 137.
Guhasena I, 216 ff. II, 122 f.
Guhya I, 147.
Gulma II, 222 f.
Guṇa I, 116. III, 151.
Guṇādera I, 191.
Guṇāḍhya I, 159 ff. 179 ff. 184. 188 ff. II, 118 ff.
Gupta I, 136.
Gurjara I, 62.
Guru III, 120.

Hachhachandra III, 204.
Halabhṛit II, 357. 370.
Halāyudha I, 332. III, 202. 214. 219. 236.
Hanumān I, 30. 292. II, 296. 301.
Hara I, 200. II, 245.
Hara (lex.) III, 219.
Hara kā pairi II, 364.
Haraswāmī I, 253 f.
Hārāvali III, 212. 220. 245.
Hari I, 9. 72 f. 92. 104. 107. 114. 119. 288. II, 5.
Hari (king) I, 158.

Haridvadra I, 72. 166. 306. II, 358 f. 364.
Hariharapura I, 81.
Hariharavāya I, 81. III, 192. 213.
Haripura I, 62. 81.
Hariśchandra I, 46. II, 163.
Hārīta III, 47 f.
Harivanśa I, 26. 278. 288. II, 358. III, 174.
Harsha or Harshadeva I, 152 ff. II, 111 f.
Harydāca I, 307.
Hasta I, 319.
Hastamukta II, 209.
Hasti I, 312.
Hāstinapura I, 30. 122. 162. 228. 230. 279 ff. 311 f. II, 293.
Hāsyārṇava II, 315.
Hātakeścara I, 45.
Havishmān I, 127. 154.
Hazár afsána II, 104 ff.
Hemachandra II, 341. 380. III, 127. 160. 222 ff. 279 f. 234. 240 ff.
Hemādchārya III, 224.
Hemanta II, 372.
Hidimba I, 296.
Himāchala II, 58.
Himālaya I, 105. 112. 160. 169. 185. 189. 196. 239. 242. 279. 287. 330. 332. 340. II, 121. 129. 187. 318. 323. 326 f. 332 f. 357. 361. 364. 368 ff.
Himāvat I, 151.
Hiraṇvati II, 308.
Hiraṇyabāhu I, 351.
Hiraṇyagarbha I, 146.

Hiraṇyagupta I, 172. 177 f.
Hiraṇyaka II, 30.
Hiraṇyakaśipu I, 32. 34. II, 183.
Hiraṇydkṣha I, 34. 58.
Hissa nāma III, 88;
Historia septem sapientum II, 96. 100 ff.
Homa I, 84. 216.
Homai II, 107.
Hosain bin 'ali II, 08.
Hosain mirza II, 94.
Hotri I, 120. III, 353.
Hridika I, 299.

Ikshwāku I, 25. 46. 127. II, 187.
Ildvrita varsha I, 29.
Indra I, 14. 26. 28. 32 f. 36 f. 41 f. 45. 105 f. 112. 125. 127. 140. 162. 192. 198. 200. 211. 226. 243. 273. 279. 287. 293. 295. 312. 318. 333. 341. II, 5. 9. 21. 23 f. 29 f. 234. 316 f. 321 f. 342. 353. 360 f. 368. 372. 377. III, 96. 124. 341. 343.
Indradatta I, 163 ff. 174 f. II, 131. III, 170.
Indradyumna I, 13.
Indrapramati I, 129.
Indraprastha I, 261. II, 293.
Indrdyudha I, 300.
Indumati I, 47.
Irugapa III, 213. 228.
Īśopaniṣhad III, 113. 320.
Īśvara I, 10. 20. II, 368. III, 134. 142. 145.
Itihāsa I, 112. 139 f. 354.

INDEX.

Jaffir II, 33.
Jagannátha I, 13 f. 18. 49. 60. 72. 79.
Jagannátha (jur.) III, 52. 72. 78. 85 f.
Jagannátha kshetra I, 82. 128.
Jahdnddr I, 169.
Jáhnari I, 239.
Jahnu II, 333. 359.
Jaimini I, 59. II, 30. III, 196.
Jaina I, 26. 76 f. 375. II, 20. 50 ff. 76. 196. 380. III, 183. 210. 213. 222 ff. 324.
Jalandhara I, 54. 67 f.
Jalaukd I, 383.
Jalaodhaka II, 35.
Jamadagni I, 59. 106. 127. 192. 196. 308. 334. II, 366.
Jambaedn I, 102.
Jambaratí I, 102.
Jambudwipa I, 32.
Jamnd I, 55. 112. 162. 215. 281. 293. 319. II, 337. 361. See Yamuná.
Jana I, 40.
Janaka I, 16. 49. II, 316. 364. III, 105.
Janamejaya I, 131. 192. 278. II, 60. III, 212.
Janani II, 35.
Janárdana I, 332.
Jangama tirtha I, 39.
Janma III, 124.
Janmdshikami I, 102.
Jarásandha I, 116. 137.
Jaláddhara kosha III, 232 f. 240.
Jaidya I, 42.

Jdtidharma III, 117 f.
Játinirnaya I, 97.
Jayd I, 162. 183. II, 117.
Jayadeva II, 370.
Jayadratha I, 310.
Jayantí I, 70. 102.
Jayapura III, 230.
Jayasena I, 198.
Jayasinha I, 274. II, 264 f.
Jimútaváhana III, 14. 16 ff. 27. 47. 53. 72. 78. 84.
Jina I, 26. II, 51. III, 225.
Jiral II, 391.
Jiva I, 151.
Jnána III, 121. 144.
Jnánakulúla III, 326. 329.
Jnánayoga I, 43.
Jnápaka II, 35.
Jneya III, 144.
Jyeshthá deri I, 59.
Jyotirciddbharana III, 169.
Jyotisha III, 316. 322.

Kachhapa II. 380.
Kaddlí I, 111. III, 183.
Kadamba II, 373 f.
Kádambarí I, 157.
Kadrú I, 201.
Kaikeya I, 296.
Kailása I, 57. 71. 106. 160. 198. 330. II, 316. 323. 326 f. 366. 368 f.
Kaiiabha I, 14. 30.
Káka II, 33.
Kákolúkika II, 33 f.
Kákolúkíya II, 9. 34.
Kakzha II, 303.

362 INDEX.

Kakutmini I, 63.
Kala II, 240.
Kald I, 101. II, 384.
Kála II, 24.
Kálagupta II, 167. 178.
Kalahakanlaka II, 256. 258.
Kalakhala II, 358.
Kálanemi I, 30.
Kálanjana II, 156.
Kaldnsa I, 101.
Káldpa I, 183. III, 202.
Kaldrúpa I, 102.
Kalaśa I, 158. II, 111.
Kálasútra III, 96.
Kdlatoya I, 132.
Kaldrati I, 110 f.
Kálayavana I, 138. 355. II, 167. 177 f.
Káli I, 101. II, 169. III, 242.
Káliddsa I, 40. 191. 344. 346. II, 152. 310 f. 314 f. 323. 329. 340. 359 ff. 372. 399. III, 168. 173 ff.
Kálikd purána II, 352. III, 46 ff. 54.
Kalila wa damna I, 180. II, 4. 10 ff. 86 ff. 132 ff.
Kálindararmá II, 213.
Kálindí II, 174.
Kalinga I, 136 f. 240. 291. 323 ff. II, 262 f. 264. 369. III, 174.
Kalinga (lex.) III, 204.
Kalingasena II, 128.
Kaliyuga I, 15. 71. 73. 118. 130. 132. 152. III, 192.
Kalpa I, 23. 138. 144. 148 f. 210. II, 322. 372. III, 316.
Kalpasthána I, 274.

Kalpasundari II, 212 ff.
Kalpasútra III, 229. 320 f.
Kalydna saptami I, 28.
Káma II, 8. 163. 171. 182. 192 ff. 211. 216. 218. 273. III, 140. 346.
Kámadera I, 35 f. 227. 356. II, 217. 394.
Kámdkhyd I, 89. 48. 77. 79.
Kamala II, 391.
Kamald I, 102.
Kámalatá II, 78.
Kámamanjarí I, 359 ff. II, 120. 195. 202 f.
Kámandaki I, 354. II, 306 ff.
Kámandakíya II, 170.
Kámapála I, 352 f. 366 ff. II, 160. 161. 189. 222. 225 ff. 236.
Kámarúpa I, 242. II, 78. 213. 322.
Kámboja I, 292.
Kámpilya I, 44. 308.
Kámabhúti I, 179 ff.
Kandda I, 59.
Kanakalekhá II, 262. 265.
Kanakarekhá I, 244. 255. 262.
Kanakavati II, 254 ff.
Kanakhala I, 166. II, 358 f.
Kandrka I, 18.
Kánchanamdlini I, 55.
Kánchí I, 42. 68. II, 250. 342.
Kanchuki II, 35.
Kandarpa I, 95.
Kandarpaketu II, 13.
Kandu I, 14.
Kandukdvati I, 371. 373. II, 242 f. 246. 260 f.
Kandukotsava II, 242.

INDEX.

Kámsa III, 48.
Kamsa I, 113. 116. 293. 299.
Kántaka I, 363 ff. II, 205 ff.
Kántimati I, 367 ff. II, 223 ff.
Kántipuri I, 136.
Kánwa I, 181. II, 80. 364.
Kanydkubja I, 186. III, 215.
Kanyápuri I, 136.
Kapála I, 27.
Kápálika II, 294. III, 193.
Kapila I, 42. 52. 135. II, 249.
Kapilá I, 38. 390.
Kapila tirtha I, 13 f.
Kardlí I, 163.
Karapála II, 35.
Karapatra I, 386.
Karéri I, 163.
Karaíaka II, 12. 139.
Karburd I, 390.
Kardama I, 124. 150.
Kardama I, 374 ff. II, 263. 265. 269.
Karkaíaka II, 197.
Karma III, 120. 124. 132 ff. 141. 152. 329.
Karmakánda III, 326.
Karmayoga I, 43.
Karmi III, 120.
Karña I, 26 f. 285. 292 f. 297. 303. 319 ff. 338. II, 296.
Karñalekhá I, 373 ff. See *Kanakalekhd*.
Karña parva I, 293.
Karñánuta II, 210.
Karpura II, 147.
Karpúra III, 174.
Kártaviya I, 309.

Kártaviryárjuna I, 105.
Kártika I, 66. 68 ff. II, 397.
Kártika máhátmya I, 64 ff. 80.
Kártika vrata I, 69.
Kártikeya I, 64. 105. 164. 183. II, 171. 234. 240. 352 f. 366. III, 194.
Káruska I, 127.
Káia I, 151.
Kashmír I, 137. 158. II, 111 f. III, 194. 226.
Káií I, 42. 60. 138. 271. 366 f. II, 189. 223. 225. 342.
Káiíkhańda I, 40. II, 342.
Káiindíhaiarmaňa III, 234. 237.
Káiípuri I, 136. II, 221.
Káiírdja I, 273.
Káiíciruddcalí III, 211.
Kaiyapa I, 11 f. 30. 33. 46. 67. 105. 108. 126 f. 130. 150. 209 f. 310. II, 157 f.
Kaía I, 163.
Kaíá II, 18.
Kaídha I, 216. 219. 223. 225.
Kathámrita nidhi II, 79.
Kathánaca I, 152.
Kathá sarit ságara I, 157. 167. 351. II, 99 ff. 108 ff. 342. III, 175. 177.
Kathopanishad III, 321.
Kátyáyana I, 90. 165. III, 16. 47 f. 67 f. 175 ff. 179. 202. 221. 311. 321 ff.
Kaumdra I, 148.
Kaumárabhritya I, 274 f.
Kauntrya III, 113.
Kaurava I, 308. III, 115.

Kauśámba mańdala I, 163.
Kauśdmbí I, 162 f. 192 f. 195 ff.
  215. 226. 239. II, 60. 113. 121.
  129. 156.
Kaushdrara III, 107.
Kautilya I, 354. II, 170.
Kdreri I, 60. 241. II, 169. 251.
Kdreri mdhátmya I, 85.
Karirdja I, 183.
Karya I, 154.
Kdrya I, 119. 343.
Káryádaráa I, 346.
Káya I, 275.
Kdyachikitsá I, 274 f.
Kdydrohańa kshetra I, 149.
Kdyastha III, 221.
Keddra I, 115.
Kekaya I, 44.
Kenopanishad III, 320.
Kerala I, 241.
Keralotpatti III, 190. 195.
Keśara II, 378 f.
Keśava II, 302. III, 221.
Keśi I, 110.
Khanati II, 219.
Kharra II, 380.
Khali vatśara II, 221.
Kinnara II, 316. 365. 368.
Kinśuka I, 302.
Kirttiśira II, 186.
Kirttiśena I, 180.
Kirttisinha III, 205.
Kokila III, 174.
Kolapura I, 62.
Konkańa II, 281.
Konkaśa III, 201.
Kośala II, 19 f. 282. 288.

Koshadáśa I, 371. II, 245 f. 261.
Koshddhyaksha II, 35.
Koshiapdla II, 53.
Koti II, 303.
Koliratha I, 72.
Kratu I, 127. 150.
Krauncha II, 366.
Kridama I, 108.
Kripa I, 308. 313. 322.
Kripá I, 308.
Kripáńa II, 301.
Kripararmd I, 192.
Krishńa I, 11. 14. 16. 26. 53. 60.
  63. 65 ff. 89 ff. 132 ff. 142. 206.
  284 ff. 313. 326. 345. 352. II.
  192. 296. 308. 328. 355. 357 f.
  III, 97. 102. 107. 112 ff. 342.
Krishńá (river) I, 60. 68.
Krishńá (leech) I, 390.
Krishńa dvaipdyana I, 121. 123.
  128. 140. 278. III, 335.
Krishńajanma khańda I, 93. 107—
  118.
Krishńa rdya I, 318.
Krishńa svdmi III. 126.
Krita III, 48.
Kritaghna I, 167.
Kritdnta III, 153.
Kritararmd I, 299. 303.
Krita yuga I, 152.
Kritrima III, 47 f. 57.
Krittiká II, 242. 352.
Kshapańaka III, 168.
Kshdra I, 382. 388.
Kshatriya I, 137. 140 f. 244. 302.
  334. II, 366. III, 94. 166.
Kshemankari devi I, 22.

INDEX. 365

Kshepaṇi II, 301.
Kshetra III, 144 ff.
Kshetraja III, 47.
Kshetrajña III, 144 f.
Kshīrasvāmī III, 138, 203 f.
Kubjd I, 38.
Kukkura I, 220.
Kulachandra I, 183.
Kuladharma III, 117 f.
Kuladwīpa I, 352.
Kulapālikā I, 361 f.
Kulastrī III, 118.
Kultūka bhaṭṭa III, 45.
Kumāra II, 5.
Kumāragupta II, 281.
Kumārapāla III, 210.
Kumārasambhava II, 315.
Kumārasvāmī I, 164, 166, 174, 183.
Kumārikā khaṇḍa I, 183, III, 197.
Kumārila bhaṭṭa III, 194 ff.
Kumbhīpāka III, 96.
Kumuda II, 328.
Kunda II, 356, 373 f.
Kuṇḍala I, 35.
Kunjara I, 37, 39.
Kuntala II, 280 f.
Kurdi II, 79.
Kūrmadāneshtra III, 96.
Kūrma purāṇa I, 25, 145, 148 f.
Kuru I, 290 ff. 336, II, 293, 307, 356 ff. III, 103, 115, 118, 120.
Kurujāṅgala I, 290, 308.
Kurukshetra I, 35, 37, 290, 308, II, 308, 356 f. III, 115.
Kurush II, 98.
Kuruvaka II, 373, 376.

Kuśa I, 47 ff. 51 f. II, 360.
Kuśadwīpa II, 341.
Kuśika I, 149, III, 221.
Kusumadhanved II, 282.
Kusumapura I, 253, 351, II, 223.
Kuṭaja II, 319.
Kuthdrikd I, 386.
Kuvalaydnanda I, 344.
Kuvalayāśva I, 42.
Kuvera I, 41, 110, 162 f. 210, 213, II, 50, 61, 117, 225, III, 312, 316 f. 322 f. 365, 368, 372, 377, 379 f.
Kuveradatta I, 361 f. II, 198 ff. 202, 255 f.

Labdhapratiśśa II, 44.
Labdhapraśīdama II, 44.
Labdhapraśamana II, 2, 44.
Laghupatanaka II, 28.
Lakshmaṇa II, 315 f.
Lakshmī I, 25, 56, 59 f. 62, 65, 70, 76, 101 ff. 165, 214, II, 50, 58, 266, 380.
Lakuli I, 149.
Lalita indra keśari I, 18.
Lāngali II, 357.
Lāngora narsinh deo I, 18.
Lankā I, 14, 29, 41, 47, 207 ff. II, 391.
Lāla I, 241, 855, II, 175 ff.
Latakana misra III, 237.
Ldiydyana III, 321.
Lava I, 47, 51 f.
Lavaṇa I, 47.
Lechhaka I, 235, 237, 242.
Laya II, 66, 78.

Lekha I, 154.
Lekhana I, 382.
Likucha II, 270.
Lūd I, 147.
Lādvati II, 231. III, 229.
Linga I, 37. 61. 63 f. II, 57. III, 201. 341.
Linga purāna II, 522. III, 122.
Lobha III, 117.
Lodh II, 378 f.
Lohajangha I, 206 ff.
Loka I, 40 f. 73. 98.
Lokāloka I, 39.
Lokāyatika III, 151.
Lomaharsha I, 88.
Lomaharshana I, 9. 15. 23. 130. 140. 278.
Lomaśa I, 55.
Lopa III, 208.
Lopamudrā II, 224.

Madana III, 174.
Madanamanchukā II, 138. 158.
Mādhava I, 240 ff. II, 156.
Mādhava (comm.) III; 172. 192 ff. 221 f. 226. 250.
Mādhavī II, 214 ff. 376.
Mādhavī (lex.) III, 204.
Mādhavīya dhātuvritti III, 192.
Madhu I, 14. 30. 32. 42. 71. 127. II, 58.
Madhumādhavī III, 201.
Madhupura II, 71.
Madhusrā III, 242.
Madhusma II, 71.
Madhvāchārya I, 30. 143. III, 182.

Madhya II, 303.
Madhyabhedī II, 306.
Madhyamika III, 194.
Madra I, 285. 299 ff. 338 f. II, 296.
Mādrī I, 279. 297. 325.
Madura II, 79.
Magadha I, 126. 162. 168. 215. 230. 285 ff. 307. 351. II, 6. 121. 160 ff. 177. 211. 236. III, 187.
Māgadha I, 133. 135. 141. 327.
Māgha I, 54 ff. 62. 102. 153.
Māgha kāvya III, 250.
Māgha māhātmya I, 80.
Mahābalipura II, 369.
Mahābhārata I, 6. 31. 36. 42. 43. 55. 63. 99. 108. 116. 199. 122. 133. 137. 139. 141. 144. 192. 277 ff. 316. II, 34. 138. 241. 293. 298. 300. 307 f. 356. 358. 366. III, 16. 102. 111. 117. 178. 274. 303. 323. 327. 336.
Mahādeva I, 101. 149 f. 160. 170. 179. 335. 341. II, 346. 366. III, 113.
Mahādeśa I, 88. 77. 355. II, 57. 157. 162. 177.
Mahālakshmī I, 65. 70.
Mahāmāyā I, 45. 58.
Mahānadī I, 90.
Mahāndiaka I, 189. 345.
Mahānidrā I, 59.
Mahānubhāva I, 127.
Mahāpadma II, 380.
Mahāpralaya II, 392.
Mahāprasthānika parva I, 287.
Mahar I, 40.

Mahdrdshira I, 376 f.
Mahdratha II, 294. III, 116.
Mahdsena I, 229.
Mahat I, 10. 23. 148.
Mahdtala I, 45.
Mahdtattwa I, 145 f.
Mdhdtmya I, 17. 91. 92.
Mahdvira III, 229.
Mahdyogi I, 149.
Mahdyuga I, 121. 128. 149. 151. 153.
Mahendra I, 240 f. 309 f.
Mahendrdditya II, 158.
Mahehcara I, 36. 159 f. II, 162.
Makehcara (jur.) III, 47.
Maheicara (lex.) III, 127. 172. 215 f. 223 f.
Mahidhara I, 198. III, 205.
Mahilaropya II, 7. 10 f.
Mahishdsura I, 29.
Mdhishmati I, 39. 62. 69. 377 f. II, 282 f.
Maind II, 386.
Maindka II, 266.
Maithild III, 14.
Maithili II, 391.
Maitreya I, 88. 120. 121. 130.
Makara I, 58. II, 45. 47. 146. III, 285. 306. 380.
Makaradanshird I, 211.
Makaranda II, 156.
Makaravyuha II, 306.
Mdla II, 328 f.
Mdld I, 188.
Mdlakdra II, 389.
Mdlati I, 68.
Mdlatimddhava II, 152. 156. 341. 348.

Mdlava I, 241. 292. 297. 352. 368. II, 161 f. 164. 179. 211. 232. 377 f. 349. 352. III, 171.
Mdlavati I, 68.
Mdlavikdgnimitra II, 315.
Malaya II, 224. 231. 264.
Málika II, 35.
Nalindika II, 355. III, 203. 209. 211 f. 216. 221. 223. 231.
Ndhyacdn I, 162. 179. 184. 188 f. II, 117 ff.
Mánakála II, 173 f.
Manasd I, 101. 109.
Mdnasa I, 37. II, 326. 372.
Mdnasdra I, 356 ff. 368. II, 161 f. 180. 182 ff.
Mánasarovara II, 326. 366. 372.
Mdnasarega II, 187.
Manddkini I, 261. II, 352.
Mandala I, 64. II, 306. III, 323. 331. 337. 341. 346.
Maidaldgra I, 386.
Mandaleicara I, 31.
Mandana mitra III, 193.
Manddra II, 377.
Mandavisha II, 43 f.
Mdndhdtri I, 42 ff. 78.
Mandodaka II, 187.
Mdndúkyopanishad III, 329.
Mangald I, 103.
Mangdliká II, 205.
Manibhadra I, 224. II, 49. 51 ff. 162. 221. 236.
Manidhamus I, 132.
Manikarniki I, 366. 388. II, 221. 231 ff.
Manipushpaka III, 117.

Manjurddini I, III f. II, 282 f.
Manmaya III, 134.
Manojara I, 127.
Manthara II, 30 ff. 67. 71.
Mantra I, 56 f. 84. 97. II. 380.
  III, 315. 322. 326 ff. 335. 337 f.
Mantrayupta I, 352. 373 f. II,
  164. 262.
Mantramahodadhi I, 84.
Mantri II, 35.
Manu I, 10. 23. 114. 123. 154.
  II, 6. 356. 397. III, 29. 42 f.
  45 ff. 50 ff. 67. 71. 87. 94. 101.
  215. 321. 336. 341.
Manu (progen.) I, 89. 127. III, 327.
Manu chákshusha I, 125 ff.
Manu sváyambhuva I, 10 f. 25. 60.
Manu vairancata I, 46.
Manvantara I, 11. 25. 46. 86.
  121 f. 127. 144. 149.
Manyamána I, 151.
Marakata II, 380.
Marichi I, 9. 46. 124. 150. 359.
  II, 189.
Márisha I, 10.
Márkaṇḍeya I, 13. 28. 30. 150.
  II, 187.
Márkaṇḍeya purána II, 380.
Marutta I, 42.
Masaka III, 321.
Nasádi II, 90. 93. 97 f. 103. 106.
Mátali I, 36.
Matanga II, 157.
Mátanga II, 172 ff.
Mathurá I, 17. 111. 115 f. 136.
  204. 208 ff. 283. 294. 307. II.
  256. 342.

Mathureśa III, 207. 233.
Mati III, 154.
Maitrá II, 66. 78.
Mátrámaria III, 121.
Matsya avatára I, 23. 46. 58. 67.
Mátsya purána I, 9. 25. 46. 152.
  II, 322. 359. III, 327.
Mattakdla II, 175 f.
Maukhya I, 148.
Maurya II, 272.
Mausala parva I, 287.
Mdyá I, 30. 63. 99 f. 112.
Máyá (city) II, 342.
Mdyana III, 192.
Mayandiri I, 241.
Mdydsura I, 167.
Mayúra III, 174.
Medhá I, 125.
Medini III, 160. 204. 209 ff. 219 ff.
  231 ff. 236. 240 ff.
Medinikara III, 127. 201. 213 f.
  220 f.
Meghadúta II, 50. 152. 310 ff. III,
  250. 303.
Meghanáda I, 38.
Meghankuśa I, 62.
Mekala II, 333.
Mekalakanyaká II, 333.
Mend I, 151.
Meru I, 30. 149. 151 f. 287. 315.
  II, 332. 360. III, 142.
Mesdr I, 157.
Mi'at dmil II, 392.
Mimánsd I, 59. 190. II, 30. III,
  196. 210.
Mimánsaka III, 193.
Mitákshard I, 8. 87. III, 9. 14.

29. 47. 51. 53. 61. 73. 76. 87 ff. 91. 125. 215.
Mithild I, 353. 365 f. II, 164 ff. 189. 210 ff. 301. III, 49. 57.
Mitrabheda II, 9. 10.
Mitragupta I, 352. 371 ff. II, 189. 241 f. 262.
Mitraka I, 149.
Mitraldbha II, 9. 28. 142.
Mitraprdpti II, 28.
Mitrasarmd I, 377. II, 232 ff. 238.
Mlechchha I, 76. 118. 120. 137. 242.
Mohini I, 112.
Moksha II, 8.
Mokshadharma I, 286.
Mrichchhakati II, 158.
Mrigdnkadatta II, 151.
Mrigdrati I, 192 f. 195.
Mrikanda I, 59. 150.
Mudga I, 390.
Mudgala I, 307.
Mudrd rdkshasa I, 175. III, 324.
Mugdhabodha III, 250. 270. 274.
Muktdmukta II, 290.
Muktdphalaketu II, 158.
Mukti I, 96.
Mukunda II, 880.
Mukula III, 203 f. 206. 242.
Mülaprakriti I, 98. III, 146.
Müllasanhitd I, 130.
Mundakopanishad III, 108 f. 322.
Murala I, 241. II, 281.
Murchhana II, 66. 77.
Mürchhen khan III, 233.
Müsd khan III, 233.
Mushikd I, 391.

Nabhdga I, 127.
Ndâlyantra I, 384.
Ndga I, 45. 194. 203. 337. II, 22. 60. 130. 132. 147. 152.
Nagadvabhatta II, 80.
Ndgakanyd I, 332.
Nâgdkhya I, 311.
Naganadi II, 338.
Nagapdla II, 281.
Nahusha I, 32.
Naimisha I, 137.
Naimishdranya I, 9. 22. 71. 92. 140. 145. 278.
Naimittika III, 106.
Naiydyika III, 144. 191.
Nakra I, 385.
Nakshatra I, 153.
Nakula I, 279. 291. 297. 321. 324.
Nakula (animal) II, 53. 76.
Nala I, 381. 384. 311. II, 138. III, 303.
Nalakurrra I, 110.
Ndlijangha II, 285 ff.
Nâlika II, 239.
Ndma III, 320.
Ndmamdld III, 218. 231. 238.
Namuchi I, 59.
Nândrtha III, 223. 232.
Ndndrthakosha III, 160.
Ndndrtharatnamdld III, 240 f.
Ndndrthasangraha III, 210.
Nanda I, 109 f. 113 f. 118. 137. 165. 178 ff. II, 46. 131. III, 324.
Nandd I, 28.
Nandana I, 333.
Nandanidhi II, 380.

Nanda paṇḍita III, 14.
Nandidera I, 191.
Nandini I, 20. 47.
Nara I, 27.
Nārācha II, 299 f.
Nārada I, 42 ff. 51. 56. 62 ff. 78. 92. 97. 119. 235. 237. 241. II, 34. 386. III, 18. 21. 47 f. 67 f. 72. 90 f.
Narahari paṇḍita III, 236.
Naraka I, 126.
Nāraedkanadatta I, 192. 242 ff. II, 113. 121. 129. 138. 156 ff. 187.
Nārāyaṇa I, 10. 30. 35. 56. 60. 83. 92 ff. 118. 139. II, 161.
Nārāyaṇa chakravartti III, 207.
Narishyanta I, 127.
Narmadā I, 35. 37. 50. 60. 62. 63. 77. 81. 137. 204. 240 f. 280. II, 320. 329 f. 331.
Narttaka I, 327.
Nasr II, 23.
Nāstika I, 376.
Nata I, 327.
Navamālikā I, 379. II, 236.
Naranadi II, 338.
Narananda I, 161.
Niddna I, 270.
Nidānasthāna I, 274.
Nidhi II, 30. 380.
Nidhipālita II, 195.
Nigraha I, 384.
Nīla I, 49. 318. II, 380.
Nīlakaṇṭha I, 141. 151. III, 116. 125. 318.
Nimba II, 214.

Nimbasati II, 248. 251.
Nīpa II, 873.
Nīpdia III, 320.
Nīr III, 127. 137.
Nīrdhāra III, 150.
Nirdwandwa III, 121.
Nirguṇa I, 147.
Nirmala III, 148.
Nirukta III, 311. 316. 318.
Nirrdna III, 122. 325.
Nirreda III, 187 f.
Nirvindhyā II. 340.
Niryogakshema III, 125.
Niṣhdda I, 35. 256.
Nishadha I, 137.
Nishkha III, 151.
Niṣṣreyas III, 137 f.
Nitambavati II, 248. 256 ff.
Niti I, 86. 354. II, 6. 85. III, 151.
Nitiśāstra II, 6. 9.
Nitya III, 106.
Nivrdta III, 139.
Nivritti III, 150.
Niyodhaka I, 327.
Nrisinha I, 52 f. II, 181.
Nrisinha avatāra I, 59.
Nūshirvān II, 88 f. III, 186.
Nydsa III, 67.

Om I, 58.
Omkāra I, 37.

Pada III, 286.
Padārthakaumudi III, 207.
Pddmakalpa I, 30.
Padmandbhadatta III, 207. 232.

INDEX.

Padmanidhi II, 50. 380.
Pádma purána I, 8f. 21-82. 121. 141.
Padmavati I, 236. 238 f. 242. II, 121. 158.
Padmodbhava I, 252. II, 160. 177.
Pádukd III, 229.
Paila I, 128 f.
Paisáchi bhāshā I, 160.-184. 189. II, 119.
Paksha II, 303.
Pakshaja II, 321.
Pálaka I, 200. II, 136 ff.
Paldia I, 70.
Pallipati II, 27.
Panava III, 116.
Pánchajanya III, 117.
Panchála I, 291. 293. 297 f. 304. 307. 310 f. 395. 397. II, 219.
Pánchardtra I, 119.
Panchasikha I, 184.
Panchatantra I, 213. II, 36. 87 ff. 132. 144 ff. III, 178. 185 f.
Panchopákhyána II, 5. 78.
Pándava I, 82. 280 ff. II, 307. 308. 357. III, 103. 115.
Pándu I, 123. 228. 278 ff. II, 293. 356. 358.
Pándya I, 241. II, 78.
Pánini I, 20. 165. 169. II, 30. 32 f. 118. III, 177. 204. 206. 221. 279. 315. 318. 324. 336.
Páninya I, 174.
Parabrahma I, 83.
Parama I, 147.
Parama brahma I, 180.
Paramátmá I, 93. 120. 147.

Parásara I, 120 ff. 139. 218. II, 6. 275.
Parasurâma I, 38 f. 69. 106 f. 291. 309. 332. II, 306.
Parichitagṛdhakágama II, 77.
Parikshit I, 133. 192.
Párshada II, 35.
Paritrâta II, 219.
Paropakári I, 244 f. 254.
Párśvantíka III, 224.
Parvata II, 308.
Pareati II, 338. 340.
Párvatí I, 38. 52 f. 56. 58. 62. 70. 103 ff. 162. 332. II, 117. 352. 360. 376.
Paryāpta III, 116.
Pāśa II, 301.
Páshanda II, 57.
Páśupata I, 59.
Paśupati I, 59.
Pátála I, 11. 22. 31. 45 f. 126. 194 f. 286. II, 22. 131. 132. 173. 344.
Pátála khanda I, 8. 22. 45 - 53. 78 f.
Pátali I, 168.
Pátalipura I, 351.
Pátaliputra I, 164 ff. 185. 351. 379. II, 11. 49. 115. 133. 282. III, 231. 324.
Pátanjala I, 120. III, 109.
Pathyápathya I, 270.
Pattabandha I, 228.
Patti II, 292.
Paiśáa II, 301.
Pátúnakara III, 221.
Paulastya I, 141.

24*

Paulkia siddhânta I, 152.
Paunarbhava III, 48.
Pavitra III, 117.
Pauńdraka I, 138.
Pavrava I, 299 f.
Paushkara khańda I, 22.
Paushkara mâhâtmya I, 27. 74.
Pavitra I, 84.
Payoshńi I, 49.
Phala III, 124.
Pilpai II, 3. 86 ff. 139.
Pingala I, 90. II, 30. III, 317 f.
Pingalâ I, 390.
Pingalaka II, 12. 129.
Piśâcha I, 41. 55 f. II, 117 f. 128. 133.
Pitâmahâ II, 192.
Pitri I, 26. 111. 125. 150 f. 154. II, 389. III, 344.
Prabhanjana I, 28.
Prabhâsa I, 39.
Prabodhachandrodaya III, 139. 196.
Prachańdavarmâ I, 377 f. II, 289 ff.
Prâchetasa I, 10. 125. 340.
Pradakshińa II, 865.
Pradhâna I, 10. 23. 93. 123. 145.
Pradyota I, 230. II, 341.
Pradyumna I, 14. 116.
Prahladravarmâ I, 353. 365 f. II, 164. 166. 189. 211 f. 219 f.
Prahlâda I, 31 ff. 59.
Prahrâda I, 31.
Prajâpati I, 25. 30. 124. 126. 272. II, 192.
Prâkŕita I, 148.

Prâkŕitâ manoramâ III, 177.
Prakŕiti I, 24. 58. 92 f. 98 - 103. 128. 145 f. II, 283. III, 119. 144. 146.
Prakŕiti khańda I, 93. 98 - 103.
Pralamba I, 110.
Pramaddropya II, 23.
Pramati I, 852. 369 ff. II, 164. 189. 233.
Pramlochâ I, 14.
Prâńakara III, 221.
Prâsa II, 300.
Praśavishyadhvaṁ III, 133.
Praśnopanishad III, 329.
Praśnottaramâlâ II, 315.
Prastha II, 251.
Prastûta I, 127.
Prasûti I, 25. 124.
Pratigraha II, 303.
Prâtiśâkhya I, 164. III, 312. 317 f. 320.
Pratishthâ I, 162.
Pratishthâna I, 62. 169. 180. 185. 190. II, 120. 151.
Pravira I, 308.
Pravŕitti III, 150.
Prayâga I, 37. 55 f. 62. 72. II, 350. 361.
Priśadhra I, 122.
Prishat I, 307. 310.
Prishtha II, 303.
Prîtamâ II, 292.
Prithâ I, 279 f. 293. 312. 319. 321. 325. 333.
Prithivî I, 125. 145.
Prithu I, 11. 25. 34 f. 38. 67 ff. 125. 140 f.

INDEX. 373

Prĭthuga I, 127.
Priyadarŝ́i III, 836.
Priyamvadd II, 211 f. 215.
Prĭgarrata I, 124. 127.
Protkalabhŕitya II, 35.
Pújyapdda III, 229.
Pulaha I, 127. 150.
Pulastya I, 23. 26. 30. 127. 150.
Pulindn I, 135. 180.
Pulinda I, 136. 204. 215. 228.
Pumdn I, 99.
Puṅ́darika II, 328.
Puṅ́darikamukhi I, 320.
Pumira II, 219 f.
Puṅ́yaka vrata I, 103.
Puráṅa I, 1—155. 178. 181 f. 350. 354. 366. II, 29. 170. 329. 336. 351. III, 46. 95. 97. 111. 115. 127. 209. 306 f. 342.
Puráṅa sanhitá I, 130.
Puráṅa sarvasva II, 318. 320 f. 359.
Purandhara I, 127.
Puri I, 17.
Púrṅabhadra I, 367 f. II, 222. 223 f.
Purohita II, 35. 274. III, 176.
Puru I, 89. 127. 291.
Púru I, 36 f. 299.
Purúravas I, 4l. 151.
Purusha I, 24. 58. 99. 127. III, 119. 141 f. 144. 147 f.
Purushottama I, 9. 11. 42. II, 19. III, 148.
Purushottama deva III, 211 f. 212.
Purushottama kshetra I, 13. 16 f. 49. 79.

Púrva khaṅda I, 19.
Púrva plihiká I, 342. 357.
Pushkala I, 50.
Pushkara I, 20. 27 f. 37 f. 74 f. 77. 79. II, 322.
Pushkardvarttaka II, 321 f.
Pushkariká II, 215 f.
Pushpa I, 186.
Pushpabhadrá I, 105.
Pushpadanta I, 162. 179. 184. 188 f. II, 117 f. 328. III, 176.
Pushpaka II, 23 ff.
Pushpakaraṅdini II, 311.
Pushpapura I, 351. 367. II, 211.
Pushpapuri II, 160. 162. 164.
Pushpodbhara I, 353. 355 f. II, 168. 177. 181 f. 185. 189.
Pushti I, 124.
Putraka I, 166 ff. II, 133.
Putrikaputra III, 47.

Rabhasa III, 202. 220.
Rabhasdla III, 220.
Rddhd I, 53. 70. 75. 84. 91 ff. 293. 339. III, 97.
Rddhdkánta deva III, 235.
Rádhiká I, 103.
Rágamanjari I, 362 f. II, 209 ff.
Rághava II, 327.
Raghu I, 47. II, 326 f. 364.
Raghumaṅi bhaṭṭáchárya III, 159. 163 f.
Raghunandana III, 72.
Raghupati II, 326.
Raghuvansa I, 47. 78. II, 315. 327.
Raikka III, 105 f.

Rájadeva III, 204.
Rájadharma I, 286.
Rájagiri I, 357. II, 180.
Rájagriha II, 22.
Rájahansa I, 351 ff. 366. 379. II, 160 ff. 226.
Rájanighańtu III, 235 f. 238.
Rajas III, 124 f.
Rájasa I, 9.
Rájasúya I, 79. 282.
Rájataranginí I, 182. II, 111 f.
Rájardhana I, 352 ff. II, 169. 171. 182 ff. 221. 225. 231. 241. 261. 269.
Raji I, 26.
Rajoguna I, 146. III, 147. 153.
Rákshasa I, 51. 55. 207 f. 239. 242. 333. 372. II, 41. 71 f. 78. 133 ff. 144. 236. 260 f.
Rákshasí I, 296.
Raktdíkha II, 37.
Ráma I, 14 ff. 29. 32. 46 ff. 50 ff. 60. 72. 74. 78. 106. 142. 182. 207 f. 242. 273. 309 f. 328. II, 60. 315 f. 326 f. 391 f. III, 195.
Rámachandra I, 22. 83. 309.
Rámadeva III, 174.
Rámagiri II, 815 f. 327.
Rámahrada I, 34.
Rámandíka II, 325 f.
Rámandíka vidyáedchaspati III, 208.
Rámánuja I, 78 f. 142. III, 277.
Rámasahasranáma I, 16.
Rámasarmaśa III, 237.
Rámdírama II, 372. III, 138. 166. 205 f.

Rámatarkárágliá III, 208.
Rámatírtha II, 167.
Rámdyasa I, 6. 29. 42. 47 f. 60. 83. 119. 144. 210. 277. 328. 346. II, 315. 360. 364 f. 388. III, 100. 179.
Ramayantikd II, 215.
Rámésvara I, 75.
Rámésvara sarmana III, 231.
Rantideva II, 353. 355. III, 219.
Rasa II, 66. 78.
Rdsa I, 95 f.
Rasakoila I, 17.
Rasamańtala I, 95.
Rasátala I, 45.
Rasavidyá I, 270.
Rásdyana I, 271 f.
Bathin II, 294.
Ratnagrica I, 42.
Ratnamdlá III, 213 f. 219 f. 222. 235.
Ratnapura I, 246. II, 20.
Ratnavati II, 251 ff.
Ratnodbhara I, 352 ff. II, 160. 167 f. 177.
Baurara I, 55.
Rauhisha II, 208.
Rácana I, 14. 41. 46. 48. 207 f. 210. II, 66. 316. 360.
Rdyamukuta II, 308. III, 138. 203 f. 216 f. 233.
Rerd I, 37. 241. II, 284. 331 ff.
Revati II, 358.
Ribhu III, 345.
Richas (pl.) I, 120.
Richika II, 281.
Rigveda I, 128 f. III, 309 ff. 321 ff. 332 ff. 339.

INDEX. 375

Ripunjaya II, 223.
Rishabha I, 262.
Rishi I, 9. 14. 23. 25. 52. 55. 60. 66. 69 f. 92. 104. 127. 145. 150. 278. II, 191. 333. 353. 368. 380. III, 323. 334 f.
Rishika I, 55.
Rishii II, 300.
Ritusanhdra II, 315. 325. 335. 362. 375.
Rohandchala II, 26.
Rohini I, 70. III, 183.
Rokh I, 192.
Romaharshana I, 130.
Ruchi I, 25. 124.
Rudeghi II, 93.
Rudra I, 59. 96. 127. 146. 149. 272. II, 5.
Rudra (lox.) III, 220.
Rukmángada I, 50.
Rukmi I, 116.
Rukmini I, 116.
Rumanwan I, 208 f. 215. 227 f. 230. 233. 235 f.
Rúpavika I, 206. 211 ff.
Rúpatikhd II, 135 f.
Ruchla I, 149.

Śabda III, 263.
Śabdachandriká III, 234. 237.
Śabdakalpadruma III, 285. 242.
Śabdamáld II, 380. III, 231 f.
Śabdaratndeali II, 380. III, 207. 219 f. 227. 240 f.
Śabdárnara II, 379. III, 212. 213.
Śabdárthakalpataru III, 234. 242.

Śabdasandarbhasindhu III, 234. 240. 242.
Śabdaidstra II, 8.
Śaiva I, 75. 80. 112. 114. 138. 143. 155. 378. III, 193.
Śairdgdrá I, 32.
Śaka I, 292.
Śáka III, 179.
Śakala III, 317.
Śákambhari devi I, 20.
Sakatála I, 175 ff.
Sikhá III, 317. 333.
Śákini II, 259.
Śakuntalá I, 40. 78. II, 311. 317. 364. 377. 383. III, 272.
Śákta I, 9. 109.
Śakti I, 9. 100 f. 122. III, 96 f.
Śaktideva I, 245. 255 ff. II, 126 ff.
Śaktikundra II, 250 ff.
Śaktimatí I, 181. 223 f.
Śaktivega I, 244. 268.
Śaktri I, 59.
Śaktri I, 122.
Śakuni I, 202. 218.
Śálayráma I, 49. 53. 61. 66. 78 f. 113. II, 324. III, 95 f.
Śálagráma kshetra I, 31. 43.
Śáláká I, 275. 382. 384 f.
Śálákya I, 274. 276.
Sálicdhana I, 162. 181 f. II, 120. III, 179. 182.
Śalya I, 271 ff. 285. 290. 318 f. II, 294. 296.
Salya parva I, 285.
Sambhu I, 156. 188. 212. II, 360.
Sani I, 47. 104 f.
Śanka I, 59. 67.

Śankara I, 93. 114. 244. 263.
Śankara (man's name) II, 211.
Śankarāchārya I, 178. 347. III,
105. 108. 113. 119. 122 ff. 128.
134. 139. 140. 142. 145. 150.
174. 188 ff. 210.
Śankaradigvijaya III, 192.
Śankarajaya III, 192.
Śankarasvedmi I, 246 ff. III, 190.
Śankaravijaya III, 193.
Śankha II, 360.
Śankhanidhi II, 50.
Śānkhāyana III, 321.
Śanku III, 168.
Śankhumukhī I, 390.
Śāndapāyana I, 88. 130.
Śāntanu I, 122. 291. 305. 313.
Śāntiparva I, 286.
Śara I, 303. II, 352 f.
Śarabha II, 362.
Śaradd tilaka I, 34. II, 50.
Śaradvat I, 308.
Śaras II, 373.
Śarayū I, 60.
Śārīra sthāna I, 274.
Śārnga II, 397.
Śārngadhara I, 388.
Śarydtī I, 127.
Śāstra I, 382. 385.
Śāśvata III, 219.
Śatabuddhi II, 68 f.
Śatadhriti I, 308.
Śatadru I, 127.
Śataghni II, 302.
Śatahali II, 319 f.
Śataka I, 345. II, 335.
Śatakarni I, 134.

Śatānanda I, 293.
Śatānika I, 19. 192. 272. II, 60.
Śatapatha brāhmaṇa III, 311.
326 f. 331.
Śatarūpā I, 10. 124.
Śatrughna I, 47 ff.
Śaudra III, 48.
Śaunaka I, 19. 23. 71. 92. 367.
II, 225. III, 323 ff.
Śacali II, 300.
Śavara II, 165.
Śayyddhyakṣa II, 35.
Śayyāpāla II, 35.
Śephālikā I, 387.
Śeṣa I, 39 f. 42. 45. 52.
Śeṣa (n.) I, 348.
Śikhandī I, 296.
Śikhī III, 316.
Śini I, 299. 344.
Śirīṣa II, 878 f.
Śiśira II, 373.
Śiśumāra I, 153. 329. II, 146.
Śiśupāla I, 116.
Śiva I, 12 f. 17. 19. 21. 26 ff. 42 ff.
50 ff. 90 ff. 138. 142. 145. 148 f.
151. 154. 158 f. 161. 160. 169.
174. 182. 185. 191. 212. 217.
243. 328. 330. 359. 366. 376.
II, 5. 66. 79. 116 f. 136. 157.
172 f. 192. 197. 224. 323. 344.
347 ff. 360 ff. 376. 399. III,
95 ff. 192. 176. 193. 341.
Śiva (man) I, 246 ff.
Śivalinga I, 355. II, 369.
Śivapurāṇa I, 89.
Śivarāmatripāṭhī I, 342.
Śivaśarmā I, 31.

Śiri I, 42. 292, 332. II, 251.
Soṅa I, 251.
Śrdddha I, 26. 29. 75. 124 f. 177.
 III, 12 f.
Śramaṇaka II, 20 f.
Śrāmaṇikā II, 237 f.
Śrauta III, 333.
Śrautasūtra III, 320 f.
Śrdeaka III, 224.
Śrdeaṅa I, 100. 153.
Śūdrastī I, 284. 369 f. II, 236 ff.
Śreyas III, 138.
Śrī I, 125. 241. III, 154.
Śrībhoja III, 174.
Śrīchandradeva III, 215.
Śrīdaṅdī I, 347.
Śrīdatta II, 320.
Śrīdharasvāmī III, 108. 116. 119.
 125. 130. 137. 140. 150. 155.
Śrīdhṛtisiṁha III, 212.
Śrīgdlikd I, 303 f. II, 304 ff.
Śrīkaṇṭha I, 38.
Śrīkarṇa deva III, 186 f.
Śrīkīrttidd I, 70.
Śrīkṛishṇa III, 215.
Śrīkṛishṇa tarkālaṅkāra III, 17.
 72.
Śrīkuṇḍala I, 55.
Śriṅga I, 382.
Śṛiṅgabhuja II, 134 ff.
Śṛiṅgagiri III, 180.
Śṛṅgāratilaka II, 315.
Śṛñjaya I, 119. 235. 307.
Śrīpativarmā I, 183.
Śrī palimān I, 180.
Śrīraṅga I, 58. 60. 81.
Śrīśaila I, 62. 85.

Śrishṭi khanda I, 22—30. 32. 73 f.
 76 ff. 141.
Śrotasya III, 128.
Śruta III, 128.
Śrutabodha II, 315.
Śrutadhara III, 170.
Śrutārthā I, 180.
Śrutdyus I, 25.
Śruti III, 97. 128. 316.
Subhadisiri III, 88.
Śūdra I, 56. 114. 136. 175. 292.
 III, 48. 94. 113. 133. 255.
Śūdraka I, 367. II, 225. III,
 185. 197.
Śuka I, 53.
Śukasaptati I, 157. II, 108.
Śukra I, 26. II, 6. 275.
Sunakśepha III, 327.
Śūraka III, 186.
Śūrasena I, 292 f. II, 256.
Śvaita I, 149.
Śveta I, 29. 148 f.
Śvetadvīpa I, 58. 118.
Śvetalohita I, 149.
Śvetaśikha I, 149.
Śvetāsya I, 149.
Śyenayūha II, 306.

Sabhāparva I, 262. II, 34.
Saddīra I, 53. 60. 62.
Sadyumna I, 127.
Sagara I, 42. 324. II, 207. 359 f.
Sāgaradattā II, 282.
Saguṇa I, 147.
Sahadeva I, 272. 291. 297 f. 324.
Sdhasānka III, 215. 291.
Sdhasānka charitra III, 216.

Sdhasika I, 111.
Sahasrabuddhi II, 63 f.
Sahasrdñika I, 199 ff. II, 60.
Nahasrdrjuna I, 55.
Sahishṇu I, 127.
Sahotha III, 48.
Sahya I, 68.
Sainti II, 300.
Sakalyḍña I, 147.
Sdkarmikd I, 230.
Sakaíaryúha II, 307.
Samddhiyoga III, 122.
Sdmaveda I, 128 f. III, 300 ff. 332 ff.
Samugabhushaña III, 231.
Sdmaydchdrika sútra III, 521.
Samudra I, 14.
Samudra (jur.) I, 59.
Sdmudrikd I, 300.
Sdmudrikd vidyd I, 234.
Samcaraña I, 308.
Samrartta III, 106.
Samratsarika II, 35.
Sdnanda I, 96.
Sanatkumdra I, 63.
Sandanta I, 384.
Sandhi II, 16 f. 26. 345. III, 160. 261. 283.
Sandhyd I, 69. II, 345. 347. III, 103.
Sandipani I, 115.
Sanga III, 125 f.
Sangama III, 192.
Sanghdta III, 146.
Sangraha I, 159.
Sangrdma I, 158. II, 111 f.
Sanhitd I, 119. 129 f. III, 283. 312. 328. 362. 334 f. 347.

Sanjaya II, 341. III, 115 f. 154.
Sanjivaka II, 10. 19. 27. 139.
Sanjñd I, 12.
Sankalpa II, 41.
Sankhdchúḍa I, 109.
Sankhya III, 118.
Sankhyd III, 119.
Sdnkhya I, 10. 16. 23. 42. 99. 120. 145. III, 108 ff. 114. 118 ff. 145. 153. 193. 346.
Sankriti II, 353.
Sannidhdtryupadeshid II, 35.
Sannydsi III, 104. 111.
Sanudra III, 149.
Sanudrdvaritta III, 212. 218.
Saphara II, 350.
Sapiñda III, 47.
Sapiñdikaraña III, 57.
Saptasati III, 178. 219.
Sdrasundari III, 207.
Sarasvati I, 19. 39. 101 ff. 165. 205. II, 5. 9. 109. 184. 356 f. 361. III, 194.
Sarasvati prakriyd III, 343.
Sarga I, 118. III, 150.
Sdrikd II, 386.
Sarvabhauma II, 328.
Sarvadhara III, 204.
Sarvdnanda III, 204.
Sarvanukrama III, 323.
Sarvatmd I, 147.
Sarvatobhadra II, 307.
Sarvavarmd I, 189.
Sdñkya II, 231.
Sdta I, 182.
Sdtavdhana I, 181 ff. 190 f. II, 120. III, 172.

Sati I, 112. 161. 368.
Satrdjit I, 112. 132 f.
Sattwa I, 100. III, 124 f. 152 f.
Sattwaguńa I, 147. III, 125. 147 f.
Sáttwika I, 16.
Satya I, 40.
Satyabhámá I, 66. 68 f.
Satyaka I, 299.
Sátyaki I, 299. II, 308.
Satydsháḍha hirańyakeśi III, 321.
Satyararmá I, 353 f. II, 160. 169.
Satyavān I, 42.
Satyarati I, 127. 312.
Satyavrata I, 57. 257.
Saubhadra I, 301.
Saubhari I, 45.
Sauddsa I, 46.
Saugata III, 194.
Saumya I, 154.
Sauptika parva I, 286.
Saura purdńa I, 8.
Saurdshira I, 62. 68. II, 254.
Sauvirsa I, 274. 393. 396. 388.
Sauti I, 22. 279.
Sautra III, 248.
Sauvira I, 292. 200.
Savara I, 353.
Sávarikd I, 390.
Sávarńi I, 88. 130.
Sávitri I, 28. 76. 96. 101. 103.
Sáyańa III, 192. 311. 328.
Sendmukha II, 292.
Sendpati II, 85.
Sendsbdd II, 96. 98.
Sendebdr II, 95. 99 ff.
Seravа I, 382.
Shdhjthán III, 257.

Shahnáma II, 90.
Shashthi I, 101. 103.
Siddha I, 374. II, 327.
Siddhántakaumudi III, 126 f. 184. 206. 238. 245. 250. 279.
Siddhi II, 60.
Siddhíndga II, 60.
Simanta II, 161.
Simantini II, 164.
Simúpdla II, 35.
Sindbad II, 78. 98. 104.
Sindhu I, 242. 291. 300. 340.
Sindhudatta II, 282.
Sinhaghosha I, 367. II, 208 f. 226. 233.
Sinhásana dwátrinśati II, 108. III, 170. 178. 183.
Sinhásan battisi I, 157.
Sinhasena I, 304.
Sinhararmá I, 279. 357 ff. II, 166. 182. 208 f. 221. 241. 261.
Siprá I, 246 ff. II, 57. 338. 340. 343.
Sitavarmá I, 352. II, 160. 169.
Skanda I, 30. 117. II, 352.
Skandopura III, 188.
Skánda purdńa I, 21. 40. 85. 181. II, 41. 358.
Skandha I, 32.
Smriti II, 195. III, 97. 128. 316.
Soma I, 16. 41. 149. 290. III, 343 f.
Soma (lex.) III, 221.
Somadatta I, 160. 180. 313. 353. 355. II, 170. 174. 181. 189.
Somadeva I, 157 ff. II, 10. 108. 111. 123. III, 175. 179.

Somapa I, 154.
Somaraśmi II, 157.
Somaśarmā I, 31 ff. II, 69 ff. 78.
Somillaka II, 31.
Somodbhara II, 333.
Sparśa III, 121.
Sthalī devatā II, 205.
Sthāna II, 66.
Sthānachintaka II, 36.
Sthavaratīrtha I, 39.
Sthira III, 91.
Srīdhana III, 23.
Striparva I, 285.
Subāhu I, 49.
Subandhu I, 178. II, 311. III, 174. 177.
Subhadrā I, 14. 296. 300.
Subhōnka III, 219.
Subhard I, 65.
Subhūti III, 204.
Suchandra I, 111.
Suchi I, 127.
Sūchi I, 357.
Sūchimukha II, 302.
Sudhanvā III, 195.
Sudhārdā I, 151.
Sughosha III, 117.
Sugrīva I, 52.
Suhma I, 371. II, 211. 242.
Suhotra I, 312.
Sukald I, 31.
Sukhardtri I, 65.
Sūkta III, 312. 323. 334 f. 337. 341 ff.
Sulakshanā II, 227.
Sumada I, 18.
Sumanas I, 33.
Sumanta I, 128.
Sumantra I, 352. II, 160. 161.
Sumati I, 51. 88. 130. 312. 352. II, 8. 160. 161. 170.
Sumedha I, 127.
Sumitra I, 52. 352. II, 160. 161. 162. 223.
Sumridika I, 19.
Sunanda I, 40 ff.
Sunda I, 55.
Sundareśwara II, 79.
Supadma III, 207. 232.
Suprajñā I, 72.
Supratīka I, 19. II, 328.
Sarabhi I, 103. II, 354.
Suratamanjarī II, 187.
Sūrya I, 8. 61. 97. 274. II, 149. III, 185.
Sūryaprabha II, 130. 132.
Sūryaraka II, 209.
Sūryavatī II, 111 f.
Suśarmā I, 185.
Suśruta (med.) I, 39. 273. 276. 286. 301.
Suśruta I, 352. II, 160. 161. 162. 282.
Sūta I, 2. 30 ff. 52. 54. 66. 69 ff. 82. 88. 92. 119. 130. 140 ff. 327.
Sutala I, 45.
Sūtra I, 92. III, 248. 279. 311. 315 f. 318. 320 f. 323 ff.
Sūtrasthāna I, 273.
Sūtyā I, 140.
Suvarna I, 115.
Suvarnavatī II, 11.
Suvrata I, 33.
Suvritta II, 167. 178.

Svadhá I, 68. 101. 103.
Svedhá I, 101. 103. 125.
Svara II, 66.
Svarga I, 55 f. 72. 211. 257. 341.
II, 2L. 321. 342 ff. 353 f. 360.
365.
Svargakhańda I, 22. 77 f.
Svargdrohańa I, 287.
Svdrochisha manvantara I, 126.
Svasti I, 101.
Svastika I, 384.
Sváyambhuva I, 124. 127.
Svedyambhuva manvantara I, 124.
Svayamdutta III, 48.
Svayamvara I, 281. 393 ff.
Syntipas II, 96 ff.

Tabari II, 92.
Tairyaksrotas I, 148.
Taittiríya I, 121.
Taittiriya áranyaka III, 328.
Taittiriya sanhitá III, 332.
Taittiriya upanishad III, 329.
Tála II, 66. 78.
Taláṭala I, 45.
Tálayantra I, 384.
Támaliptá II, 261.
Tamas III, 124 f.
Támbúlardhaka II, 35.
Tamoguńa I, 146. III, 147. 154.
Támraliptdá I, 216.
Támralipti I, 216 f. 219. 226.
Tantra III, 95 ff.
Tántrika I, 83 f. II, 50. 380.
Tapas I, 40.
Tapaní I, 127.
Taptamudrá I, 56. 80.

Taptí I, 241. 355. II, 332. 394.
Táraka I, 30. II, 352.
Tárapála III, 221.
Táráralí I, 367. 369. II, 169.
224 ff.
Táráratí I, 324.
Túrendra III, 174.
Tarka I, 120.
Taithrá, Taithrí II, 18.
Tattva III, 135.
Tejas I, 145.
Tejaspura I, 49.
Tejasvarga I, 143.
Tikásarvasva III, 201.
Tila II, 320.
Tilottamá I, 55. 111. II, 192.
Tirtha I, 12 f. 27. 35. 38 f. 77.
85 f. II, 358.
Tírthakhańda I, 22.
Tiruvikramadeva III, 188.
Tittibha II, 17 f. 140.
Tomara II, 300.
Trayi II, 272.
Tretáyuga I, 152.
Trigartta I, 222.
Trikándašesha III, 126. 202. 211 ff.
220. 240 ff.
Trikándaviveka III, 208.
Trikárchaka I, 386.
Trilochanadeva I, 183.
Tripeṭí I, 81.
Tripura II, 365.
Trishṭubh III, 143.
Trivikramasena II, 153.
Tryambaka II, 236.
Tulasí I, 53. 57. 66 f. 72. 72. 81.
101. 103. 107. 118. III, 92. 95 f.

Tuida I, 38 f.
Tunga I, 34.
Tungabhadrá I, 62. 81.
Tungadhanved I, 371. 373. II,
242. 261.
Turushka I, 242.
Tushli I, 121.
Túlindma I, 157. II, 242.

Udaya I, 123.
Udayana I, 191. 194 f. II, 60.
121. 341 f.
Uddiaka I, 70.
Uddhata II, 65.
Uddhava I, 115.
Udgatd I, 121.
Udyogaparva I, 284. II, 308.
Ugrasena I, 115 f.
Ugrairaras I, 22. 140.
Ujjayini I, 77. 196 ff. 214 f. 239.
241. 246 ff. 344. 355 f. II, 57.
121. 154 f. 157. 173 f. 179 ff.
240. 257. 314. 339. 341 f. 344.
352. III, 165 ff.
Und I, 12. 20.
Unddi III, 237 f.
Unddikosha III, 237.
Upahdravarmd I, 353. 365 f. 375.
II, 166. 189. 210.
Upajati III, 143.
Upakośá I, 168 ff. II, 113.
Upamanyu I, 59. 192.
Upanayana III, 55.
Upanishad III, 106. 257. 312. 328 ff.
345.
Upaparva I, 296.
Upapurána I, 2. 22. 112.

Upasarga III, 320.
Upasunda I, 55.
Upaydja I, 326.
Uras II, 318.
Urddhapundra I, 57.
Urddhasrotas I, 148.
Uru I, 125. 127.
Urvasi I, 41. II, 281. 314 f.
Usanas I, 62. II, 6.
Ushd I, 117.
Ushmapa I, 154.
Utkala I, 12. 17.
Utkarsha I, 158.
Utpalinikosha III, 202. 212. 218.
Utathala I, 256. 265.
Uttama I, 127.
Utidnapáda I, 124. 127.
Uttara II, 294.
Uttarakhanda I, 8. 19 ff. 48. 53-62.
Uttararámacharitra I, 51.
Uttarasthána I, 274.

Váchaspati II, 6. III, 212. 221.
Vadiia I, 886.
Vágbhatta I, 273. 384 ff. III, 221.
Váhana I, 182.
Vdhini II, 232.
Vahni I, 110.
Vaideha I, 239.
Vaidya II, 81.
Vaijayanti III, 221.
Vaikarttana I, 323.
Vaikrita I, 148.
Vaikuntha I, 40 f. 55. 58. 72. 74.
113.
Vainateya II, 229.
Vaiśikha I, 71.

INDEX.

Vaidikkamdkdimya I, 71.
Vaišampāyana I, 129 f. 278.
Vaišeshika I, 59, 120.
Vaishnava I, 9. 24. 31. 53. 57 f.
  62. 66. 68 ff. 83 ff. 90. 98. 107 f.
  111. 119 ff. 143. 148. III, 92.
  189. 278.
Vaitarana II, 282.
Vaišya I, 35. 55. III, 94. 113.
Vaitdlika I, 227.
Vaitaraṇī I, 17. 241.
Vaivasvata I, 11. 13. 25. 127.
Vaivasvata manvantara I, 121.
Vdjasaneyi sanhitā III, 332.
Vdji I, 129.
Vdjikaraṇa I, 274. 276.
Vajra II, 302. 307. 371.
Vajrandbha I, 11.
Vaka I, 110. II, 25. 32. 324. 337.
  III, 182.
Vakdulapratyaya II, 32.
Vakil al bahr II, 13.
Valabhi II, 254. 256.
Valaka II, 238. 324.
Vallabhacharya I, 120.
Vallabha paṇḍita III, 172.
Vallala paṇḍita III, 172.
Vallalasena III, 172.
Vālmīki I, 17. 51 f.
Vāmadatta II, 150.
Vāmadeva II, 164. 167. 169. 171.
Vāmalochand II, 175.
Vāmana II, 328. 267.
Vāmana avatāra I, 59. II, 362.
Vāmana purāṇa II, 352. 366. III, 47 f.
Vana I, 117. III, 174.

Vananadi II, 338.
Vanoparva I, 333.
Vdnaprastha III, 102.
Vaṇia III, 331.
Vardka avatára I, 59. 121.
Vardhakalpa I, 121. 149.
Vardhamihira II, 16. III, 168.
  173. 184 ff.
Vdrdka purāṇa II, 352.
Varaṇd I, 85.
Vdrdṇasī II, 221.
Vararuchi I, 162. 165. 170. 174.
  178 f. 183 f. II, 46. 118. III,
  163. 170. 173 ff. 202. 208. 219.
  324.
Varddhamāna I, 244. 255. 263.
  267. II, 13. 126 ff. 138.
Varga III, 321.
Vārkshadas I, 151. 154.
Varna II, 66. 78. III, 51.
Varnasankara I, 141. 301.
Varnaviplavandša III, 211.
Varaka I, 164 ff. III, 176.
Vārtā II, 272.
Vdrttika III, 177. 324.
Varuṇa I, 41. II, 18. III, 343.
Vasanta II, 173.
Vasantabhdnu II, 277. 280 f. 286.
Vasantaka I, 203. 205 f. 211. 236.
Vāsara I, 200.
Vāsavadattā I, 196. 210. 203. 205 f.
  213. 226 f. 230. 236 ff. II, 121.
  156. 213. 341 f. III, 172.
Vdshkala I, 129.
Vasishtha I, 16. 28. 54. 57. 60 ff.
  82. 120 ff. 127. 150. II, 365.
  III, 42. 53.

Vāsishika I, 150.
Vāsu I, 102. 127.
Vasudatta I, 163.
Vasudeva I, 108 f.
Vāsudeva I, 14. 16. 138. 294. 339. III, 142.
Vāluki I, 39. 46. 180. 195. 337. II, 22.
Vasumān I, 127.
Vasumati II, 160. 163 f. 211.
Vasumitra II, 200.
Vasunemi I, 195.
Vasundhara I, 377. II, 282.
Varupālita II, 195.
Vāsupūjya III, 221.
Vasurakshaka II, 270.
Vasurakshita II, 282.
Vasusakti II, 7.
Vasushena I, 333.
Vaṭa I, 70.
Vatsa I, 191 ff. 226 ff. 268. II, 60. 113. 121 f. 123. 156. 341.
Vatsandga II, 234.
Vātsyāyana I, 39 f. 42. 45. 52. 187.
Vāyu I, 41. 130. 140. 279.
Vāyu purāṇa I, 7. 140-155. 174. II, 322. 333. 366. 389.
Veda I, 67. 68. 92. 94. 97. 101. 128 f. 140. 145. 147. 151. 164. 273. 313. 330. 340. 354. II, 21. 196. 240. 290. III, 42. 103 ff. 108 ff. 127. 129 f. 142. 149 ff. 192. 248. 255. 257. 305 ff.
Vedakumbha I, 185.
Vedānga III, 312. 316.
Vedānta I, 59. 86. 120. 126. 147.

II, 396. III, 105 ff. 109. 114. 120. 153. 191 f. 346.
Vedāryāsa I, 121. 128. 149.
Vegardu II, 187.
Veḍā II, 149.
Vena I, 25. 84 f. 38. 125. 141.
Veṇī I, 68. II, 388. 391.
Venkaiddri I, 60. 81.
Venkatagiri I, 58.
Vetāla II, 133. 154.
Vetālabhaṭṭa III, 168.
Vetālapanchavinśati II, 108. 153 f. III, 170. 178. 183.
Vetasa I, 164.
Vetravati II, 337.
Vibhīshaṇa I, 14. 20. 207 ff.
Vibhūtachaddāsi I, 23.
Vibhūti III, 142 f.
Vichitravīrya I, 123. 291.
Vidarbha I, 376. 878 f. II, 270. 277.
Videha II, 210.
Vidita II, 337.
Vidura I, 123. 313 f. 321.
Vidūshaka II, 133.
Vidvān II, 93.
Vidyādhara I, 41. 54. 236. 243 f. 260 ff. 358. II, 113. 121. 127 ff. 156 ff. 187.
Vidyādharī I, 266. 268. II, 127 ff. 156.
Vidyākaramiśra III, 234.
Vidyāvinoda III, 174.
Vidyeśvara II, 182.
Vigraha II, 17.
Viguṇa III, 133.
Vihāra II, 51. 76. 145.

Vikdrabhadra II, 271. 277.
Vijaya II, 79. III, 151.
Vijayanagara I, 91. 343. II, 106. III, 192. 213. 228.
Vikarma III, 135.
Vikarna I, 291.
Vikarttana I, 333.
Vikalavarmā I, 365. II, 211 ff.
Vikrama I, 157. II, 154. III, 168. 170 ff. 186.
Vikramacharitra I, 157. 181. III, 169 f. 388.
Vikramāditya I, 157. 181. II, 108. 153. 158. 314. 339. III, 166 ff. 174. 180 ff. 199. 212. 215. 221.
Vikramaśila II, 158.
Vikramorvaśī II, 152. 314 f.
Vikriti I, 128. 148.
Vikundala I, 55.
Vildsini II, 36.
Vimardaka II, 157. 212 f.
Vīnā II, 60. 242. 386 f.
Vinaid I, 209. 301.
Vindvatsa II, 60.
Vindyaka I, 348. III, 171.
Vinayavati II, 225.
Vinda II, 294.
Vindhya I, 28. 49. 75. 162. 202. 204. 214. 239 f. 255. 352. 369. 376. II, 20. 152. 179. 234. 242. 270. 282. 328 ff. 354.
Vindhyaka II, 20.
Vindhyavāsinī I, 163. 179. 184. 204. 371. II, 242. 284. 372.
Vindulekhā I, 266 f.
Vindumati I, 266 f.

Vīrabhadra I, 50.
Vīracharitra I, 157.
Viraja I, 127.
Viraja tīrtha I, 13.
Viraketu II, 175.
Viramani I, 50.
Vīramitrodaya III, 47. 67. 73. 91. 94.
Viraśekhara II, 187.
Virasena II, 281.
Virdi I, 22.
Virdia I, 284. II, 294.
Virdiaparva I, 284.
Virūpaka I, 360. 863. II, 203.
Visālā II, 341.
Visālākshā II, 275.
Vishnu I, 9 f. 13. 15. 18. 23 ff. 40 ff. 53. 56 ff. 90. 95 ff. 147 ff. 161. 208. 211. 213. 255. 283. 306. 309. 340 f. 376. II, 15. 19. 127. 150. 174. 366 f. 397. III, 148. 150. 227. 342.
Vishnu (Jur.) III, 47 ff. 69.
Vishnugupta II, 272.
Vishnu purāna I, 3. 7. 10. 15. 25. 31. 59. 71. 116. 120—139. 141. 144. 163. 289. 308. II, 6. 322. 358. 366. 869.
Vishnuśarmā II, 8. 6 ff. 48. 74 f.
Vishnuvardhana III, 227 f.
Visokadwddali I, 26.
Visokavarmā II, 219.
Viśravana I, 882.
Viśruta I, 352. 376 ff. II, 164. 182. 269 ff.
Viśvadeva III, 343.
Viśvakarmā I, 13. 19. 96 f. 110. 210. III, 346.

Viśvaketu I, 44.
Viśvakosha III, 204. 212. 214 ff. 221. 223. 232. 234. 239 ff.
Viśvāmitra I, 127. 273.
Viśvaprakāśa III, 214 ff. 220. 236.
Viśvarūpa I, 118.
Viśvasena I, 115.
Viśveśvara I, 85. 181. 366.
Vitala I, 45.
Vitankapura I, 236.
Vitasti I, 32.
Vitunda I, 88.
Virddabhangdriśara III, 20. 27.
Virddachintāmaṇi III, 18. 47. 73.
Virddaratnākara III, 18.
Viriṃśati I, 290.
Vopadeva III, 184. 206. 238. 250. 292.
Vopālita III, 212. 212.
Vrata I, 28. 86.
Vriddha kārita I, 54.
Vriddhakshetra I, 300.
Vriddhipatra I, 386.
Vrihadbala I, 11.
Vrihadīshu I, 308.
Vrihaspati I, 26. 59. 110. 140. 211. II, 6. III, 44. 49. 51. 67. 90. 94.
Vrihaspatisaṃhitā III, 20.
Vrihatkathā I, 157. 159. 163. 204. 221. II, 10. 12 ff. 60. 109 ff. III, 175. 177 f. 183. 220.
Vrihatsaṃhitā III, 185.
Vrihimukha I, 286.
Vrindā I, 68. 115.
Vrindāvana I, 53. 60. 70. 95 f. 108. 110. 115. 118. II, 328.

Vrishabhānu I, 70. 109.
Vrishasena I, 302.
Vrishni I, 312.
Vritra I, 34. II, 29.
Vritrāsura I, 28.
Vrittāgra I, 380.
Vritti I, 182. III, 121.
Vyadhana I, 382.
Vyādi I, 163 ff. 174 ff. III, 176. 202. 212. 221.
Vyāghradatta I, 304.
Vyākaraṇa III, 316.
Vyākhyāmrita III, 204.
Vyākhyāpradīpa III, 206.
Vyākhyāsudhā III, 204.
Vyāpdīraya III, 133.
Vyāsa I, 9. 15 f. 22 f. 31. 38. 52. 62. 71. 82. 68. 92. 121. 123. 128. 130. 140. 144. 278. 291. 313. 340. II, 6. III, 196.
Vyavahāra III, 87.
Vyavahāramātrikā III, 92.
Vyavahāramayūkha III, 47. 54. 67 ff. 91. 94.
Vyavahārātattva III, 94.
Vyavasthā III, 19. 23.
Vyūha I, 58. II, 305 ff.

Yādava I, 132 f. 287.
Yādava (lex.) III, 221.
Yadu I, 80. 108. 132. 299. 304. 312. 352.
Yahya II, 93.
Ydja I, 326.
Yajña I, 124. III, 136.
Yajña (name) I, 135.
Yajñadatta I, 166.

Yajñaśri I, 135.
Yâjñavalkya I, 87 f. III, 44. 47 f. 69. 91. 332.
Yajñavati II, 182.
Yajurveda (white) I, 128 f. III, 309. 311 f. 317. 325. 326. 332 ff.
Yajurveda (black) III, 321. 332.
Yaksha I, 69. 162. 182. 224. 356. 374 f. II, 117 ff. 147. 169. 180. 224. 266 f. 312 f. 316 f. 319. 327. 345. 368. 373 f. 882. 386. 394. 396. 399.
Yakshini I, 367. 369. II, 227. 372.
Yama I, 34. 41. 44. 64 f. 69. 304. 376. II, 6. 24. III, 345.
Yama (Jur.) I, 59. III, 47 f.
Yâma I, 124. 298.
Yamadwitiyâ I, 65.
Yamagitâ I, 130.
Yamund I, 60. 332. II, 10. 332. 370.
Yantra I, 382 f. 387. II, 301.
Yantramukta II, 299.
Yâska III, 311. 318.
Yaśodâ I, 102 ff.

Ydtaydma III, 151.
Yathârtha II, 198. 202 f.
Yati II, 66.
Yavana I, 292. 366. 371 f. II, 219. 246 f.
Yayâti I, 36.
Yoga I, 15. 43. 143. 145. 149. II, 131. III, 108 ff. 118. 121 f. 142.
Yogakaraṇḍikâ I, 220.
Yogânanda I, 175 ff. II, 131.
Yogandharâyaṇa I, 196 f. 203. 205. 213. 228. 230. 233. 235 ff.
Yogaśâstra III, 109.
Yogeśvara I, 147.
Yogi I, 16. 143. 246. II, 57 f. 131. 153. III, 111. 119 f.
Yogini II, 133.
Yojana I, 214.
Yudhishthira I, 279. 286 ff. 316. 324 ff. 337. 340. II, 34. 307 ff.
Yuga I, 15. 45. 129. 151. II, 322.
Yugandhara I, 201.
Yuvarâja II, 35. 177. 226.
Yuvarâjya II, 220.
Yuyudhâna I, 292. II, 308.

ADDITIONAL NOTE to Vol. II, p. 16, and Vol. III, p. 185.

We are indebted to Dr. Kern, of Benares, for the following quotations from the text of the Brihatsanhitâ:

मावापत्ये श्वभे निन्ने इत्येव पातले वसुधा ।
केमाचिय्कख्यवता कापालमिय भनं धर्षी ॥

रोहिणीयकटमर्दनमग्नो यदि भिनत्ति रुधिरोऽथवा स्विद्यी ।
किं वदामि यदृगिदृशावरे अद्य देवमुपयाति संचयम् ॥
रोहिणीयकटमर्द्दनसंस्थिते चन्द्रमण्डलरवीक्षिता अदाः ।
क्वापि यान्ति विमुवाचितायमा: सूर्यतप्तपिठराद्बुपाचिन: ॥

The couplet beginning यदि भिन्ते is not found in any of the seven MSS. he has consulted. See also Böhtlingk's "Indische Sprüche", Nos. 1886 and 2648 f.

From the printed edition of the Vikramârkacharitra (Madras: 1861) we add the following two stanzas as a supplement to Prof. Benfey's note (Pantschatantra, II, p. 393):

उत्तरम वराहमिहिरेण ।
चर्कसुतेन हि अये श्रीमद्गुरुव रोहिणीयकटे ।
द्वादशवास्त्रामहि नहि वर्षति वर्षाणि वारिदो निजगाम ॥
रोहिणीयकटमर्द्दसूनुना भिनत्ते रुधिरवाहिनी हरित् ।
किं ब्रवीमि नहि वारिसागरे सर्वतोऽत्र उपयाति संचयम् ॥
मतान्तरे ।
यदा भिनत्ति मञ्जो ऽयं रोहिकायकटं तदा ।
वर्षाणि द्वादशाब्दं वारिवाहो न वर्षति ॥

See Böhtlingk, L l., Nos. 2354 and 2367.

CORRECTIONS.

Vol. I.

Page 68, line 19 and 22 read Krishṇá
- 77, - 12 - Kámákhyá
- 79, - 5 - Kámákhyá
- 103, - 2 - Goloka
- 112, - 30 - Vrihaspati
- 116, - 19 - Rádhá
- 119, - 19 - Puráṇas
- 123, - 2 - Páṇḍu

CORRECTIONS.

Page	line		read	
127,	22		read	Viśwámitra
127,	23		-	Bharadwája
129,	19		-	Yájnavalkya
129,	24		-	Taittiríya
137,	2		-	Nishadha
152,	25		-	Tretá
154,	22 and 26		-	Várhishadas
154,	23, 26, 27		-	Ushmapas, Ájyapas
154,	25		-	Somapas
157,	10		-	Sáliváhana
158,	28		-	Sangráma
179,	8		-	Badariká
179,	11		-	Badarikásrama
228,	16		-	Pándu
260,	15		-	Golden City
273,	19		-	Viśwámitra
274,	2		-	Sárira
295,	3		-	Śrinjaya
297,	6		-	Bharadwája
307,	31		-	Śrinjaya
310,	9		-	Brahmá
312,	23		-	Ajámídha
313,	27		-	Parásara
348,	20		-	Vijayanagara
351,	20		-	Pushpapura
857,	10		-	Púrva
364,	18 and 25		-	Chandravarmá
372,	22		-	Dákiní
372,	26		-	Pachisí
377,	2		-	Máhishmatí

Vol. II.

Page	line		read	
26,	23		read	Rohanáchala
47,	29		-	from
77,	8		-	áveshihí
120,	23		-	Sáliváhana

CORRECTIONS.

Page 133,	line 28	*read*	chháditaṁ
- 164,	- 11	-	Mitragupta
- 209,	- 19	-	endeavouring
- 209,	- 22 and 29	-	Chandravarmá
- 210,	- 11	-	Chandravarmá
- 221,	- 4	-	Chandravarmá
- 248,	- 17	-	Dhúminí
- 243,	- 19	-	Nitambavati
- 315,	- 8	-	Ṙitusanhára
- 354,	- 16, 19 and 24	-	Charmanwati
- 364,	- 24	-	Káṅwa
- 372,	- 2 and 24	-	Airávata
- 394,	- 21	-	Śálagrama

Vol. III.

Page 25,	line 28	*read*	पिछड़ोऽम्बरः
- 96,	- 15, 19 and 24	-	Brahmá
- 108,	- 13	-	Śankara
- 108,	- 13	-	Śrídhara
- 108,	- 14	-	Sánkhyas
- 127,	- 24	-	Medinikara
- 128,	- 15	-	Śrotavya
- 128,	- 16	-	Śrota
- 141,	- 23	-	adhyátma
- 177,	- 14	-	Manoramá
- 183,	- 21	-	Śáliváhana
- 213,	- 13	-	Vijayanagara
- 240,	- 12	-	Prayoga
- 291,	- 11	-	Átmanepada

www.ingramcontent.com/pod-product-compliance
Lightning Source LLC
Chambersburg PA
CBHW020108010526
44115CB00008B/746